DATE			

MAX WEBER'S
POLITICAL
SOCIOLOGY

Recent Titles in Contributions in Sociology
Series Editor: Don Martindale

Contemporary Issues in Theory and Research: A Metasociological Perspective
William E. Snizek, Ellsworth R. Fuhrman, and Michael K. Miller, editors

Nationalism and the Crises of Ethnic Minorities in Asia
Tai S. Kang, editor

History of Sociological Thought
Jerzy Szacki

Management and Complex Organizations in Comparative Perspective
Raj P. Mohan, editor

Methods for the Social Sciences: A Handbook for Students and Non-Specialists
John J. Hartman and Jack H. Hedblom

Cult and Countercult: A Study of a Spiritual Growth and
a Witchcraft Order
Gini Graham Scott

Poverty in America: The Welfare Dilemma
Ralph Segalman and Asoke Basu

Politics, Character, and Culture: Perspectives from Hans Gerth
Joseph Bensman, Arthur J. Vidich, and Nobuko Gerth, editors

Ethnicity, Pluralism, and Race: Race Relations Theory in America
Before Myrdal
R. Fred Wacker

Civil Religion and Moral Order: Theoretical and Historical Dimensions
Michael W. Hughey

Countercultural Communes
Gilbert Zicklin

The Adventure of Reason: The Uses of Philosophy in Sociology
H. P. Rickman

MAX WEBER'S POLITICAL SOCIOLOGY

A Pessimistic Vision of a Rationalized World

Edited by RONALD M. GLASSMAN
and VATRO MURVAR

Contributions in Sociology, Number 45

Greenwood Press
Westport, Connecticut • London, England

Library of Congress Cataloging in Publication Data
Main entry under title:

Max Weber's political sociology.

(Contributions in sociology ISSN 0084-9278 ;
no. 45)
Bibliography: p.
Includes index.
1. Weber, Max, 1864-1920—Political science—
Addresses, essays, lectures. 2. Weber, Max, 1864-1920—
Sociology—Addresses, essays, lectures. 3. Political
sociology—Addresses, essays, lectures. I. Glassman,
Ronald M. II. Murvar, Vatro (date) . III. Series.
JC263.W42M39 1984   301'.092'4   83-1678
ISBN 0-313-23642-9 (lib. bdg.)

Library of Congress Catalog Card Number: 83-1678
ISBN: 0-313-23642-9
ISSN: 0084-9278

First published in 1984

Greenwood Press
A division of Congressional Information Service, Inc.
88 Post Road West
Westport, Connecticut 06881

Printed in the United States of America

10 9 8 7 6 5 4 3 2 1

CONTENTS

MAX WEBER'S POLITICAL SOCIOLOGY

INTRODUCTION

Ronald M. Glassman and Vatro Murvar

Max Weber left us with a set of pessimistic predictions about the emergent structure of modern society—predictions which haunt us today. He warned that bureaucracy would become the predominant mode of administration in both the economy and the polity and that bureaucracy, because of its intrinsic structure, could become the infrastructure in a system of authoritarian domination. Pursuing his analysis to its logical conclusion, Weber warned that bureaucracy could overwhelm parliamentary democracy, paradoxically, the system he spent his life helping to institutionalize in Germany.

Weber offered little hope to optimistic dreamers. He not only predicted the probable decline of parliamentary democracy, he also insisted that socialism, as an alternative system of economy and polity, would be doomed to an even more rapid decline. In Weber's view, socialism would degenerate into a more insidious form of bureaucratic despotism. Socialism demands more planning than capitalism and therefore generates a larger bureaucracy; socialism also fuses economic and political power, inadvertently establishing the administrative bureaucracy of the state as supreme.

Hopes for both parliamentary democracy and for classless socialism shatter against the rock of authoritarian bureaucracy. Weber's pessimism extended beyond the effects of bureaucratization to include certain "unintended" negative effects of the rise of rational science heralded with such enthusiasm by the enlightenment thinkers: The causally related decline of magic, ritual, and the religious world view would produce in contemporary individuals a general "disenchantment" with the world. Such disenchantment could lead to a kind of cynical withdrawal into a world of private hedonism; public responsibilities would be left to the technical managerial experts of the all-pervasive bureaucracy.

Even Weber's one hope, that of charismatic leadership—the leadership that could possibly preserve democracy and save us from bureaucratic domination—founders on the rock of rationalization. For according to Weber's own projection, charisma could hardly flourish in a "disenchanted" world.

Why does the amount of administration in contemporary society continue to increase dramatically, and why should the mode of administration become a "new iron cage of serfdom"?[1]

Weber believed that the demands of a mass society, linked to a technologically sophisticated economy, necessarily would lead to an enormous degree of coordination and management. When he toured the United States in the period before World War I, he was quick to observe that although the United States did *not* have an administrative state or a bureaucratic economy as yet, the continental size of the United States and the increasing complexity of its economy eventually would produce the need for such structures.[2] The passing of time has more than demonstrated that theory. And, although we may despair over the growth of bureaucratic organization in government and corporations, we have not, at this point in history, devised an adequate alternative. Until we do, we must watch the process of expansionary bureaucratization unfold as Weber maintained that it would.[3] The giant transnational corporation and the top-heavy administrative state have now become fixtures of mass technocratic-industrial society.

Why is this necessarily problematic? Weber in his typification of modern bureaucracy, although praising its rationality and longevity, warns of its inherent authoritarian nature.[4] Bureaucracies exhibit a hierarchical structure of authority, a chain of command not unlike that of the modern military organization. Hierarchical authority is antagonistic to processes of "collegial authority" (councils of equals) and individualism that are central to democratic institutions. The bureaucratic hierarchy is controlled by an "elite" of top mangers who make decisions with the technical advice but without the consent of those below them in the hierarchy.[5] Finally, bureaucratic rules and red tape are not laws.[6] They are not debatable and are not subject to amendment. These rules, as well as decisions made by the elite, are not subject to open discussion or to constitutional interpretation and limitation as laws are.

What Weber saw as an ideal typification of bureaucratic organizational structure was a new form of despotic domination.[7] This form of domination is subtle in that it controls decision making and negates civil liberties without resort to a secret police or conquering army.

But we do have parliaments and we do have courts. Why should bureaucracy overwhelm these institutions? Weber believed that the specialized experts organized into smoothly functioning units by the bureaucratic managers would provide these elite managers with a decision-making ability foreign to the parliaments and the courts.[8] He foresaw the dilemma that contemporary congresses would face when presented with problems beyond their collective expertise. There is a continuing trend toward the abdication of decision making by the elected representatives of the people and toward the increasing importance of nonelected decision makers.

In Sweden, when one takes a tour of the capital, one's guide is likely to state openly that the *national planning board,* rather than the parliament, makes most of the important decisions. At the same time, Americans decry the fact that nonelective White House staff, with newly coined managerial titles seem to be running the show in conjunction with the heads of key government bureaus and corporations.

And what of socialism, the alternative to "oligarchic democracy" and the great hope of Marxist intellectuals? Weber stated flatly that socialism would demand even more bureaucratization than would democracy, as has already been discussed. He further stated that this bureaucracy would be fully fused with the politico-military might of the state.[9] A planned economy is a managed economy, and a managed economy is a bureaucratic economy. If capitalist economic units were *eventually* to become bureaucratized, socialist economic units would be bureaucratized in their inception.[10]

Further, the separation of economic power from political power in the Western capitalist nations was, for Weber, a key element in the preservation of democracy.[11] Defenders of capitalism (and its concomitant class inequality) from Locke[12] to Hayek[13] have used this argument. However, Weber was not an apologist for the capitalist rich; he simply understood the potential power of the state.[14] It seemed clear to him that if an economic planning bureaucracy were fused with the military and police power of the political state, the emergence of a despotic system would increase in likelihood. This is precisely what he predicted for the Soviet Union shortly after the triumph of the Bolsheviks.[15]

Contemporary social democrats and some contemporary Marxists have been seeking ways to combine a socialized economy with some form of political democracy. Perhaps they will succeed—Sweden is *not* despotic, and Solidarity *has* recently demanded civil liberties and democratic participation in Poland. But Weber's warning stands as a beacon to the social democrats, just as it stands as a beacon to capitalist democrats, who seek to steer clear of the dangers of authoritarian bureaucracy.

If the "rationalization" of the organizational structure of society worried Weber, so too did the rationalization of thought. The thinkers of the enlightenment heralded science as the "savior" of humankind. They enshrined "reason" as the loftiest of human gifts. Weber shared their positive view of the role of reason and science in the progress of human beings. He was even optimistic about the possibility of creating a value-neutral social science in a value-relative world.[16]

The problem he perceived was inherent not in science itself but rather in the "unintended effects" science would produce. If the thinkers of the enlightenment envisioned the rational, secular-scientific world view as *the* liberating force for humankind, Weber foresaw that the decline of magical, ritual, and theological elements from everyday life that would follow the advent of the scientific world view would leave the average individual "disenchanted" with the world.[17]

From his viewpoint, the world lacked meaning and justice. The function of religion is to provide humans with a coherent, shared meaning system, a set of rituals to calm existential fears, and a theological answer to the question of why humans must endure injustice and suffering.[18]

Marx and Durkheim shared with the philosophers of the Enlightenment a negative ("opiate," "cohesive") view of religion, whereas Weber took an original broader approach. While Weber accepted Marx's opiate function in all instances in which religion sanctified and legitimized corrupt and brutal political regimes, he objected to Marx's generalization that religion always and everywhere performed that function alone. He documented many instances in which religious leaders and movements performed a revolutionary and reform function.[19] Basically agreeing with Marx, Durkheim postulated that there can be no society without the cohesive, opiate function; this only religion can supply. While not needed by the enlightened elite, religion is necessary to control the masses of uneducable humanity for no laws could do it without religious sanctification.[20] To this end Durkheim actively promoted "civil religion" to replace traditional religions. In contrast to Marx and Durkheim, Weber analyzed religious phenomena with scientific neutrality, seeing its significance in satisfying a basic human need.

To Weber, the combination of rationalization and religious decline meant a disenchantment with the world that would in turn result in a cynical withdrawal of the individual from the public sphere and a retreat into the private sphere of personal hedonism. Both the citizen's role and the relatively humanistic ethics of world religion would be abandoned in favor of a personal, private orientation to pleasure, and society as a whole would be left to the mercy of the "soulless" managers and technicians of the bureaucracy.[21]

What solution did Weber find for the tragic fate he envisioned for humanity? How could his contemporaries break out of the "iron cage"? In his moments of ultimate pessimism, Weber always turned to his own vision of hope—the *charismatic leader*.[22] Believing that parliamentary democracy was no match for rationally organized bureaucratic expertise and that the purely rational approach to the world led to a disenchanted withdrawal from it, he hoped that if a form of charismatic leadership were *institutionalized* within a carefully delineated system of legal authority, that perhaps such charismatic leadership—by the nature of its irrational social bond—would rouse contemporary individuals out of their withdrawal and hedonism and draw them back into the public fray.

Weber further hoped that such charismatic leadership might provide a check to the power of bureaucracy by uniting the power of the people against it. The charismatic plebiscitary presidency became Weber's final hope and plebiscitarian democracy his major political commitment.[23]

One might ask whether the irrational power of charisma could really be contained within a framework of law. One certainly should also wonder whether Weber could have maintained his faith in the charismatic plebiscitarian presidency if he had lived through the Hitler-Mussolini dictatorships.[24] Charismatic leaders may not always be a force for good—the Attilas and Hitlers stand side by side with the Moseses and Gandhis in human history. And legal authority, no matter how firmly institutionalized, may not always be able to contain the assertions of extra-legal presidential powers.

Having just criticized one of Max Weber's few optimistic conceptions, let us add that Weber himself became despondent about his own deus ex machina. In the end, he came to believe that in a rational, disenchanted world, even *pure* charismatic leadership would be impossible to establish.[25] Rather, *institutional charisma*—the charisma of high offices and giant organizations, the charisma that stood people in awe of kings and empires—would again emerge as the dominant form.[26] In such a setting, pure charisma cannot flourish, and the gates of the new iron cage once more close around the individual. As we in the West now witness the utilization of "manufactured" charisma by the public relations image makers of the mass media,[27] and as we see the cult of personality promulgated for the same purpose in the East, the haunting pessimism of Weber's view begins to overwhelm us. At this point in history, it has become clear that both liberal and radical thinkers alike had better come to grips with Weber's views if they wish to create a world that differs from his dreary vision.

The essays in this volume, with the exception of the one by Hans H. Gerth, were originally presented at the Max Weber Colloquium held at William Paterson College, October 30 and 31, 1980. These essays focus on Weber's political analyses. Are his views grounded in a realistic appraisal of social development, or are they linked to his enmeshment with the tumultuous history and culture of pre-Nazi Germany? Reinhard Bendix, Hans Gerth, Regis Factor and

Stephen Turner, Ernest Kilker, and Vatro Murvar debate this issue. What of Weber's out-of-hand dismissal of socialism? Is his appraisal well founded, or is it part of his non-Marxist, multi-causal, historical sociology and his own philosophy of life? Dennis Wrong, Lawrence Scaff, and Zoltan Tar discuss this question.

On the process of "rationalization" itself, Jose Casanova, Roslyn Wallach Bologh, and Robert Antonio present their views. Casanova, focusing on recent German scholarship, suggests that rationalization is the central theme unifying all of Weber's work. Bologh points out that the process of rationalization was, for Weber, the source of all the paradoxical dilemmas that have emerged in the modern world. She enumerates and analyzes these "Weberian" dilemmas. Antonio focuses on the problem of bureaucracy as a system of domination. He contrasts Weber's typi-fication of bureaucracy to that of Talcott Parsons, establishing key differences between these two viewpoints—differences that lead to two very different assessments of future development.

Finally, Stanford Lyman discusses Weber's conception of charisma as a force for social change in history, William H. Swatos, Jr., then describes the possible decline of "pure" charisma in a "rationalized," "disenchanted," "media-messaged"[28] world, and Ronald M. Glassman focuses on the attempts to "manu-facture" charisma through the use of the mass media.[29]

The collection of essays here presented is preceded by a prologue written by Reinhard Bendix that provides us with a touching personal view of Weber's greatness as a social scientist. The volume concludes with an epilogue by Vatro Murvar that reminds us—as Bendix reminds us in the prologue—that Weber was human, not an idol or a supreme master, and that he expected his posterity to take him seriously by extending and criticizing his work.

It is hoped that this anthology will produce a response from scholars, not merely in terms of the theoretical aspects of Weber's work but also in terms of the potentialities for the practical pro-duction of institutional and societal change of a more positive and hopeful nature than was experienced by Max Weber.

NOTES

We would like to thank the members of the Sociology Department, the Continuing Education Department, and the administration of William

Paterson College for their enthusiastic support of this project.

1. Many contemporary students of Weber, especially in Germany, reject Parsons's translation of *"ein stahlhartes Gehäuse"* as "an iron cage." Parsons was influenced by John Bunyan's *The Pilgrim's Progress* (1678) when he chose this term in his translation. (See "Letter from Talcott Parsons," *Sociological Inquiry* 51 [1981]: 35-36.) Instead the terms "metal cloak" or "shell of bondage" are suggested. Vatro Murvar argues that the "iron cage" metaphor is bias-laden and plainly journalistic overkill which will not last. (Vatro Murvar, ed., *Max Weber Today—An Introduction to a Living Legacy and Selected Bibliography,* Max Weber Colloquia and Symposia at the University of Wisconsin [Brookfield, Wis., 1983], pp. 10ff., 16.) Ronald M Glassman feels that "iron cage" is very evocative of the potential despotic structure of bureaucracy. For the proper intent of Weber's expression, see Max Weber, *Economy and Society,* ed. Roth and C. Wittich (New York: Bedminster Press, 1968), pp. 1402-03.

2. For a discussion of Weber's American visit, see Marianne Weber, *Max Weber: A Biography,* tr. and ed. Henry Zohn (New York: John Wiley, 1975). See also Vatro Murvar, "Social Justice, the U.S.A. and Max Weber," forthcoming.

3. Weber, *Economy and Society,* pp. 956-1003.

4. Ibid., pp. 990-98.

5. Ibid., pp. 223, 990-98.

6. Ibid., pp. 956-58. Cf. pp. 641-729 on Law.

7. Ibid., pp. 990-98.

8. For a discussion of Weber's alleged pessimism about democracy, see articles by Regis A. Factor and Stephen P. Turner and by Ernest Kilker in this volume. For a more optimistic view see Vatro Murvar's Epilogue.

9. Max Weber, *Socialism,* tr. H. F. Dickie-Clark (Durban: University of Natal Press, 1967). See also "Socialism," in Max Weber, *Selections in Translation,* ed. W. G. Runciman and trans. E. Mathews (Cambridge, Eng.: Cambridge University Press, 1978).

10. Weber, *Socialism*; and Max Weber, *The General Economic History* (New Brunswick, N.J.: Transaction Books, 1981).

11. Weber, *Economy and Society,* pp. 74-202, 271-84. See also Friedrich Hayek, *The Road to Serfdom* (Chicago: University of Chicago Press, 1944).

12. John Locke, *Treatise on Civil Government* (New York: Cambridge University Press, 1960), pp. 21-41.

13. Hayek, *The Road to Serfdom.*

14. Weber, *Economy and Society,* pp. 941-54; 1006-104.

15. This will be discussed in detail in the Epilogue to this volume.

16. Max Weber, *The Methodology of the Social Sciences* (Glencoe, Ill.: The Free Press, 1949), pp. 1-47.

17. For a discussion of Max Weber's conception of "disenchantment," see the article by William H. Swatos, Jr., in this volume.

18. Weber, *Economy and Society,* p. 518.

19. Karl Marx, *The Jewish Question* (New York: Pathfinder Press, 1970). Vatro Murvar, "Toward a Sociological Theory of Religious Movements," *Journal for the Scientific Study of Religion* 14 (1975): 229-56. See also Vatro Murvar, "Integrative and Revolutionary Capabilities of Religion," in Harry M. Johnson, ed., *Religious Change and Continuity: Sociological Perspectives* (San Francisco: Jossey-Bass, 1979).

20. Emile Durkheim, *Suicide* (New York: Free Press, 1951). See also Emile Durkheim, *The Elementary Forms of Religious Life* (New York: Free Press, 1954).

21. Max Weber, *The Protestant Ethic and the Spirit of Capitalism,* trans. Talcott Parsons (New York: Charles Scribner's Sons, 1958), pp. 155-85.

22. Controversies around the concept of charisma are abundant, but to relate it to Nietzsche's *übermensch* is unwarranted. See Walter Kaufmann, *Nietzsche,* 4th ed. (Princeton, N.J.: Princeton University Press, 1974), pp. 3-9, 43, 441-47, 486, for the forgery of Nietzsche's last writings including letters by his sister Elisabeth Förster-Nietzsche and for the subsequent Nazi glorification of Nietzsche based on her fabrications.

23. Wolfgang Mommsen, *The Age of Bureaucracy* (Scranton, Pa.: Harper & Row, 1977).

24. Ronald Glassman, "The Negative Aspects of Charismatic Leadership," paper presented at the Eastern Sociological Association Meetings in New York, 1980. (Available upon request.)

25. See the article by Swatos in this volume. See also Ronald Glassman, "Conflicts Between Legal and Bureaucratic Authority," in Arthur J. Vidich and Ronald M. Glassman, *Conflict and Control: The Challenge to Legitimacy of Modern Governments* (Beverly Hills, Calif.: Sage Publications, 1979).

26. See the article by Ronald Glassman in this volume. See also Edward A. Shils, "Charisma, Order, and Status," *American Sociological Review* 30 (1965).

27. Ibid.

28. Marshall McLuhan, *The Medium Is the Message* (New York: Bantam Books, 1967); Marshall McLuhan, *Understanding Media* (New York: McGraw-Hill, 1965).

29. For reasons of length, a section on "Legitimate Domination" was not included in this work. See Weber, *Economy and Society,* pp. 941-1364; Mommsen, *The Age of Bureaucracy;* Vidich and Glassman, *Conflict and Control;* and Jurgen Habermas, *Legitimation Crisis* (Boston, Mass.: Beacon Press, 1973).

PROLOGUE

WHAT MAX WEBER MEANS TO ME?

Reinhard Bendix

Our meeting at this colloquium is to deal with Max Weber's political sociology, broadly understood. The topics of the papers announced for our meeting cover a wide range so that the overall title is somewhat nominal. But all of us share a common interest in Weber's work, which we find stimulating, but which each of us develops in his own way. In this sense there are many "usable" ideas in that work, even though it does not offer an overall theory. Recently, in Berkeley, someone gave a talk on Max Weber's theory; I did not attend, but I wondered what he meant. In this respect Weber is a much more uncomfortable classic than either Marx or Durkheim. For these reasons my talk today is addressed to the question: What does Weber stand for if his work cannot be identified with a specific theory? I will try to answer this question in personal terms, my ventures or adventures with Weber's work. That way, I do not implicate anyone else. Other versions are possible, but naturally I prefer mine.

Since I use this personal approach, it is perhaps of interest that I never read a line of Weber during the first 22 years of my life in Germany. In fact I received a copy of *Wirtschaft und Gesellschaft* from a girlfriend as a going-away present in 1938, when I emigrated from Berlin to America. If the native Americans among you discovered Weber during your student days, so in fact did I—at the University of Chicago. I had the unread book on my bookshelf in those days. I studied under Louis Wirth, who had recently translated (together with Edward Shils) Karl Mannheim's *Ideology and Utopia,* and since Mannheim combined the influences of Marx and Weber, so eventually did I.

My first effort to understand Weber grew out of a preoccupation with historical materialism. In the 1920s, Berlin had been heady with political turmoil and intense discussions of Marxism. Though my father was a Social Democrat, what stood out in my mind was his critique of Marxism. There were politically oriented discussion groups already in the Gymnasium (the German high school), and so I set out to examine for myself what my father criticized. I still remember the way the question was posed, as far as I was concerned. According to historical materialism, the organization of production influences our thought. How did it do that? Remember, I was completely untutored. In 1933 I was thrown out of school because I refused the Hitler salute (my father was in prison at the time). And although I had started reading about such questions by 1931 under the promptings of my father, I best remember reading learned works late at night during the first years of Hitler, a lonely and seemingly incongruous effort to keep the menace surrounding me at bay. For a time I struggled with Kant and Hegel; somehow the more difficult the text, the greater the effort and the more insulating the effect. No doubt there was a bit of misplaced bravado here too. But I wearied of these abstractions, and in an effort to discover how life experiences influence thought I discovered, if that is the word, John Dewey's *Human Nature and Conduct,* the life-history approach of Charlotte Buehler and several works on child psychology.

There is no need to go into detail, but recently I had occasion to summarize the results of these initial explorations, and they bear on what Weber has meant to me. Of course, I could not have formulated matters in this fashion at the time; my summary is best understood as a description of the ideas with which I was struggling. But remember that, abstract as these preoccupations were, they had an immediate bearing on my situation. My father had been expelled from the Berlin Bar Association in 1933, he rejected the idea of emigration and attempted instead to make a living as a legal counsellor outside the courts—until he was arrested in 1935. He was released from Dachau two years later on condition that he emigrate within two weeks to a non-European country. My parents went to Palestine in 1937.

Under the circumstances, historical materialism—the determination of the individual's life by his place in the organization of production—was not only a theoretical issue. Could my father succeed in his attempt to continue his legal work? Could I find a job despite the anti-Jewish policies of the Nazis? And though I did, what would become of my intellectual interests, which I pursued without any prospect of regular study, since all Jews had been barred from the universities? These questions are asked after the fact; at the time one lived from one day to the next, hoping to make it somehow—despite all the signs pointing to nowhere.

In the late evening hours I read Dewey's *Human Nature and Conduct,* to test my endurance perhaps, to practice English—and, yes, to find a way of coping with historical materialism. Dewey made clear that much of our conformity consists in the habits we learn in order to function. I was sure he could not have had my situation in mind, but the routines of getting through each day in the accustomed ways certainly helped under Hitler. It was much harder to see how these habits of conformity were also the basis of making choices of one's own.

I think this is where belief came in. I certainly wanted to believe that choices were still open to me, though my situation indicated otherwise. Put it down to my age: I was 17 when Hitler came to power, 22 when I emigrated. My father was 56 and 61 in those same years. He had a stake in defending his belief in the law to the last; I did not. On the contrary: I had wanted to emigrate in 1933 on no promise or prospect of any kind; what held me back was my father's determination not to be separated from the only roots he knew. Obviously, there were few American undergraduates during the 1930s who were reading John Dewey with such thoughts in mind.

Over the years, the question has stayed with me even as the circumstances which had made them so urgent receded into the background. The view that men act as their social roles dictate was certainly prominent in the teaching of sociology at the University of Chicago. Were personal choices then a mere illusion? In the late 1950s I put this question to Alfred Kroeber, who had studied culture and American Indian tribes all his life. I wanted to know whether the anthropological portrayal of simple societies was misleading when it showed the meticulous conformity to traditional patterns and little else. For example, in a dance everyone present understands the dominant pattern, but it might not be true that everyone also understands the consummate skill of an individual dancer which is surely needed, if by minute and highly intricate variations peculiarly his own he shows off *his individual mastery and the dominant pattern* at one and the same time. Kroeber quickly agreed and indeed pointed out that the dominant cultural pattern was really the precondition for the display of individuation. Anybody can do the expected, but to do that and still distinguish himself shows the real master.

In my studies at Chicago I learned that social theorists do not ignore this phenomenon, they "merely" underemphasize it. In Georg Simmel's view, an individual's many group affiliations and social roles allow the person to assert himself to a degree, for he is not fully beholden to any one of them. (This prompted me later on to translate "Die Kreuzung der sozialen Kreise," one chapter of his *Soziologie,* which I rendered in English somewhat irreverently as "The Web of Group-Affiliation.") In George Herbert Mead's analysis the organic basis of all behavior allows the person to react in his own terms to the standardized expectations of others. In his approach to role playing, Erving Goffman designates as "role distance" the capacity of the individual to differentiate between his social performance and his own concerns as a separate being. Certainly, much social life runs along customary lines and there are many people whose lives consist in little else; yet even they hold occasional surprises for us. As Tony Tanner has written in his book on Joseph Conrad's *Lord Jim,* incidentally one of my favorite books from my years in Berlin:

But although we are all role players for much of the time we spend with other people, there will obviously be a difference between those people who are unaware of the fact—who disappear into their roles, as it were—and those who are at all times quite aware that the particular role they are performing in any one particular situation is not to be identified as their whole self, that they have facets and dimensions of character which cannot always be revealed on every occasion. The former type of person may sometimes appear to be something of an automaton, incapable of reflection and detachment, while the latter type may often wish to make a gesture of disengagement from the roles he is called upon to play, to indicate that he has not become mindlessly imprisoned in those roles. [Tony Tanner, *The Reign of Wonder* (Cambridge University Press, 1968), p. 253]

Every social theorist of note is aware of this, and it may be more a matter of temperament than of science how much emphasis this individual dimension receives. Yet the drift of social history is to attribute this capacity for "disengagement" to some social force in turn. Emile Durkheim's account of nineteenth-century individualism is a good example, for in his view individualism is as much a byproduct of group pressures (collective representations) as the collectivism and conformity of an earlier time. But even if individualism too is socially caused, that truism does not nullify the phenomenon of individualism. Sociologists not only misrepresent Durkheim but the society they study if they recognize "real social forces" only in collective determinants. Bennet Berger and I argued some years ago for the validity of this dual emphasis in an article entitled "Images of Society and Problems of Concept Formation in Sociology" (Reinhard Bendix, *Embattled Reason* [New York: Oxford University Press, 1970], pp. 193-211).

In Max Weber's work this double emphasis appears explicitly. At the end of *The Protestant Ethic* he states that it is not his aim "to substitute for a one-sided materialistic an equally one-sided spiritualistic causal interpretation of culture and history." This passage has been quoted frequently. But it has not been noted nearly as often that this programmatic declaration is identical with Weber's definition of "action" and "social action" in the first paragraph of *Economy and Society*. The relevant sentence reads: "We shall speak of 'action' insofar as the acting individual attaches a subjective meaning to his behavior—be it overt or covert, omission or acquiescence. Action is 'social' insofar as its subjective meaning takes account of the behavior of others and is thereby oriented in its course." Of course, most of our actions blend "action" and "social action" in Weber's sense of that distinction. But still the distinction remains between our individual capacity to make sense of what we do and our tendency to do that within the framework of what others (but then which others?) expect of us. One may call that capacity the spiritualistic side and our conformity with expectations the materialistic side. The two go together, but this "togetherness"—what Weber often called the unbroken continuity of all gradations—should never be considered an argument against making distinctions.

All this does not seem to have anything to do with political sociology, but it does. After a debate with or about Spengler (I do not remember which), Weber is reported to have said that no one of his generation could reach intellectual maturity without having come to terms with Marx and Nietzsche. Marx and Nietzsche were reductionists, the one considering the organization of production, the other the struggle for survival, the ultimate determinant of human history. Weber devoted much of his attention to the social consequences of economic behavior and organization, but he entitled his last series of lectures in Vienna on the sociology of religion "A Positive Critique of Historical Materialism." And although his emphasis upon the unavoidable struggle between conflicting value positions reveals an influence of Nietzsche's will to power, Weber emphasized (in his first studies of farmworkers in East Elbia) that the desire for emancipation from personal subservience counted for more to these workers than the economic loss they incurred by moving to the city.

At the risk of oversimplifying a complex issue, I shall restate Weber's position in terms of its Marxian and its Nietzschean components. From Marx he took the emphasis on the economy; a great deal of his work is devoted to the causes and consequences of economic behavior. From Nietzsche he took the emphasis on the struggle for survival; a great deal of his work is devoted to showing that men make their history in ever-recurring contention with other men and that in these contentions all sides are prompted by material interests which symbolize the role of force and by ideas and values which point that force in one direction or another. Weber rejects the reductionist philosophy of both Marx and Nietzsche. Neither the organization of production nor the struggle for survival appears to him as an "ultimate determinant," even in the long run. He wants to give equal emphasis to ideas and interests, to social conformity and individual commitment, not because these opposed promptings are ever of equal weight, but because they are ever-present. Weber also rejects the utopianism of a total reorganization of society, whether it be by Marx's proletarian revolution or by Nietzsche's men that are larger than life, his so-called *Uebermenschen,* of whom some echoes are still found in Weber's own concept of charisma. (I have no proper translation of *Uebermensch* since the term *superman* has been preempted by the comic strips and the movies.)

In all of his work, Weber was concerned with the chances of individualism and rational choice in a world of power struggles, bureaucratic organization and capitalist enterprises which militates against these chances. But as I look back, I am most impressed by his anti-utopian approach. It is best not to put a party label on this way of looking at the modern world but to think of Weber's work in more abstract terms. Not the least of the many Weber paradoxes seems to be that by his whole manner he resembled some Puritan divine, if not some Old Testament prophet, who were surely utopians, whereas his whole work tends in an anti-utopian direction. I want to formulate this "message" of Weber's work as I came to perceive it in working my way through his writings.

The personal sense of an individual's action is a force in society, however it may be caused. Social scientists who neglect this part of the evidence abandon the legacies of the enlightenment as do those followers of Marx and Freud who fail to distinguish between caused and unavoidable behavior. Contemporary evidence as well as considerations of intellectual strategy support the old-fashioned view that studies of social determinants must not neglect individual differences. The numerous and often unknown dissenters in fascist Germany and Soviet Russia who have defied these regimes were and are such individualists. When writers and scientists in the Soviet Union prove themselves capable of challenging not only supreme power but also the apparent consensus of the entire population, it seems wrongheaded that some theorists in the West make social forces appear overwhelming. It seems just as wrongheaded for men of ideas to minimize the individual's capacity for innovation, when a full acceptance of that view would destroy the importance these same men attribute to science. I could not be content with these contradictions or with a history of social theory which consists of mutually exclusive emphasis on society and the individual, like a pendulum whose every swing in one direction necessitates an opposite swing of equal amplitude.

In the end, these intellectual impulses led me to my interpretation of Weber's work. It seems to me that Weber promises an end to that swing of the pendulum. He offers an anti-utopian view of the social world which is nevertheless open to its possibilities of development. Karl Loewith put it very well when he wrote some two generations ago:

Even the extreme casuistry of [Weber's] conceptual definitions in *Economy and Society* has not only the meaning to capture and determine reality in definitions, but, at the same time and above all, the opposite meaning of an open system of possibilities. ["Marx and Weber," in *Gesammelte Abhandlungen* (Stuttgart: W. Kohlhammer, 1968), p. 66]

Weber's approach does not lead to a benign view of the human condition, nor does he have all the answers. But his definition of human action encompasses with equal emphasis man's quest for subjective meaning and his compliance with the expectations of others. His definitions of class and status group do the same for man's acquisitiveness and his quest for honor and power over others. His definitions of morality do the same for actions guided by a sense of responsibility for the outcome and those guided by a surpassing conviction which disregards all questions of consequences. Indeed, his writings reveal polarities of this kind so repeatedly that I have come to think of them as the theoretical core of his work. This conceptual device is quite ancient and it is not confined to the Western tradition. But in Weber's hands it acquires two meanings which have been of special importance to me.

One of these consists in a comparative historical perspective not only as a methodological device but as a view of man and society. Every human achievement, every social fact or historical situation allows a conceptual formulation only by emphasizing certain attributes while neglecting or excluding others. Hence every formulation bears within it "the seeds of its own destruction"—a phrase I borrow from Marx which I apply, however, at the conceptual level, a practice he would not have condoned. Accordingly, the study of man and society cannot rest content with the observation of any one set of facts without at least noting their cultural, chronological and other limitations. Sooner or later, such limitations will provoke contrary tendencies, what has been conceptually excluded will reassert itself and before long new constellations will become the focus of attention.

What is here said of conceptual formulations applies to intellectual positions more generally. I think Weber might have agreed, but I just do not know. I think that every intellectual position exacts a price; for every insight that is won, certain other insights are forgone, left out, underemphasized, or whatever the appropriate expression may be. Kenneth Burke once wrote that every way of seeing is a way of not seeing, and that the poor pedestrian capacities of the fish are best accounted for by his excellence as a swimmer. Something like that is at work in Weber's casuistry, his anti-utopian position, his use of comparative historical materials in preserving our sense of the indeterminacy of the human condition. The price Weber paid for his indeterminacy, his openness to human possibilities, which is revealed by his casuistry, by his comparative panorama of man in history, that price consists in Weber's work being a rather poor guide to positive ideals of political structure. Note his emphasis that to him political questions are problems of institutional technology. Note also his comment that no definition of the state can be substantive (he says the definition must be formulated in terms of administrative organization) because that would imply specific policies, whereas history shows that states have pursued all kinds of policies including the most contradictory ones.

But if this is a limitation, then it is also associated with one of Weber's great strengths. By this I mean the dialectic character of his types of domination. Here are interpretations of *charisma* and *bureaucracy* to show that these concepts have a peculiar quality which makes them specifically suitable for the comparative studies which are central in Weber's work.

Let us begin with charismatic authority. We know it is characterized by the extraordinary quality of a personality, but the existence of this quality, and thus the phenomenon of charisma in general, is based on the belief which the person endowed with charisma shares with his followers. This definition gives rise to a peculiar uncertainty: The charismatic personality believes his extraordinary qualities to be derived from objective experiences, as in the case of the prophet who must speak because a higher power compels him to do so. But only the prophet perceives this higher power as an objective experience. To all others this perception seems at first a subjective statement or declaration, until eventually they let themselves be convinced of the extraordinary nature of the prophetic experience. It is a rare occurrence if the consciousness of a prophet and of a mass of people coincide. More often, only the prophet is convinced of his calling and mission, and he finds only a few disciples or believers. It happens still more frequently that a people in need searches for a charismatic personality who could alleviate their suffering; but either none can be found or only a pretender appears, in which case the outcome is that improvements prove illusory or utter despair sets in. You can see that the type of charismatic authority offers in reality a wide field for research and should not simply be vulgarized as a label. The applicability of the concept, as a task for research, should really be universal.

Parallels with other types of authority are easily stated. We know that traditional domination is based on the sancity of partriarchal authority and traditional norms, which include the personal arbitrariness of the master. It may be true that the arbitrariness of the master is limited by tradition; but since everything is based on established usage and oral consent, the limits of arbitrariness are determined only in real life, such that they can be scientifically investigated solely on a case-by-case basis. The problems of the traditional type of domination are the following: The arbitrariness of the master, which is justified in principle, comes into conflict with traditional rights all too easily. Then the question arises whether the subjects remain unconditionally obedient by suffering arbitrary transgressions of traditional rules or when they finally repudiate obedience by invoking ancient rights.

Conditions are similar if we consider the concept of legal domination, with which Weber connects the differentiation of formal and substantive rationality.

Thus these definitions of concepts contain a fundamental vagueness or uncertainty, which can only be removed from case to case by interaction of the ruler with his subjects. It is in this openness to developmental possibilities which are compatible with a type that I see the generalizability of Weber's concepts. As mentioned earlier, this openness makes every ideal type into a research program. This is also the reason why the actual formulation of a concept, like state or class, should come at the end and not at the inception of an investigation, as Weber emphasized at the beginning of his chapter on the *Sociology of Religion*. In this sense the ideal type of the social sciences is at first only an approximation or sketch; its precise meaning can be determined only by means of apropriate investigations.

I would now like to use the concept of bureaucracy to demonstrate a little more fully the historical limitations of a concept as well as its more general applicability. Of course one can, depending on the intentions of the research, stress one or another of these aspects.

Weber points out that he has the specifically modern form of administration in mind. Consequently, "bureaucracy" is limited to Western Europe and even more specifically to Prussia, all the more so as this bureaucracy is understood only as the executive organ of legal authority. The purpose of this historically limited concept is to contrast it to other forms of administration, such as Weber cited, for example, in his analysis of the Chinese bureaucracy. However, Weber's definition of the concept of modern bureaucracy appears in categorical form, which seems to suggest its general applicability. How can one reconcile this general claim with the historical limitation of the concept? I maintain that Weber's concept of bureaucracy also contains a dialectical element.

The well-known formulation seems to present bureaucracy as an "iron cage." Each administrative position is precisely circumscribed by its official duties, a position in the hierarchy, a salary fixed by contract, full-time employment, and so forth. All functions of bureaucratic work seem to be fixed, and yet Weber allows an element of uncertainty to enter even into this "cage." This element is the technical qualification of the official. Technical and bureaucratic qualifications, however, mean nothing else—despite the many examinations and controls—than that one has to rely on the experience and good judgment of the qualified official. The same is true of experts in any other context. The sense of specialized qualification lies in the expertise which the layman can use to his benefit only through consultation or employment of a certified professional. Weber sufficiently stressed the discrepancy between expert officials and political laymen. He also pointed out that technically qualified officials can make a secret out of their knowledge in order to avoid unpleasant or inappropriate controls. Technical qualification means not only technical know-how but also knowledge of official forms, procedures, appeal channels, precedents—all things to which the official has ready access and things which can, as we all know, easily degenerate into a special "technique" of bureaucratic abuse. Thus at the center of Weber's concept of bureaucracy lies an element of uncertainty, which lends itself to specific investigation, as this is the only way we can come to grips with the different meanings of this concept, even *within* the

European cultural sphere.

Having examined some of the ways in which one can speak of a dialectical use of concepts in Weber's work, I want to conclude with a comment on its anti-utopian orientation. Fascism and communism are two versions of the utopian mentality. However dissimilar in ideology, both assume that man and society are subject to total manipulation. If either racial identity or the organization of production is the ultimate determinant of history, then whoever controls these factors is capable of directing history. In both cases the consequences of utopia have been so abhorrent that I, for one, came away with a fundamental distrust of utopianism. To my mind, Weber's conceptual polarities provide a block against utopian tendencies without downgrading the consideration of alternatives. Such considerations are essential, for this is obviously not the best of all possible worlds, but neither is it the worst. Differences between democracy and a one-party dictatorship, between a technology used for benign or malignant ends, make a fundamental difference in our lives, even though many defects remain associated both with democracy and benign technology. But there is a genuine choice between a careful consideration of those differences, on one hand, and a summation of all real defects into one apocalyptic vision. Utopians set so high a goal for the future that nothing present is worth preserving, and it is this all-or-nothing posture which Weber's approach condemns as self-defeating. For if every human condition has limits and invites or provokes countervailing tendencies, then a utopian society is one without limits and hence without alternatives. Weber's whole work shows (though not in so many words) that a society without limits is not a possible human achievement, though he himself notes that aiming for the impossible is sometimes needed to achieve the possible. The point is that utopians militate against the possible by demanding the impossible as the *only rational* course in a *totally irrational* world. Weber's work means to me that it is more human and more predictable to continue our struggle with the imperfections of rationality, that this attitude keeps open more chances for the opportunities of individual choice compared with the prospects of unremitting manipulation. It is for all that a sober view of the human condition, anticipating adversity, and he would not have it otherwise. Sixty years after his death, who can honestly say that he was mistaken?

PART I

Ideology

Liberalism and Conservatism in Max Weber's Political Thought

1

MAX WEBER'S POLITICAL MORALITY

Hans H. Gerth

Since World War II, Max Weber has become as influential and controversial as Karl Marx was before the conversion of the latter's thought into dogma by one-party socialist states. Karl Jaspers, the psychiatrist and existentialist philosopher, saw in Weber "the philosopher of our time." Others have called him the bourgeois Marx. If labels are necessary in this age of slogans, we might call him "the Jeremiah of Imperial Germany."

Ever since his visit to the United States in 1904, Weber deeply feared that Germany, and hence Europe, might well become divided under the respective influences or suzerainty of the United States and Russia. Yet "his existence," to quote Jaspers again, "was support for all those who face the future without illusions, who are active while life is granted them and who are hopeful so long as not all is lost."

Germany is a country with a history of repression, discontinuities and the forgetfulness of its own past. When in 1959 the German Sociological Society celebrated the first half century of its existence, not a single paper was devoted to its founder and most preeminent member. But at the 15th meeting of the Society, in May 1963, a storm of controversy raged over Max Weber and his legacy. Talcott Parsons celebrated Max Weber as the debunker of illusionist habits of thought and as a sociological realist without ideologies. Wolfgang Mommsen, the author of *Max Weber und die Deutsche Politik*, on the other hand, criticized Weber for being a

Lecture given at Hokkaido University, Japan, 1964. Reprinted from *Politics, Character, and Culture: Perspectives from Hans Gerth*. Edited by Joseph Bensman, Arthur J. Vidich, and Nobuko Gerth (Westport, Conn.: Greenwood Press, 1982).

theoretician of "national" and "power" politics. Mommsen thus implied that a politics not concerned with power is possible. It is indeed one of the liabilities of an impotent German liberalism to dichotomize and polarize *Gesinnungspolitik* and *Machtpolitik,* the politics of conscience and power. The latter was attributed to an evil Bismarck and the former to a morally superior but politically impotent liberalism. Mommsen is reported to have surpassed even Raymond Aron, who in his criticism evaluated Weber as a social Darwinist justifying imperialism and the plebescitarian rule of a charismatic leader. Weber allegedly thus prefigured fascism and Hitlerism.

Similarly Herbert Marcuse tended to telescope history by stating "the seizure of power by the bourgeois class means the democratization of the still pre-bourgeois state. The political immaturity of the German middle classes, however, raises a cry for caesarism. Democracy corresponding to capitalistic industrialization threatens to tilt into plebescitarian dictatorship; bourgeois rationality calls forth irrational charisma."

As in the case of Marx, one can, a few decades after his death, read into Weber's work diametrically opposed points of view. Some intellectual historians and ideologists take the position that, since this is true, they can avail themselves of whatever is useful in their predecessors' work for their own use and consign the rest of the work to oblivion. Thus Nikolai Bukharin, in his text *On Historical Materialism,* acknowledged the "mass of valuable" material Weber's work provided him.

Against Marxism, Weber raised the essential objection that Marxism was reductionist, that it views and interprets all cultural phenomena as being expressive of and determined by economic processes and class struggle. Weber rejected this view and maintained the position of causal pluralism in the attempt to explain social and structural phenomena. As an example, Weber argued that European feudalism arose in response to the threat of the armies of crusading Arabian horsemen invading France from Spain.

Weber attributed the rise of the economic basis of feudalism, i.e. economically expendable, rent-based manorial landlords, to the extensive confiscation of church lands by Charles Martell. Martell did this for military reasons. He needed an army of economically expendable but self-equipped knights. These were to displace the then current peasant militia.

In arriving at such an explanation, Weber used the concept of an "unanticipated totality," the idea of structural whole, an ideal type of feudal society, which had specified "requirements." He thus posited a teleological completion of the dimensions entertained in his initial concept.

The same historical phenomenon can be seen as the product of an infinite number of causes, all of which in their own right lead together often to unwilled and unanticipated consequences from the standpoint of their original intentions. Yet when we look backward from the known result, we can see, as in the case of the rise of feudal society, the concatenation of a series of causes leading to a common result. In a purely causal analysis, a thousand and one senseless events, decisions, ideas and subjective intentions would seem to lead to utterly fortuitous and contingent results. And in a purely teleological perspective these would serve the purely unitary *ex post facto* ends of the theorist.

This teleological perspective stood behind Christian teleological faith as it was secularized by Hegel in his philosophy of history and his *Phenomenology of the Mind.* Hegel felt himself to be contemplating the end of history, which he conceived as the progress of man toward reason and freedom. Hence, with the French Revolution and, later, the British Reform Bill of 1832, little of qualitative importance remained to happen before the end of history was achieved. Time, i.e. history, was fulfilled: the World Spirit had all but completed its work.

This Hegelian way of thinking entailed two assumptions. A distinction was made between mere intelligence and reason. Mere intelligence meant only insight into the value of instrumental efficiency and the concatenations of cause and effect. Mere intelligence entails only the knowledge of segments, aspects, of reality and never a conception of the totality of man's fate and experience. Knowledge of the totality requires, under this mode of thought, more than segmental causes of events: It requires an understanding of the meanings of man's estate as a whole.

Hegelian philosophy was, in addition, not oriented to cosmology and nature, not to the objective time of the celestial universe but to time as man experiences it in human history; in his life cycle and in the time spans of social collectivities, including the family, national states and social and cultural systems. It is the time of human memory and hope. While the objective time of the celestial universe is often called chronometric time, time as experienced is called "Kairos," historical time, i.e., the time of human decision. Thus nations have their own heroic time and stretches of time when nothing essential seems to happen or even when time seems to shrink and stand still. During crucial time periods, as during revolutions and war, when national identity and cohesion seems to be at stake, very much seems to happen in so short a time period that time looms large in memory and in the collective organization of memory that is historiography.

Weber, following these aspects of the Hegelian legacy and absorbing a century of work in German social science, saw the diverse causal chains of history culminating in two master trends, rationalization and bureaucratization.

Progressive rationalization had led to industrialism and to the formation of large-scale bureaucracies in increasingly complex business organizations and in the nation state. The latter was the framing organization of the unitary territorial political organization.

He conceived of capitalism as embodying two central dimensions. The first was based upon the organization of legally free labor oriented to the profitable production of goods and in their exchange in a market. Secondly, he saw capitalism as a preindustrial and universal phenomenon oriented to and depending upon political opportunities for profit. The first type accounted for the institutionalization of man's workaday life. It required, Weber emphasized, a rationally calculable and enforceable law, a dynamic technology and science and, hence, the elimination of magic and the dissolution of kinship cohesion.

Weber was convinced that the emergence of capitalism could not be adequately explained in terms of purely economic factors such as the availability of precious metals during the age of discovery and the availability of free labor through the dispossession of the English yeomanry during the enclosure movement when landlords shifted from crop raising to the grazing of sheep.

Weber felt a specific type of man was necessary for modern capitalism to emerge, one who was sober, rational-minded and given to hard work. Magical gifts of grace, i.e., religious dualism in standards had to be abolished in favor of a single standard of Puritan asceticism and to devotion to a workaday life in order to remake the world. Ostentation derived from, among other things, success at work had to be depreciated. This included the devaluation of luxurious living, the reinvestment of funds in rent-yielding landed estates, in race horses, and the purchases of Italian violins during the grand tours of the scions of aristocratic families. What counted was profitable reinvestment in productive enterprises. Piety was the god-willed service to give homeless men and vagrants the god-willed opportunity to prove themselves in their daily life as god-fearing servants pursuing their calling.

Weber's still controversy-provoking study, *The Protestant Ethic and the Spirit of Capitalism,* served, at the beginning of the century, to make essentially these points. His comparative studies of Ancient Eastern civilizations, especially of India, China and the Near East, seemed to fortify his thesis. While in the Oriental civilizations, some individual factors were more favorable to the development of capitalism than in Europe, there was always one or more essential factor lacking. Especially lacking was the training of men for an ascetic vocational way of life in the workaday world.

In contrast to this rational workaday capitalism with its demand for sober rationality, political capitalism, Weber's alternative type of capitalism was age-old and could be found throughout history all over the world. Political capitalism is oriented to securing profit opportunities from government. Examples are the "tax farmers" of ancient Rome, the privileged chartered company like Warren Hastings' East India Company, the venture and booty capitalism of Pizzaro, Columbus, the Fuggers, Cecil Rhodes and the purveyors and purchasers of American government during the Civil and post-Civil War era. Political capitalism, Weber felt, was in his era staging a gradiose revival on the basis of industrialism.

Weber, in the style of classical liberalism, separated politics and economics. He was, however, convinced that the merger of politics and economics was unavoidable in eras of chronic warfare. He further feared that this merger would continue during his time with no accountability to publicly elected and sufficiently strong parliamentary leaders. He strongly criticized emerging romantic glorifications of the "corporate state." He thus criticized fascism

before it emerged. "Propagandists of anti-parliamentary ideas,"
he wrote,

fancy that the state would then be the wise agent controlling business. The
reverse holds. The bankers and capitalist entrepreneurs, so much hated by
them, would become the unrestrained masters of the state. Who in the
world is the state besides this cartel machinery of large and small capitalists
of all sorts, organizing the economy when the state's policy-making
function is delegated to their organizations? . . . The profit interest of
capitalistic producers represented by cartels would then exclusively
dominate the state.

To Weber, the only practical way of organizing an industri-
alized nation under a democratic constitution was through the
competition between the complex bureaucracies of corporate
capitalism and mass organized trade unions, farmers and congeries
of other class interest groups, all under a rational civil service
controlled by a relatively strong and competitively selected party
leadership. It is often forgotten in our telescoping of time that
Weber wished to see a powerful executive leader in control over the
army who was supported by the only party with strength in 1919,
the Social Democratic Party. Weber knew Friedrich Ebert, the
saddle maker from Heidelberg who became the first President of
the Weimar Republic. Weber's concern was to make the office of
President strong enough to safeguard the newly achieved democratic constitution. He also wished the German Republic to have a
sufficiently strong central core to ensure national cohesion at a time
when the particularism of the separate states of Germany threatened to dismember the nation. Finally, Weber hoped to safeguard
Germany from Russian domination. Karl Marx considered Russia
to be the main menace. This posture of both Weber and Marx was
in the tradition of the democratic liberalism of 1848 and was
opposed to the policy of Bismarck and the Junkers.

Weber's attitude to the executive reflects the change in German
liberalism away from such older models as British constitutionalism and French parliamentary democracy to that of the American
solution of presidential responsibility. This, in turn, reflected
Weber's conception of democracy. Weber considered the personal
regime of the Kaiser a great misfortune and a primary cause of
policy blunders contributing to the imperialist division of the
world.

In 1919 Weber examined German political life with a critical eye in order to assess the prospects of democracy. He was a monarchist who felt that hereditary kingship had the advantage of removing the center of national identification from competitive struggles for party leadership. He was a nationalist when young, but ended as a left-wing liberal and as a politically homeless man. He sympathized with the socialists without being a socialist, yet he criticized them for lacking imagination and passion. He dismissed the communists for lacking political realism and, despite their heroic, utopian but self-deluding posture, for wishing to transfer Leninist conceptions of politics into the entirely different political context of Germany.

When the Berlin Soviet, the council of workers and soldiers, was constituted, the soldiers of Potsdam voted for their officers as delegates. The soldiers were peasants and, accordingly, monarchists, conservative and god-fearing haters of Rosa Luxemburg and Karl Liebknecht, the founders of the German Communist Party. Their delegates were not even allowed access to the speaker's platform at the meetings of the Berlin Soviet. Weber considered their slogan, "a united front of workers and soldiers," a deceptive imposition based upon the Russian situation as applied to a German context which had radically different class and loyalty constellations.

The election results in Germany as recorded in the census volumes, published since 1871, would record the relative success of democratic monarchist parties during the 1920s and even during the great depression. These would bear out the conclusion that Weber had a more realistic appreciation of the facts of German political life than that of even high-minded communist intellectuals. One of these was Ernest Toller, who returned from the war in which he, a Jew from Silesia, had volunteered. Toller was a talented communist poet and playwright who in a short time became famous. At the end of the war, when the Communist Party established a Soviet Republic in Bavaria, Toller was its President. A Bavarian regiment returning from France made short shift of the Bavarian Soviet Republic. A thousand Bavarian communists were convicted by a military tribunal and executed. Toller was one of those arrested. Max Weber addressed the military tribunal and succeeded in snatching Toller from the fusillade.

Thomas Mann and Rainer Maria Rilke made depositions for Toller and French socialists pleaded on his behalf, but the soldiers of the tribunal had undoubtedly never heard of Mann and Rilke, nor would they be impressed by French socialists. Weber, on the other hand, donned his officer's uniform and presented himself to the tribunal as an officer of the Imperial Army. He surely knew how to address them. Weber wrote to his wife Marianna, "I had hardly spoken more than ten minutes when the tribunal broke out into laughter. I knew I had won."

Weber as a young man had been a first-rate jurist, and served in the Berlin courts. He knew how to prepare and plead a case; and Toller's death sentence was commuted to confinement in a fortress. In 1933, Toller fled Germany and came to the United States via Holland, but committed suicide in despair in 1939. Toller was one of the many veterans who were students before whom Weber delivered his famous lecture, "Politics as a Vocation."

The Toller defense is only one incident that demonstrates Weber's freedom from anti-Semitism. His circle at Heidelberg included Georg Lukacs, Emil Lederer and Georg Simmel. He repeatedly fought against anti-Semitism and pan-Germanic ideologies on the public platform, in the press and before the German Sociological Association; and he repeatedly opposed the social Darwinist racist interpretations of the events of the time. He considered race, the constancy of nature, a reductionist idea infinitely worse than the reductionism of such Marxists as Karl Kautsky. The latter, Weber allowed, adduced at least a meaningful, changeable order of things into intellectual discourse.

Yet, as we have noted, Weber argued that propositions about causal significance of economic factors had to be determined in their respective situations. As a total explanation of man's estate, economic determinism was to him simply metaphysics.

Weber's overwhelming fear from 1904 onward was that "world power might be divided between the decrees of Russian officials on the one hand and the conventionalism of Anglo-Saxon society on the other with, perhaps, a dash of Latin reason thrown into the latter. To divide world power thusly meant to control the future of cultural development."

The impending defeat of Germany caused Weber to reread the Bible and to write his essays on Ancient Judaism. Weber saw King Solomon's aspirations to act on the stage of world politics with an economically weak base as a vanity comparable to the Kaiser's megalomania during the post-Bismarck period of his "personal regime." The great prophets of doom of the fourteenth to eighth centuries B.C. therefore intrigued Weber especially. In them he discovered the birth of conscience, the inner-directed man. Unlike Freud, he saw this internal mechanism as an acquisition of the mind emerging in a specific historical and social situation of anguish and not as the product of an archaic, prehistoric past based upon the supposed frustration of a band of brothers-in-crime, committing patricide while vying for the love of their mother and subsequently creating the incest taboo.

The Old Testament prophets, whom Weber identified with, acted as solitary men in the name of God. They served as the conscience of their people and their time. They found the inner strength to stand up against false prophets who made their living off religion and who did not have the religious conviction necessary to sacrifice themselves, if need be, for it. John the Baptist made such a sacrifice in the face of the temptations of a dancing Salome. Von Hoffmannsthal and Richard Strauss placed the drama of the prophet and his temptress on the opera stage during this period of Weber's life. But Weber identified most with Jeremiah, the prophet of doom. He envisioned, in anguish, in "Politics as a Vocation," the future of his people as one of a "polar night of darkness."

Yet Weber did not believe in hero worship, nor in a Russian savior. He felt that the age of prophecy was forever past as that of charioteering military heroes and heroism. Similarly he believed that charismatic heroes and saviors belonged to preindustrial societies that had neither rational bureaucracies nor democracies.

Weber felt that revolutionary "cult of reason" taken by Robespierre during the French Revolution was the last genuine form of charisma that had emerged in charisma's fateful course through history. Neither Bismarckism nor Bonapartism appeared to him as genuine charisma. Weber considered modern charisma to be a deception, an apolitical appearing phantasmagoria created by despotic men who were out of step with the demands of an age that was in the process of fundamental democratization. These processes included the downward leveling of feudal nobilities into agrarian capitalists who retained feudal pretensions. It included the upward rise of a broad, literate level of working men in an age of bureaucratic industry and mass armies.

Weber was vehemently opposed to academic men who increasingly exploited their privileged academic positions as pulpits for political prophecies and world views. In the face of this trend Weber advocated the "value neutrality of science." He fought against special pleading in the classroom before captive audiences of intellectually helpless and disarmed students. Weber attempted to separate the role of scholar from that of political man.

Dying in 1920, he was spared the nightmare of the great depression, the rise of totalitarian fascism and nazism with their personality cults of il Duce and Der Fuehrer and their despotic armies and total war.

He died with these words on his lips: "The real thing is the truth."

2

WEBER, THE GERMANS, AND "ANGLO-SAXON CONVENTION": LIBERALISM AS TECHNIQUE AND FORM OF LIFE

Regis A. Factor and Stephen P. Turner

England obsessed the Germans, and academics of bourgeois origin in particular. At the time of the revolutions in 1848, England had everything that Germany did not—a unified nation, an empire and therefore a leading place in world politics, modern industry, a bourgeoisie that shared in ruling the nation, and a legal structure in which a minimum of basic rights were assured. Thus England became a source of inspiration and a model. She also became a source of self-doubt for Germans. It is not too much to say that England produced a form of *ressentiment* in Max Scheler's sense: The Germans, finding the values evident in the English model impossible to achieve in Germany, rejected the model and denied these values or denied that the English had really achieved them. This peculiar braided strand of jealousy, denial, and admiration, mixed with a certain amount of misunderstanding and misinterpretation of English life, runs through German thought from the 1840s to World War II.

Max Weber was a part of this tradition of admiration, misperception, and envy. As a student in Berlin, he attended the lectures of Rudolph Gneist on German state law and Prussian administrative law (Mayer, 1956, p. 27). Gneist, one of the most influential juristic thinkers of the century, was a student of the English constitution and English law, which he presented to Germans as an example from which to learn.

The distinctively German contribution to nineteenth-century liberalism, the idea of the *Rechtsstaat,* grew in part out of meditations on England such as Gneist's. The lesson of England, for these jurists, was that England was a nation of laws, while Germany was a nation of men. The men who ruled in fact were bureaucrats and the police, who were granted a great deal of discretion under the law. The discretion itself appeared to the German liberals to be symptomatic of the lack of freedom in Germany. The remedy appeared to be control over this discretion by law, and this aim was an innovation in the liberal tradition, which had not previously been concerned with restraining a bureaucracy but with controlling a legislature or a monarch (Hayek, 1960, p. 202). The *Rechtsstaat* ideal was put into practice in the 1860s and 1870s in Germany, under the influence of Gneist, by the creation of a system of separate administrative courts with powers of review (p. 201).

The cornerstone of the *Rechtsstaat* had no sooner been laid than the change of intellectual climate that led to the creation of the welfare state and "monarchical socialism" took place. In this climate, the detailed implementation of the idea of the *Rechtsstaat,* which required not just a new judicial structure but the construction of a detailed set of specific rules governing the actions of the bureaucracy (to which legal appeal could be made), was not possible. The new tendency was to widen the loopholes and expand the sphere of discretionary authority to deal with the new tasks of government, thus subverting in practice the original aim of the change. Weber was an unhappy witness to this entire sequence.

WEBER ON THE BRITISH STATE SYSTEM

Like other liberals, Weber never tired of comparing the British system to the German system. To Germans who regarded parliamentary democracy as un-German, he was characteristically contemptuous.

We do not want to hear the nonsensical talk about the contrast between the "West European" and the "German" ideas of the state. We are dealing here with simple questions of [constitutional] techniques for formulating national policies. For a rational politician the form of government appropriate at any given time is a technical question which depends upon the political tasks of the nation. It is merely a regrettable lack of faith in

Germany's potentialities when it is asserted that the German spirit would be jeopardized if we shared useful techniques and institutions of government with other peoples (1978, p. 1383).

He was similarly contemptuous of the social policy views which, according to Hayek, destroyed the *Rechtsstaat* by expanding the role of the state. In his 1895 inaugural address, Weber had complained about the "stereotyped yelping of the ever growing chorus of social politicians of the woods and fields" (1980, p. 447). In his wartime essays he blamed Bismarck, who, he said, "in imitation of certain American practices, believed that he could create a positive attitude toward the state, and political gratitude, by granting welfare benefits out of public funds or compulsory private funds. A grave political error: every policy that ever banked on political gratitude has failed" (1978, p. 1391).

Weber was always quick to remind Germans who had contempt for English political forms of the world power the English state had attained: "Is this a 'night-watchman state' that managed to attach to itself, despite its very small population, the best parts of all continents? How philistine is this hackneyed phrase that betrays so much of the resentment of the *Untertan*" (1978, p. 1407). Parliament in particular, Weber believed, had been a means of attaining the kind of political leadership that enabled Britain to become a great power (1978, p. 1428), and he sought to copy the features which he concluded made parliament a "nursery for leaders." When Weber played an important political role for the only time in his life, as a member of the postwar constitutional commission, he fought for the inclusion of a provision granting powers of investigation to parliamentary committees, which, he believed, was one of the features of the British parliamentary system bearing on the production of leaders.

These borrowings are impressive and have led many readers to mark Weber down as an admirer of the British. But Weber made some important remarks that fit poorly with any simple form of this interpretation. The importance of the remarks is borne out by the fact that Karl Jaspers, who was close to Weber, repeated them over the years. As we will see, they reflect a theme common in the German liberal tradition.

The remarks were made during the war and are Weber's most extensive formulation of his thoughts on the precise nature of Germany's historical task as a world power. It is well to recall that the goal of making Germany a world power is a major theme in his political thought from the start of his career. Weber said that a people organized as a great power had different tasks than peoples like the Swiss, Danes, Dutch, or Norwegians. The Germans have a particular responsibility for the disposition of the future of culture. Today, Weber claimed, the world faces the prospect of being divided up between the "*Reglements* of Russian bureaucrats on the one hand, and the conventions of Anglo-Saxon 'society' on the other, possibly with a little Latin 'raison' added." Because of our weight as a nation, Weber said, we have an obligation to throw ourselves against these two forces. To refuse would be to become Swissified, to become one of the "little peoples" of the world. Such struggle, he said, is the unavoidable demand of great-power status. "Pacificism, after the fashion of American Ladies (of both sexes!) is truly the most fatal cant" (1971, p. 143).

BRITAIN IN WEBER'S WELTPOLITIK

David Beetham objects to the interpretation which claims that Weber's remarks reflect a desire to compete with Russia and England by extending German power, and he has attempted to explain the statements in a way that moderates them. "If it had been the extension of Germany's power, and prestige through power, that had been Weber's goal, one would expect this to have been most clearly demonstrated at the point of Germany's maximum territorial gains, when it seemed that she was winning the war" (Beetham, 1974, p. 139). In fact, Beetham points out, Weber was critical of annexationist demands. He believed that the earlier occupation of Alsace-Lorraine had led to the permanent enmity of the French, and any future attempt at annexation would, similarly, turn out to be a source of weakness and not a source of strength.

Beetham construes this as evidence of maturation from the views of his inaugural speech of 1895, in which peace is described as phony. The mature Weber, Beetham says, believed that war and politics operate differently, and that statesmanship may achieve what war cannot. He remained committed to the value of having Germany count in world politics. But he recognized that this end could best be secured by political alliances. The cultural value that could be achieved through international politics by Germany was the protection of the small states and their cultures. "What," Weber asked, "would become of the independence of the Scandinavians, the Dutch, the people of Tessin, if Russia, France, England, Italy, did not have to respect our armies? Only the balance of the great powers against one another guarantees the freedom of the small states" (quoted in Beetham, 1974, p. 142).

Beetham concedes that this appears to be "merely a plausible rationalization of Germany's involvement in the war" (1974, p. 142). Beetham also concedes that Weber was aware that there were important *Realpolitik* considerations against the proposals of the extreme annexationists. Yet Weber's own proposals were scarcely less extreme. Although he was against any "annexations" and against any German settlement outside German frontiers, he wanted a customs union with Poland, Lithuania, and Latvia, "the right for us to build and garrison fortresses (north of Warsaw), also to build strategic railways; the same conditions for Austria south of Warsaw" (quoted in Mayer, 1956, p. 75).[1] For the west, he proposed permanent military occupation of Luxembourg; occupation for a period of twenty years of Liege and Namur until Belgium fortified and defended Ostend and her southern frontier. As Mayer remarks, "It is open to doubt whether Weber's war aims were *de facto* much different as compared with the war aims of the *Alldeutsche*. More subtle they certainly were" (Mayer, 1956, p. 75).

FREEDOM AND CULTURE IN WEBER'S IMAGO MUNDI

Weber repeated the slogan that pictures German culture as threatened by Russia and England and varied it in other contexts; Jaspers recalled it years later as "the Russian whip and Anglo-Saxon convention" and wrote as if it was at the center of Weber's political *imago mundi* (1957, pp. 55-56). The slogan derives from Treitschke's "Russian knout and the English money bag," and in his time, the slogan divided the Anglophiles from the Anglophobes. Although Treitschke was not, many of the older generation of liberals, including Theodor Mommsen and Lujo Brentano, were admirers of the English. Those in Weber's generation, and especially Weber's politician friend Naumann, were bitterly anti-English.

"If anything in world history is certain," Naumann wrote in 1900, after coming under Weber's influence, "it is the future world war, that is, the war of those who seek to save themselves from England" (quoted in Sheehan, 1966, p. 184). Such sentiments were a constant source of friction during the brief time of Brentano's political cooperation with Naumann. In 1907 Naumann told Brentano, "I want to remain in harmony with you but there are things about which almost the entire younger generation [i.e. the generation including Weber and Meinecke] thinks differently." Brentano was more of an Anglophile than the "younger generation," and this generational shift in Germany liberalism was a significant development. But Brentano, for all his admiration for the English, was not free of these ideas. He too expressed fear of the "transfer of the center of culture to the United States and the hegemony of Russia in Europe" (Sheehan, 1966, p. 187).

Such fears were part and parcel of the nineteenth-century German liberal tradition. The image of the world contained in the slogan had gradually become a standard element of the German political semiotic, and, by the late date at which Weber appealed to it, it was freighted with distinctive associations. A standard formulation, complete with the main associations, might be this: Germans are free, individual, and heroic in character; Russians, Anglo-Saxons, and Americans are slavish, unheroic, materialistic and rationalistic mass men. Sombart's claim in *Heroes and Hawkers,* that the English are a vulgar and nonheroic mass, captures part of this complex of images; the notion that the English are inner slaves captures still more. Brentano, as we have seen, substituted the Americans for the English, and this too eventually became more common. In the 1920s Count Keyserling spoke of the "extraordinary likeness between Bolshevik Russia and America. The difference actually amounts to a mere difference of language: the spirit is the same. . . . Both countries are basically socialistic. . . . the rule of the animal ideal" (1929, pp. 252-53). When Weber and Jaspers appealed to these cultural images, they were understood in terms of and as part of this tradition. Moreover, their fears of the loss of heroism or individual greatness in a mass, bureaucratic society had the effect of sharpening their denunciations of the Russian and Anglo-Saxon cultural alternatives, since these peoples were widely believed to be unheroic: in the case of the English, inner slaves; in the case of the Americans, "mass men."

Martin Heidegger appealed to a similar world image in some of his few political remarks. In his 1935 lectures, published as An *Introduction to Metaphysics,* Germany appears as the small but spiritually great nation caught between the culturally void colossi of America and Russia. These are, he said, "metaphysically the same, namely in regard to their world character and their relation to the spirit" (1961, p. 37), and this sameness consists in the fact of the demonic influence of "technology" over these nations. Technology is Heidegger's portmanteau term for the scientized ordering of the life world. Under it he would include bureaucracy, and thus there is a close similarity to Weber. When Weber spoke of the threats to freedom, it was the inevitable rise of bureaucracy that he regarded as the greatest threat, and this gives us an inkling of what he meant by *freedom.*

In Heidegger's later works, man's enslavement to technology is taken as a matter of fate, and liberalism is held to be a last foolish gasp before the total negativity of Marxism engulfs us. But Heidegger once considered national socialism to be a viable protest against this "darkening of the world," and he wrote of the world situation in a way that suggested that it was Germany's destiny (and perhaps responsibility, as the only truly philosophic modern nation) to make this protest. In the *Introduction to Metaphysics* he described "the inner truth and greatness of" national socialism in the framework of these ideas about the darkening of the world and in a parenthetical comment which was perhaps inserted later, the inner greatness of national socialism is said to be bound up with "the encounter between global technology and man" (1961, p. 166). Weber, of course, would not have seen any point to a "protest" against fate.

WEBER ON ENGLISH FREEDOM

One variant of the tradition of thinking of Germany as possessing a distinctive spirit held that Prussianism was the repository of this distinctive spirit. This variant was, however, more smug than aggressive or apocalyptic. In the light of what we have said about the peculiar mixture of feelings of admiration and envy for the English, it is interesting to note that Weber, who absolutely rejected the self-characterizing claims of Prussianism, did so by a comparison to the English.

Despite the occasional boasting of our literati, it is completely untrue that individualism exists in Germany in the sense of freedom from conventions, in contrast to the conventions of the Anglo-Saxon gentleman or of the Latin salon type of man. Nowhere are there more rigid and compelling conventions than those of the German "fraternity man." (1946, p. 390)

Weber in fact praised the English club, which, he suggested, is selective, but once a person is a member relations are governed by a strict principle of equality of gentlemen, in contrast to the "principle of pennalism" (1946, p. 388).[2] This does not amount to rejection, on Weber's part, of the ideal of freedom and individuality the Prussians claimed to meet, and it implicitly accepts the idea that the English lack inner freedom because of their conventions. But in contrast to Jaspers, he made occasional remarks that suggested something quite different—that the English had "inner strength" as individuals that the Germans did not. And this makes for a paradox.

On the one hand, Weber seems to have regarded the English as unfree. Weber, like Jaspers, hated cages or shells (cf. Turner, 1982), and when, in the face of this long German tradition, he spoke of "Anglo-Saxon convention" as a threat to be fought, one supposes that he thought of convention as a shell, as much a fetter and cage as any other. So to understand Weber we must distinguish two kinds of freedom: freedom that is strangled by convention; and freedom that is consistent with convention.

Weber repeatedly recognized English *political* freedom as a fact. In *The Protestant Ethic,* he quoted Montesquieu's remark that the English "had progressed the farthest of all peoples of the world in three important things: in piety, in commerce, and in freedom" and asked whether their commercial superiority and their adaptation to free political institutions are connected in some way with that record of piety which Montesquieu ascribed to them (1958, p. 45). He clearly believed that there was a connection, for he later remarked on

the relative immunity of formerly Puritan peoples to Caesarism, and, in general, the subjectively free attitude of the English to their great statesmen as compared with many things which we have experienced since 1878 in Germany positively and negatively. On the one hand, there is a greater willingness to give the great man his due, but, on the other, a repudiation of all hysterical idolization of him and of the naive idea that political obedience could be due anyone from thankfulness. (1958, pp. 224-25)

He found a theological basis for this "immunity" in Puritan views "on the sinfulness of the belief in authority, which is only permissible in the form of an impersonal authority, the Scriptures, as well as of an excessive devotion to even the most holy and virtuous of men, since that might interfere with obedience to God" (1958, p. 225). These views, as he was aware, differed from Lutheran opinions, which gave theological ratification to secular authority and the authoritarian state.

Yet Weber was rarely directly interested in freedom in the political sense. Typically his concern was with leadership as well—"the willingness to give the great man his due." It is noteworthy that Cromwell so interested Weber. He also interested Carl Schmitt, for reasons that derive from a common German perception of Cromwell as a great dictator. Schmitt finds Cromwell's deep hatred of Spain to be the key to his greatness, for by defining Spain as "foe" and orienting his whole being to the struggle against Spain, he created English world power. Weber saw in Cromwell a lesson about the connection between freedom, power, and leadership. He said that "Puritanism enabled its adherents to create free institutions and still become a world power" (1958, p. 261). To be a world power required leadership—great men given their due—and Puritanism, Weber thought, made disciplined obedience possible without the surrender of a "subjectively free attitude."

The striking thing about these comments on the English is that they do not suggest that Weber saw England as an example of the process of attaining political freedom that Germany could imitate. The free attitudes of the English are not, as Weber described them, a matter of political forms but of the religious endowment of Puritanism. This endowment cannot be readily acquired in any other way. So what Weber has given us amounts to a theory of Anglo-Saxon exceptionalism. There is no force like Puritanism which can be hoped to transform Germans, and hoping for such a force would be utopian. Perhaps political education, experience of political responsibility, and the development of a certain restraint and reserve in public life which could be imitated by the citizenry might, taken together, produce results similar to the effects of a Puritan heritage—but this would have been an extremely optimistic view, and uncharacteristically so for Weber, who was a great pessimist. So one can scarcely attribute to Weber the expectation that political education would have had any but the most superficial effects, at least on something as fundamental as the attitudes necessary for full political freedom.

Thus, England could not have figured as a model for the attainment of freedom in the sense of political freedom. Nevertheless, Weber attempted to borrow particular English state forms. If political freedom was not his aim, what was it? What *did* he expect as the consequences of the borrowing of these techniques? These questions may best be answered indirectly.

THE PROBLEM OF BORROWING: SPENGLER'S CRITIQUE

We have quoted Weber's remarks on those who objected to the borrowing of English institutions. What were their objections, and how do their views compare with Weber's?

The most famous formulation of the argument against borrowing is undoubtedly Spengler's famous pamphlet of 1920, *Prussianism and Socialism.* Spengler's attack was directed at unnamed Germans who wished to impose English institutions on Germany, among whom Weber must be numbered. The recently promulgated constitution had a number of English parliamentary features, some of which Weber specifically promoted. For Spengler, these institutions were contrary, indeed antithetical, to the German national character. So he attacked the individuals who fostered the Weimar order in terms of the general contrast between the Prussian and the English character. Much of what Spengler said is on the polemical order of Sombart's *Heroes and Hawkers.* But Spengler, unlike Sombart, was able to see the moral and religious foundations of English political life quite clearly, for Spengler had doctrinal reasons for supposing that the political ideas of nations "were the purest and most extreme expression of their wholly personal and immutable patterns of life" (1967, p. 16).

Representative assemblies in Germany, Spengler observed, are glorified beer gardens (1967, p. 7), in which the liberals especially have a taste for fomenting ideological dramas (p. 45). In Weimar, under the first Socialist government, this led to a whole political style. "Every day," Spengler said, "we can take our pick among massacres of Western capitalists—on the editorial pages" (p. 23). None of this is characteristic of the English parliamentary order. The English, he said, act without drama, and the parties are led by those who can act (p. 12). But they conduct themselves as gentlemen and can settle momentous disputes by means of private conversation and private correspondence (p. 73). The parties act in a good deal of secrecy, and their decisions involve the "dictatorial domination" of the few, but this is understood by the electorate, which elects a party to act on their behalf, not a "representative" of their will (p. 75). An Englishman, when he ignores politics, does so knowing that his interests will be cared for. The German who ignores politics does so with a feeling of complete apathy. When a Prussian or German has made use of the vote, it has often been "merely his way of expressing a vague annoyance" (p. 83).

"With us," Spengler said, "parliamentarism will always be a conglomeration of externals" (1967, p. 83). While the outer trappings of government can be chosen, the essential things cannot. In England, parliament governs according to unwritten laws evolved through long practice (p. 21). To put practices, such as the sovereignty of party leaders, into effect, one would have to be English by instinct and have mastered the English style (p. 9). The English style, Spengler observed, is deeply rooted in the English moral and religious tradition. The English Independent created a lay religion using the Bible in which one was externally free to interpret the text as one wished. Enormous self-assurance in action followed from this, as in the ruthlessness of Cromwell's soldiers who nevertheless saw themselves as a community of saints (p. 52).

Work, for the Independent, was a consequence of the Fall. For the Prussian, it is a calling, a vocation (Spengler, 1967, p. 54). For the Prussian, duty becomes the essential moral concept. In the Prussian system of obligations, it was possible to have a supreme independence of inner life. The English, in contrast, tended to have uniform tastes and a sense of common interests (p. 46). Spengler repeated the common view that this means that the English, while practically free, are profoundly superficial and are inner slaves (p. 50).

The political implications of these differences are crucial: A system like England's, which relies on private initiative and a weak state, "implies extreme independence of mind" (Spengler, 1967, pp. 54-55); a tradition in which duty is the supreme moral concept necessarily differs. The motto, " 'Do your duty by doing your work,' " Spengler said, "is for the few who wish to inject it into the community and thus force it upon the masses" (p. 54). So politics in a tradition based on "duty" aims to make the will of the individual subject to the will of the totality (p. 84). The German liberals, he pointed out, are not themselves free of this tradition: "Beneath the *Bratenrock* of the German liberal is a heart that still beats to the languid rhythm of the old *Reich,* and a soul that deplores the realities of modern civilization" (p. 86).

Spengler's prognosis for the then new Weimar order was grim. The constitution, he said, is already doomed. Parliamentarism, which requires such tact, is breaking down even in England, where it is strongest. In England, the traditions necessary for a parliamentary order cannot withstand the coming struggle between rich and poor. "The relationship between party leaders and party, between party and masses, will be tougher, more transparent, and more brazen. That is the beginning of Caesarism" (Spengler, 1967, p. 89). Weber agreed with much of this, and particularly with Spengler's remarks on what Weber called the exhibitionism of German politics.

Spengler and Weber also agreed about the workings of the English parliamentary system—about the rule of the few, the ability of the leaders, who know how to act. Their characterizations sharply differ from Anglo-American perceptions. Bryce, for example, held that democracy was "government by discussion" and considered England to be an example of this. Woodrow Wilson saw the House of Commons as a marvelous debating society—and founded debating societies in American colleges in imitation of it (cf. Eden, 1983). Weber and Spengler saw the Commons as a case of the rule of the few and control exercised privately, rather than the achievement of consensus through discussion. Cromwell interested them both for the same reasons, for his ruthlessness and the self-assurance of his followers—i.e., as a dictator. Both saw a religious foundation to the English form of political life. But here some interesting differences between the two become evident.

Weber had a peculiarly abstracted view of the conventions that make English liberal government possible. For Weber, the effect of religion is interiorized and psychological. So he treated the conventions as somehow distinct from the religious inheritance, rather than something in which the religion is, to use T. S. Eliot's language, "incarnated" (1968, p. 106). At the same time, he separated the political techniques—the liberal forms of state—from the conventions. Today we have the dubious benefit of having observed the failure in practice of many constitutions copied from the American model, and we are perhaps less inclined to separate techniques of rule from political traditions. But this was equally evident, before Weber's time, to such writers as Taine and Bagehot, who objected specifically to the notion that British forms could be transplanted to nations with different customs and traditions.

Weber is strangely sanguine on this issue. German political parties, he said,

produce from their midst responsible leaders, rather than mere demagogues and dilettantes. Parliament must be completely reorganized in order to produce such leaders and to guarantee their effectiveness; in their own way, the British parliament and its parties have long been successful in this regard. It is true that the British conventions cannot simply be taken over, but the basic structure can very well be adapted (1978, p. 1428).

For Spengler, this is a kind of butchery. Parliamentarism "without the conventions," as it would be in Germany, would be merely the enthronement of the beer garden—and for the short term, Spengler's prediction was correct. Weber hoped that the possession of political responsibility by parliament would itself lead to a political tradition of sorts, one that valued facing facts, cooperation, and rational conduct. He believed that suitable "procedures and conventions . . . will become apparent as soon as the parties are forced to pursue responsible politics" (1978, p. 1428). These words were written in wartime. In the postwar period, Weber seems to have abandoned the naive hope that parliament would come naturally to conduct itself in a responsible fashion. In this period he hedged his bets by suggesting the strengthening of the office of the president.

LIBERAL FORM
WITHOUT LIBERAL "CONVENTIONS"

Did Weber have a blind spot that prevented him from noticing and understanding the political significance of custom and convention? Or was his borrowing of liberal techniques of parliamentary and constitutional structure motivated by the expectation that these techniques, in the German setting, would produce a particular kind of regime that would be illiberal in substance because it was driven by the politics of charismatic competition between candidates for an office that was a de facto dictatorship?

The blind spot is evident in contexts other than politics. A large part of the literature in the sociology of complex organizations has been devoted to the criticism of the rigidity and limited applicability of Weber's conception of bureaucracy even to those organizations that aspire to maximal efficiency and rationality. On the theoretical level, Weber's account of bureaucracy contrasts to such figures as the great American theorist of bureaucracy C. I. Barnard, who placed enormous emphasis on "informal organization" and "organizational morals" and sharply questioned the notion of the "authority" of the executive (Wolf, 1974, pp. 71-72, 106-08, 118-21). No place is given in Weber's discussion for such considerations, because the focus is exclusively on what might be called the spoken and written rules, and the pheonomenon of discipline, as against the unspoken practices and traditions: But rules and bureaucratic technique do not necessarily outweigh and render irrelevant the unwritten portion of practice.

Weber told us what he expected to be the consequences of the borrowing of particular techniques of rule. These expectations, however, were mixed with misunderstandings of the way the techniques worked in their original American and English settings. Weber believed that the English system was in effect a dictatorship.

Nowhere in the world, not even in England, can the parliamentary body as such govern and determine policies. The broad mass of deputies functions only as a following for the leader or the few leaders who form the government, and it blindly follows them *as long as* they are successful. *This is the way it should be.* Political action is always determined by the "principle of small numbers," that means, the superior political maneuverability of small leading groups. In mass states, this caesarist element is ineradicable. (1978, p. 1414)

This element, he believed, was increasing in significance.

In the United States, equal suffrage has resulted time and again in the election, as lord mayor, of a popular trustee who was largely free to create his own municipal administration. The English parliamentary system equally tends toward the development of such caesarist features. The prime minister gains an increasingly dominant position toward parliament, out of which he has come. (1978, p. 1415)

This was an error: If there has been such a tendency in English or American politics, it has been constrained or overbalanced by other opposing tendencies.

Weber construed as "caesarist" or charismatic a set of political relations between politicians and citizens that were, in America and England, governed by convention and a code of political morality, which sharply limited the autonomy of these new "Caesars." Perhaps this misinterpretation influenced Weber's belief that the rise of a new prophet, a leader with the power which Hitler proved to possess, was not possible under modern circumstances. Perhaps it also led him to ignore the traditional liberal concern with the limitation of executive power. His constitutional proposals enhanced and expanded the power of the president, in part because he believed that the principle of charisma—in its struggle with bureaucratization, which he feared above all—needed all the help it could be given. With this step the good of a liberal democracy was interred—and the evil allowed to live on after.

NOTES

1. Beetham blandly describes this condition of permanent military occupation in these terms: Germany would need to guarantee for herself the security of the northeast frontier against Russian threats (1974, p. 141). What Weber's proposal actually amounts to is a satellite status for Poland not unlike its current relation to Russia. Naumann envisaged something similar in his *Mitteleuropa.* Weber's lack of interest in annexations thus probably reflects a fear of the dilution of German nationhood rather than

any interest in the freedom of small nations.

2. Pennalism was a system of fagging practiced on freshmen in German Protestant universities.

REFERENCES

Beetham, D. 1974. *Max Weber and the theory of modern politics.* London: Allen & Unwin.

Eden, R. 1983. *Political leadership and nihilism: A study of Weber and Nietzsche.* Tampa: University Presses of Florida.

Eliot, T. S. 1968. *Christianity and culture: The idea of a Christian society* and *Notes towards the definition of culture.* New York: Harcourt Brace Jovanovich/Harvest Book.

Hayek, F. A. 1960. *The constitution of liberty.* Chicago: University of Chicago Press.

Heidegger, M. 1961. *An introduction to metaphysics.* Garden City, N.Y.: Anchor.

Jaspers, K. 1957. Philosophical autobiography. In P. A. Schilpp (Ed.), *The philosophy of Karl Jaspers.* New York: Tudor.

Keyserling, H. 1929. *America set free.* New York: Harper & Brothers.

Mayer, J. P. 1956. *Max Weber and German politics* (2d ed., rev. and enl.). London: Faber & Faber.

Sheehan, J. J. 1966. *The career of Lujo Brentano.* Chicago: University of Chicago Press.

Spengler, O. 1967. *Selected essays* (D. O. White, Trans.). Chicago: Henry Regnery.

Turner, S. P. 1982. Bunyan's cage and Weber's casing. *Sociological inquiry, 52,* 84-87.

Weber, M. 1946. *From Max Weber: Essays in sociology* (H. H. Gerth & C. W. Mills, Eds.). New York: Oxford University Press.

————. 1958 *The Protestant ethic and the spirit of capitalism.* New York: Scribner's Sons.

————. 1971. *Gesammelte politische schriften* (3d ed., rev.) (J. Winkelmann, Ed.). Tubingen: Mohr.

————. 1978. *Economy and society: An outline of interpretive sociology* (G. Roth & C. Wittich, Eds.) (3 vols.). Berkeley: University of California Press.

————. 1980. The national state and economic policy (Freiburg address). *Economy and Society, 9,* 428-449.

Wolf, W. B. 1974. *The basic Barnard: An introduction to Chester I. Barnard and his theories of organization and management.* ILR Paperback No. 14. Ithaca, N.Y.: New York School of Industrial and Labor Relations, Cornell University Press.

3

MAX WEBER AND THE POSSIBILITIES FOR DEMOCRACY

Ernest Kilker

The inadequacy of all of the reigning accounts of Weber's political sociology and eventual advocacy of plebiscitarian democracy pivots on their failure to integrate fully his comparative historical sources and their relationship to the rest of his work. The effort here will be to demonstrate that Weber's political reasoning was not simply a product of Germany's immediate situation or Weber's supposed bourgeois values. Weber's espousal of plebiscitarian democracy and monocratic bureaucratic administration is a result of the logic and the cumulative evidence explicit in his depth historical sociology of law and sociology of domination. That evidence and logic draw certain parallels between ancient and medieval political predicaments and the situation of modern Germany.

THE COLLAPSE OF NATURAL LAW LEGITIMATION

In line with Weber's radical nominalism, his formal typology of legitimate rulership focuses on legitimacy as claimed, rather than legitimacy as believed.[1] To the extent that there is a probability in fact that social action will be guided by a belief in the existence of a legitimate order, to that degree an order may be viewed as valid. Validity rests on voluntary obedience and compliance, in a word, on consent. Actual consent may rest on a wide variety of motives, including fear, coercion, the expectation of material benefits or prestige, habit, convention or the sheer lack of a compelling alternative. Regardless, every regime, no matter how structured, seeks to cultivate a belief, no matter how formed, in its legitimacy. Weber lists four and later three "inner justifications" for compliance. The former reads as follows:

The actors may ascribe legitimacy to a social order by virtue of:

  a. tradition: valid is that which has always been;
  b. affectual, especially emotional, faith: valid is that which is newly revealed or exemplary;
  c. value rational faith: valid is that which is deduced as an absolute;
  d. positive enactment which is believed to be legal.

Such legality may be treated as legitimate because:

  a. it derives from a voluntary agreement of the interested parties;
  b. it is imposed by an authority which is held to be legitimate and therefore meets with compliance.[2]

These formal grounds of legitimacy correspond to traditional, charismatic, natural law, or democratic and legal forms of authority. However, in later presentations, the original four bases of legitimacy are conspicuously reduced to three.[3] "Value rational faith" (for example, democracy and natural law) is dropped from the later discussion, a fact of enormous theoretical and practical significance. As Weber argued, natural law, which underpinned the usurpation and eventual constitutionalization of subjective rights inhering in individuals, was the last of the cosmological justifications which sought to curb or to supplant the positive law of the sovereign by appeal to the higher eternal order of nature and reason.[4] It is in the name of this higher order, in lieu of religious norms or revelation, that revolting groups regardless of their political or religious persuasion made their claims: "We hold these truths to be self-evident, that all men are created equal and are endowed with certain inalienable rights." Natural law variants also provided the philosophical foundation of economic freedom.

As Weber was quick to point out, the ideal claims of natural law lagged far behind its actual influence on conduct. Instead of being purely "rational," it became, in large part, instrumentally expedient. Class relations in natural law ideology reflected the substantive justification of inequality rather than the formal rationalistic freedom of contract.

THE COLLAPSE OF DEMOCRATIC LEGITIMATION

What about democracy? According to Weber, the power to command may appear in "innocent garb," as if the ruler were a mere servant of the people.[5] This phenomenon is seen in its purest form in so-called *immediate* democratic administration. The form of administration is called democratic for two reasons:[6] first, all are considered equally qualified to conduct public affairs; second, the scope of command is kept to a minimum. Administrative roles are rotated or determined by lots or assigned for short periods. All important decisions are reserved for the determination of the whole group. The current administration need only prepare and carry out resolutions and current business in accord with the instructions of the general assembly.

According to Weber, this kind of administration occurs under the following conditions: The organization must be local or otherwise limit the number of members, the social positions of the members must not differ, the administrative functions must be relatively simple and stable, and there must be a certain minimum development of objectivity determining ways and means.[7]

However, as soon as a democratic administration is made the object of political struggle, it loses its most attractive feature—its minimal amount of domination.[8] A political party, after all, is an organization whose very purpose is to fight for the powers of domination, and consequently it *internally* assumes a dominational structure, no matter how hard it tries to conceal this fact.

In sum, Weber argued that the universal political subject of immediate democracy is not possible except in small closed communities of social equals. Immediate democracy and government by amateurs are inadequate beyond a certain limited size.[9] Direct democracy is an unstable structure. Every development toward economic differentiation increases the probability that political administration will fall into the hands of the wealthy.[10] Their capacity for political action is based on the fact that they are "economically care-free." Further, once a group grows beyond a certain size, administrative needs cannot be satisfied by rotation, lot, or anyone an election might designate. As Weber put it, "As soon as mass administration is involved, the meaning of democracy changes so radically that it no longer makes sense for the sociologist to ascribe to the term the same meaning as in the case discussed so far.[11]

It is necessary at this point to follow Weber's historical examples, in which democracy was seen as more than a mere means but as an end in itself, a way of life, a total ethic. The examples he lists include the Greek polis, the early Italian city-states, and the Swiss cantons.[12] Yet, in each instance, democracy as a "value rational" faith gave way under the simultaneous strain of class and status struggle and the need for continuous administration to the "law of the small number"—rule by a plebiscitarian leader, a group of notables, or hereditary oligarchy.

In ancient Greece, initially, law was the charismatic creation of law prophets, but "before long" new law was that of the *ekklesia* (assembly). In Athens, the *demos* was actually asked each year whether new laws should be maintained or amended.[13] Democracy, as an end in itself, as a "value rational" idea, as the "rule of the people," was here instituted in one of its historically purest forms. However, and for Weber this is historically decisive, the real political leader created by the fully developed democracy in Periclean Athens was the demagogue.[14] The demagogue's power rested not upon law or office but entirely upon personal influence and the trust of the *demos*. Such a leader's position was neither "legitimate" nor "legal," though the entire constitution of the otherwise leaderless democracy was tailored to his existence. The "demagogue," once a respectable orator presenting questions for deliberation to the people, now took on his familiar modern meaning—a rabble rouser promising anything in order to achieve power.

Turning to the examples of the medieval urban communes, Weber noted that the medieval city was a condition of possibility for both modern capitalism and the modern state.[15] It also provided comparative historical reasons for Weber's pessimistic views on the technical limits of the historical possibility of direct or immediate democracy. Again, he argued that the universal political subject of immediate democracy is not possible except in small closed communities of social equals. Immediate democracy and government by amateurs is inadequate beyond a certain limited size; any "rationalization of interaction" inevitably leads in an authoritarian direction

—the law of small numbers, the iron rule of oligarchy.[16] The introduction or realization of gross economic and social inequality, the
increase in the complexity of administration, changes in the means
of warefare, the demands of everyday economic life, the confrontation with and possible contribution of religious authority, the
appeal of a Caesar to small tradesmen and workers—all are recurrent Weberian political themes, and all contributed to the demise of
the medieval urban commune.

In addition, it must be recalled that, although most communes at
their outset paid lip service to political equality and the general
assembly, these formless bodies, usually instigated by resident
nobles or rich burghers, quickly gave way to consuls, again usually
nobles or rich burghers, who had the time and the confidence to
organize and to act. The general assembly remained, but as an
echo, not a voice—the public's only choices being acclamation or
riot.[17]

Democracy rapidly gave way to a hereditary oligarchy which,
lacking a broad base of support, was forced to yield considerable
power to an impartial and imported *podesta*. The *podesta* was an
elected official "called" in from another community to solve the
problem of unity. In fact, it was the institution of the *podesta*
which led to the propagation of Roman law in Italy. In order that a
foreign-born *podesta* might administer justice, it was necessary that
the applicable law be codified, rationally elaborated, and inter-
locally somewhat standardized.[18]

The *popolo,* an alliance of professional associations or "arts,"
formed in self-defense against the ruling oligarchy. It formed a
subcommunity which was run by the *capitano popoli*, with help
from representatives of the guilds. When the *popolo* achieved
political dominance in the commune as a whole, it attempted in
turn to exclude the nobility from the exercise of political power and
legal rights. The end result of this process was rule by a tyrant.

In the case of the Swiss cantons, the rule is still democracy—a
show of hands on everything from the election of a cantonal president to the passing of a new law. But even in this case, if you look
at the lists of presidents, you find that certain families have
controlled these offices from "time immemorial."[19] Although a
democracy in law, these cantons are actually run aristocratically,

because not everyone can take an office without ruining themselves professionally. In the case of Zurich, the solution to the problem of status struggle was again the plebiscitary leader, "as if Zurich was imitating the Italian system of *podestas*."[20]

As a democrat, Weber was a pragmatic liberal. Democracy was a method and a means: it was not an end in itself. It was a method of selecting leaders, and it was a means both of giving their rule an aura of legitimacy and of including all politically significant segments of the population in the political affairs of the nation. However, it was not the proper means for deciding ordinary political issues. Such issues inevitably required *compromise* arrived at through negotiation rather than a vote.[21] The classical democratic doctrine, as we have already thoroughly demonstrated, was hardly one Weber could "believe" in. The theory of the "sovereignty of the people," the "will of the people," the "wisdom of the people," were all utopian fictions whose desire was the abolishment of the dominance of men over men—in Weber's view, a this-worldly impossibility.

PROBLEMS OF FORMAL LEGAL LEGITIMATION

The basis of legal authority rests on rational grounds, including a belief in the "legality" of patterns of normative rules and the right of those elevated in authority to issue commands. Every body of law consists essentially in a consistent system of abstract rules, which are applied to particular cases.[22]

However, according to Weber, such a procedural justification is hardly as compelling as the old natural law conceptions:

In consequence of both juridical rationalism and modern intellectual skepticism in general, the axioms of natural law have lost all capacity to provide the fundamental bases of a legal system. Compared with firm beliefs in the positive religiously revealed character of a legal norm or in the inviolable sacredness of an age-old tradition, even the most convincing norms arrived at by abstraction seem to be too subtle and highly intellectualized to serve as the bases of a legal system. The disappearance of the old natural law conceptions has destroyed all possibility of providing the law with a metaphysical dignity by virtue of its immanent qualities. In the great majority of its most important provisions, it has been unmasked all too visibly indeed, as the product of technical means of a compromise between conflicting interests.[23]

THE PLEBISCITARIAN LEADER

In his discussions of state administration, ostensibly in the service of the irrational values of a nation, Weber's sociological work is a litany extolling the advantages of monocratic bureaucratic administration.[24] In the process, his critique of direct democracy and deliberative collective discussion is brutally pessimistic and unsparing. Calculability and technical rationality become a major yardstick by which all political processes are measured, the definitive standpoint from which everything else is assessed.[25] Monocratic bureaucratic administration is indispensable for the needs of mass administration. The only choice, as Weber structures it, is between bureaucracy and dilettantism. Only by reversion in every field—political, religious, and economic—to small-scale organization would it be possible to any considerable extent to escape the influence of bureaucracy.[26] The principle of collegiality which was ostensibly advanced as a means to promote objectivity and integrity in leadership had, as Weber saw it, everywhere given way to the technical superiority of monocratic organization.

But what of the potential power of the average individual political subject in the categorical framework of Weber's political sociology? It is fair to say that the possibility of such a subject is eclipsed from the outset. Rather, there are only inactive and normally inert masses who, in terms of party politics and the play of interests, are merely objects of solicitation—so many votes on election day.[27]

Consequently, the proposal of the plebiscitarian leader as the solution to Germany's problems of order and unity and his positioning on the top of the bureaucratic administration was not based on Weber's "personal values" or short-term trends, or a desperate turn in response to the haggling of parliamentary committees during the first few weeks of parliamentary rule in Germany, or a political imitation of Nietzsche's *übermensch*. Rather, it was based on the comparative historical evidence, as Weber saw it. However, Weber expected his plebiscitarian leader to obey the law. The plebiscitarian leader would sit on top of a monocratically run bureaucratic administration, itself resting on a system of formal legality. The leader would be elected directly by the people to whom he would be directly responsible. The legitimacy of such a charismatic leader would extend only as far as his own "success." The parameters of his leadership would be determined by the requirements of formal legality and the dependence of the welfare of the masses on a certain degree of bureaucratic traditionalism. In Weber's framework, any talk of a renewal of freedom and political participation is utopian, and any "rationalization of interaction" inevitably leads in an authoritarian direction.

Weber's purpose, however, was not to promote and accelerate bureaucratization but to find a way to animate and channel it in the direction of compelling national goals. Bureaucracy could not be controlled from below, only from above. A decentralization of authority would only impoverish the prospects of the nation and exacerbate the already chaotic political situation. How, then, to prevent the bureaucrats from soullessly inheriting and desiccating the future?

It is from this rock bottom of political despair that Weber raises the plebiscitary leader. This ancient comparative historical type, born of class- and status-ridden democracies and demagogic politics, had independent sources of legitimacy and was not strongly integrated into the reigning hierarchical order. The fundamental significance of the plebiscite for Weber was that it produced a charismatic authority which concealed its authoritarian element. The plebiscitarian leader seemed to be dependent on the will of those over whom he had authority. However, he was actually a demagogue able to influence action by virtue of the blind devotion and trust his political followers had in him personally. Weber saw the limits of the possible and the politically successful in the contemporary period not in terms of the qualitative flowering of language and thought as in the Greek *polis* or medieval commune but in the stump speeches of the political demagogue whose impassioned rhetoric influences by emotion.[28] Such a demagogic leader would be in a position both to push a national ethic[29] in the face of the disastrous German defeat and to defend individualism in the face of the collective socialist assault. The political leader, with an independent power base grounded in the mass vote of the people, would transcend the class interests of parliament. He would be subject to recall only by a vote of the people. Parliament would serve as a school for plebiscitarian leaders, where they would test their mettle and learn political discipline through the committee system. As Wolfgang Mommsen has put it, "Formal legal constitutionalism would obviate the disadvantages of pure Caesarism."[30]

Weber had found comparative historical reasons to hope that plebiscitarian democracy could solve the problem of chronic disunity and help reorder German political and social institutions as well. Such a demogogic leader in the role of a law "prophet" could help enact progressive legislation. As Weber argues:

Prophets are the only ones who have taken a really conscious "creative" attitude toward existing law; only through them has new law been consciously created. For the rest, as must be stressed again and again, even those jurists who, from the objective point of view have been the most creative ones, have always and not only in modern times regarded themselves to be the mouthpiece of norms already existing, though perhaps latently, and to be their interpretors or appliers rather than their creators.[31]

In this way, new secular purpose and social fact must ground itself in "sacred" content if it is to achieve the social stamp of legitimacy and approval. Eventually, Weber seems to apply this insight to the problem of German leadership. He endows the plebiscitary leader with the charisma of a this-worldy prophet and puts him in a position where he can take a "consciously creative attitude toward the law," that is, create the meanings embodied in his own ultimately personal value commitments.

NOTES

1. Joseph Bensman, "Max Weber's Concept of Legitimacy: An Evaluation," in *Conflict and Control,* ed. Arthur Vidich and Ronald Glassman (Beverly Hills: Sage, 1979) pp. 17-48.

2. Max Weber, *Economy and Society,* 2 vols. (Berkley: University of California Press, 1978), p. 36. Weber, of course, explicitly admitted that he was building on Jellinek's work on constitutional theory in developing his own sociological typology. Jellinek writes of the *practical value* of such a typological approach:

From the viewpoint of the practitioner, the type proves to be a heuristic instrument, since it is feasible, with a high degree of probability, to draw certain inferences from the type for the life of the individual state. The applicability of the same type points to an analogous course of similar politics in the future. When we speak of the lessons of history, we have in mind—whether we know it or not—the typical element in human affairs. Only because similar events repeat themselves under similar conditions can history become our schoolmistress. Only because the functioning of the state has constants in its flux is scientific politics possible, that means, a theory of the intelligible structure of the state. (G. Roth and R. Bendix, *Scholarship and Partisanship* [London, 1971], p. 261)

3. Weber, *Economy and Society,* p. 215.

4. Max Weber, *On Law in Economy and Society* (New York: Simon & Schuster, 1954), pp. 284-300.

5. Ibid., p. 330.

6. Ibid., p. 330.

7. Ibid., p. 331.

8. Ibid., p. 333.

9. Max Weber, *Weber: Selections in Translation,* ed. W. G. Runciman (Cambridge: Cambridge University Press, 1978), p. 243.

10. Weber, *Economy and Society,* p. 949.

11. Ibid., p. 951.

12. Ibid., pp. 295-96.

13. Ibid., p. 1314.

14. Ibid., p. 1314.

15. Max Weber, *The City* (New York: Free Press, 1958), p. 181. Weber never completed his contemplated work on the modern state.

16. Max Weber, *The Theory of Economic and Social Organization* (New York: Free Press, 1964), pp. 412-13.

17. Weber, *City,* p. 122.

18. Weber, *Economy and Society,* p. 1275.

19. Max Weber, "Socialism," in *Max Weber: The Interpretation of Social Reality,* ed. J.E.T. Eldridge (New York: Scribner's Sons, 1971), p. 194.

20. Michael Mollat and Philippe Wolff, *The Popular Revolutions of the Late Middle Ages* (London: George Allen and Unwin, 1973), p. 70.

21. Weber, *Economy and Society,* p. 1455.

22. Weber, *Theory,* p. 131; Weber, *On Law,* p. 63.

23. Weber, *On Law,* p. 298.

24. Weber, *Theory,* p. 337.

25. David Beetham, *Max Weber and the Theory of Modern Politics* (London: George Allen and Unwin, 1974), pp. 274-75.

26. Weber, *Theory,* p. 338.

27. Ibid., p. 408.

28. Weber, *Economy and Society,* p. 1129.

29. Marianne Weber writes:

In those weeks Weber was ready to do anything for the nation and to assume the leadership of youth, but there was no one to follow him. It was not really surprising that his national ethic fell flat with the young pacifists and communists, who were hoping for a turning point in world history in accordance with their beliefs. But that there was no reaction from the young people with traditional attitudes had to be taken as a crushing symptom of a complete moral exhaustion caused by the war. (*Max Weber: A Biography,* trans. Harry Zohn [New York: Wiley and Sons, 1975], p. 631)

30. Wolfgang Mommsen, "Max Weber's Political Sociology and His Philosophy of World History," *International Social Science Journal,* 17, no. 1, (1965), p. 40.

31. Weber, *On Law,* p. 320.

Marxian and Anti-Marxian Themes in Max Weber's Political Sociology

4

MARX, WEBER, AND CONTEMPORARY SOCIOLOGY

Dennis Wrong

The failure of our multiple particular researches conducted with increasingly precise and complex methods to cumulate into a coherent overall vision of the world largely accounts for the immense flowering of interest in recent years in the so-called classical sociologists. This new interest has been especially pronounced in the cases of Marx and Weber, both of whose work was preeminently historical in focus, guided by what the Marxist philosopher Karl Korsch called the "principle of historical specificity."

A major theme of recent discussions of Weber has been his relation to Marx and Marxism, discussions that have revised the simplistic view of Weber as an "idealist" critic of Marxist "materialism" based on *The Protestant Ethic and the Spirit of Capitalism,* the first of Weber's major writings to be translated into English and to become widely known. The Parsonian interpretation of Weber exaggerated the differences from Marx in many areas and sometimes tended to present Weber as a kind of anti-Marx. One of the first overviews of Weber's sociology in English antedating Parsons's 1937 discussion in *The Structure of Social Action* was that of Albert Soloman, whose writings on Weber are largely remembered for his description of Weber as the "bourgeois Marx" and his later claim that Weber's sociology was "a long and intense dialogue with the ghost of Karl Marx." The label retains a certain appositeness, but the characterization of Weber's sociology is not really tenable. Weber's stature in the Anglo-American world has become so great that Marxists and neo-Marxists today are prone to try to assimilate him to Marx, seeing him as expanding upon a number of themes first adumbrated by Marx which have become more salient in this century, such as the greater bureaucratization of capitalism and the state and their increasing interpenetration. This perspective was ably presented by Hans Gerth and C. Wright Mills in their introduction to the first book-length selection in English of Weber's sociological writings, which appeared in 1946. In more recent versions, one sometimes detects an inclination to dispose of Weber by annexing him to an essentially Marxist outlook, but that Weber and Marx are less at odds than was formerly believed, at least at the level of their substantive interpretations, seems to me to be undeniable.

Some Marxists of a doctrinaire cast of mind, unable simply to dismiss Weber as a bourgeois ideologue—though efforts to do so continue—have tried to cope with him by claiming that his most valuable ideas are directly borrowed from Marxism. On the other hand, disillusioned Marxists or neo-Marxists, whose hopes have been irretrievably shaken by two world wars, the creation in Russia and elsewhere of new political and social tyrannies in the name of Marxism, and the stolidly non-revolutionary temper of the working class in capitalist countries, have often tended to cannibalize Weber, drawing heavily on his vision while reformulating it in more congenial neo-Marxist or Hegelian terms. I have in mind particularly the original Frankfurt School theorists. As Raymond Aron, the man who introduced Weber into France, wrote of Herbert Marcuse's famous attack on Weber at the 1964 Heidelberg conference honoring the centennial of Weber's birth:

Have events proved Max Weber wrong. . . ? It is quite obvious that they have borne him out, as even Herbert Marcuse admits. . . . Herbert Marcuse cannot forgive Max Weber for having denounced in advance as a utopia something that up to now has indeed turned out to be utopian: the idea of a liberation of man by the modification of the system of ownership and a planned economy.[1]

That is what sticks in the craw of Marxists to this day even more than Weber's ironic definition of himself as a "class-conscious bourgeois." For he engaged Marxists on their very own terrain with superior intellectual resources, often reached similar conclusions about past and contemporary history, and yet unreservedly rejected their historical optimism. Marxism, even in the complex and subtle variants that are influential in Western universities today, remains a political faith affirming the unity of theory and practice, however unconsummated that unity is presently conceded to be by "Western" Marxists shorn of any illusions about the oppressive practice of all existing Communist states. Although Weber died just a few years after the Bolshevik seizure of power, he foresaw almost immediately that it would prove to be a historical disaster for the Russian people, producing "mounds of corpses."[2]

Weber was equally blunt in rejecting the revolutionary means as well as the utopian ends cherished by Marxism: "He 'who wishes to live as modern man,' even if this be 'only in the sense that he has his daily paper, railways, electricity, etc.,' must resign himself to the loss of ideals of radical revolutionary change: indeed he must abandon 'the *conceivability* of such a goal.' "[3] Recent events in France in 1968, in Chile and Portugal in the 1970s, and the appearance of what has come to be called "Eurocommunism" have in different ways powerfully confirmed this conclusion. Today's "Marxists of the chair," a species at long and welcome last becoming established in the American university, often expound a Marxism that owes more to non-Marxist thought than to the original doctrine. In particular, the eschatological hopes invested in the proletariat have been considerably diluted or abandoned to the point where some latter-day self-described Marxist theoreticians remind one of the death-of-God theologians who made a brief stir in the 1960s. They have tacitly accepted the diagnosis of modern industrial civilization that Weber advanced with bleak but unsurpassed clarity over sixty years ago. Yet Marx remains for them an iconic figure while Weber continues to arouse their ambivalence.

Western Marxists who long ago rejected the world of the Gulag Archipelago often remain reluctant even to acknowledge that world as *a* form of Marxist "praxis," if not the only imaginable one. Self-declared Marxists, after all, rule states containing over a third of the world's population, whereas Weberians control no more than a few professorships. An American Marxist professor once complained to me rather bitterly of an eminent colleague: "He thinks it fine to love Tocqueville, but you're not supposed to love

Marx.'' Such an attitude was certainly not uncommon in American sociology until fairly recently, but I could hardly refrain from remarking—though I did refrain—that in the world at large people have been killed for not loving Marx, or for not loving him in the prescribed way. To be sure, people have also been killed for loving him, though not quite as many; the numbers in both cases, however, run to the millions. But no one has ever been killed for not loving Tocqueville or Max Weber.

Twenty years ago I described Max Weber as ''the one great man we sociologists can plausibly claim as our own,'' a judgment with which I concur if anything more than ever today. But the word *plausibly* was deliberately inserted in the statement with Marx in mind, for it is possible to deny that Marx was essentially or fundamentally a sociologist but not that he was a great man who, whatever the fate of the movements launched in his name, achieved an encompassing grasp of wide swaths of human history without sacrificing, like so many of his contemporaries and his own epigoni, concrete detail to the conceptual demands of an abstract scheme. In reaction against such schemes, Weber was deeply suspicious of wide-ranging developmental theories, but the scope and depth of his own historical work achieves as much as Marx's does the level of universal history. Marx and Weber are therefore likely to continue to be linked together less as antipodal figures than as sources of inspiration for the large-scale comparative historical sociology toward which the more ambitious social scientists in a number of countries are increasingly moving now that the view that the natural sciences present an appropriate model for the social sciences to emulate has been epistemologically dethroned.

The present revival of broad comparative history which recognizes both Marx and Weber as ancestors is an interdisciplinary project involving both sociologists and historians who have overcome the traditional barriers that have long divided them. In its fidelity to the actual historical record, the new comparative history even at its most ambitious bears little resemblance to the all-embracing systems of such nineteenth-century sociologists as Comte and Spencer, who tried to impose abstract nomological straitjackets on the disorderly and variegated materials of actual history. If we turn, however, to the discipline of sociology as presently conceived in the United States, Weber's influence is considerably more pervasive than that of Marx.

Let us assess Weber's impact on American sociology, considering it in relation to the established specialties of the field rather than according to the natural lines of division in his work that have been carefully drawn by recent Weber scholars.

FORMAL ORGANIZATIONS

It is scarcely an exaggeration to say that the very existence of formal organizations as a specialty stems from Weber's conception of bureaucracy. Weber, of course, did not invent the concept of bureaucracy: Hegel and Marx used it, Saint-Simon at least implied it, and such nineteenth-century novelists as Gogol, Balzac and Dickens (not to speak of Kafka early in the present century) satirized it. Weber's achievement was to extend it from the realm of government to other areas of social organization, to identify bureaucratization as a master trend in modern society, and—most important to American sociologists—to define it formally as a generic type of social structure. American social scientists took the Weberian model as a point of departure for the empirical observation and analysis of a huge variety of special-purpose organizations which, not surprisingly, were often found to deviate from the attributes of the model.

Apart from legitimating a new field of empirical research, the early users of Weber's concept were actuated by two extrasociological aims. First, the Weberian model could be used to defend the welfare state of the New Deal—and even the idea of "socialism"—against its conservative political opponents, who made an epithet of "bureaucrat" in their diatribes against "red tape," desk-warming civil servants feeding at the public trough and the like. Weber's emphasis on the *efficiency* of bureaucracy as a means to the achievement of clearly defined collective goals served as a defense against its detractors: "The decisive reason for the advance of bureaucratic organization has always been its purely technical superiority over any other form of organization. The fully bureaucratic mechanism compares with other organizations exactly as does the machine with nonmechanical modes of production."[4] At the same time, Weber's insistence that bureaucratization was not confined to government but encompassed the corporate economy as well drew the sting from the arguments of the defenders of "free enterprise" against state intervention in the economy.

A second aim, following from the first, was to reformulate the idea of bureaucracy in order to make it less incompatible with the American democratic and egalitarian ethos. This involved divesting the Weberian concept of its heavy emphasis on hierarchical authority, impersonal relations and the suppression of individual initiative. The accounts by the Harvard industrial sociologists of the emergence of an "informal structure" of social relations in large organizations, modifying and bypassing the formally prescribed rules and lines of authority, were widely employed for this purpose. Weber's relative neglect of "staff" as opposed to hierarchical "line" positions in organizations and his failure to discuss the collegial ties central to the professions were also stressed in this connection, especially by Talcott Parsons.

These uses and modifications of Weber's model tended to ignore the duality of his own outlook toward bureaucracy as, on the one hand, an indispensable rational instrumentality under the conditions of modern life, and, on the other, as a "living machine" which "in union with the dead machine . . . is laboring to produce the cage of that bondage of the future to which one day powerless men will be forced to submit like the fellaheen of ancient Egypt."[5] American liberal democratic social scientists found Weber's historical pessimism, based on the fear of a trend toward total bureaucratization, no easier to stomach than did Marxists. The "counterculture" of the 1960s, on the other hand, has given far greater resonance to Weber's despair over the "iron cage" of modern society, though it often assumed oppositional stances that he would have regarded as sentimental and unrealistic.

Indeed, the negative side of Weber's view of bureaucracy has in recent years almost completely overshadowed the positive side. What one writer has called "bureaucracy baiting" has become as characteristic of the left as of the right.[6] Bureaucracy is presented as an implacable force opposing both personal freedom and popular democracy. Weber's emphasis on the essential passivity of bureaucracies, their availability to any political leaders strong and determined enough to use them, is ignored in this view. Nor has the possibility of combining democratic leadership and control with a reliable and efficient civil service, advocated by Weber in the last few years of his life, received anything like the attention given to his more pessimistic statements about the spread of bureaucratization.

SOCIAL STRATIFICATION

Marx, of course, long ago placed classes and class structures at the very center of sociological and historical analysis, and his views have loomed large in most theoretical discussion ever since. However, the Weberian triad of status, wealth and power is indispensable to the study of social inequality and class structure, although the interdependences among the three are as important a subject of investigation as the distinction itself. This has not always been recognized by American sociologists, whose quick acceptance of the triad was not free of selective distortion. The concept of "status group" is sometimes employed as a counter to the economically based Marxist concept of class, although Weber never contended that status groups were *more* important in modern society than classes, which he, like Marx, grounded in the economy, merely that they were distinguishable. Weber's emphasis on status was also sometimes invoked in support of a quite different use of the term: its equation with the prestige rankings of individuals or positions (usually occupations derived by the favored methods of survey research). But Weber wrote of status *groups,* not of status as an attribute of individuals or positions, and he did not identify status groups with a rank-order reflecting an underlying consensus on values in society. Far from implying consensus, conflict between status groups was in Weber's view just as prevalent as class conflict.

POLITICAL SOCIOLOGY

Nearly all of the classical sociologists were concerned at some level with politics, even though—or perhaps because—the hallmark of the sociological perspective, as it arose in the nineteenth century was to claim historical, causal and normative priority for society over the state. This, in conjunction with the later almost simultaneous development of political science as a discipline, retarded the emergence of political sociology as a sociological specialty.

Like formal organizations and social stratification, political sociology began to emerge as a specialty not long after publication of the first translations of Weber's sociological writings. (His many commentaries on the political issues of his time remain untranslated, as does Mommsen's important study of his political views.) Weber's concept of legitimation, his threefold typology of legitimate authority, his definitions of the state and of power and his treatment of bureaucracies as power structures (which influenced his contemporary, Robert Michels) have had a far-reaching effect on the theoretical formulations of political scientists as well as political sociologists. Weber alone of the "classical" sociologists, including Marx, did not treat the state and politics as secondary phenomena subordinate to autonomous "social forces." Of nineteenth-century social thinkers, only Tocqueville bears comparison with Max Weber in this respect, and his insights were less systematically developed. Traditional Marxism, like its bourgeois counterparts, has a dusty Victorian ring and has required strong infusions from later thinkers, including Weber, in order to retain the appearance of relevance to our time, not to speak of its embarrassments in confronting the record of the movements and regimes it has itself inspired. Max Weber of all the classical sociologists seems most to be our contemporary, for the troubled history of the twentieth century has cast doubt, to put it mildly, on the classical ascription of primacy to the social over the political. Totalitarianism has merely deviated furthest in achieving the complete ascendancy of the latter over the former.

The three specialities influenced by Weber that I have reviewed are all primarily concerned with social organization. If a sociology of economic life ever develops as a recognized specialty, it will join them in owing a large debt to Weber. The sociology of culture rather than of social organization is a larger component of the other specialties in which Weber's influence has been great. He is with Durkheim one of the two major theorists of the sociology of religion. Without reducing religious ideas to simple reflections of the social location of the classes and communities that upheld them, he explored their intimate connection with the concrete situations in which their creators and carriers found themselves. Weber was formally educated in the law and his earliest scholarship dealt with legal institutions. Since much of it remains untranslated, or has been translated only recently, his influence on the sociology of law, especially in comparative historical scholarship, is bound to increase. His writings on the sociology of music and of architecture are major contributions to these undeveloped fields.

Weber does not easily lend himself to the categorizations favored by writers of textbooks and taxonomists of sociological theories. Specious though such pedagogic labeling often is, at least a modicum of plausibility exists for calling Marx a "conflict theorist," Durkheim and Parsons "functionalists" or "consensualists," and various other people "exchange" or "phenomenological" or "symbolic interactionist" theorists. Weber fails to fit under any of these familiar rubrics or under those that stress epistemological standpoints ranging from strict positivism to pure hermeneutics. *Historicist* perhaps suits him best, but most sociologists have felt uncomfortable with the label.[7] Their historical knowledge, especially in America, has usually been limited, and in Weber they confront a man whose works, in Mommsen's words, "display an abundance of historical knowledge which has so far not been surpassed by anyone else, with the possible exception of Arnold Toynbee."[8] American sociologists have often regarded sociology as a kind of intellectual short-cut providing nomological formulae under which historical particulars can be subsumed, thus eliminating the necessity of understanding them directly in their complex particularity. Weber's vast and detailed knowledge seems to reproach sociologists for their hubris, especially since he makes little claim to derive from it universal generalizations, in contrast to Toynbee's "challenge and response" theory of civilization, which can be identified with a familiar tradition of theorizing and criticized for its vague, metaphorical character.

But Max Weber was more than a scholar of prodigious learning. Even his most specialized and objective writings communicate an underlying tension and moral passion, a "pathos of objectivity" in Gerth and Mills' incisive phrase. Moreover, he never confined himself to "scholarship as a vocation" but was constantly drawn to politics even if in the end his career as a political man was abortive. Thus he demands to be assessed according to the ultimate values that gave his life and work a unity despite the apparent fragmentation of his omnivorous intellectual concerns.

There is much justification for regarding Weber as an existentialist *avant la lettre*. To his close friend, Karl Jaspers, Weber himself was an existentialist hero, and Jaspers claimed that his own existentialist philosophy was inspired by the example of Weber as "the man who embodied human greatness," who "lived in the only way possible for a man of integrity in those times; breaking through all illusory forms he disclosed the foundations of human Existenz."[9] Weber's indebtedness to Nietzsche, generally regarded now as one of the fathers of existentialism, has been increasingly recognized by his more recent interpreters. Weber's conception of the relationship between values and knowledge can now be seen as much more existentialist than positivist. His insistence on "value freedom" or "ethical neutrality" as a prerequisite for any social science worthy of the name has long been upheld by American sociologists as the first commandment of their calling. Younger sociologists involved in the protest movements of the 1960s attacked value neutrality as a self-serving defense of professional interests, as an excuse for political indifference and simply as a sham violated in the actual research of many who proclaimed it. Neither side in this rancorous dispute, now thankfully showing signs of moving to higher intellectual ground, did justice to Weber's position, whether in claiming to affirm it or to reject it.

Weber did not argue for the exclusion of value judgments from social science because he regarded them as blind, irrational eruptions of human emotion posing a threat to the majestic authority of pure science. It was rather the other way around: He wished to preserve values as the realm of individual freedom subject to the dignity of reponsible choice uncoerced by the constraints of the world of fact revealed by science, even in the face of a full and stoical awareness of these constraints. This was, of course, a Kantian position reflecting Weber's neo-Kantian philosophical heritage. But Weber differed from the Kantians in denying that there were objective values on which rational consensus was possible. He insisted rather that there was a plurality of irreconcilable values, that the world was one of "warring gods" and that to align oneself with one of the gods meant to deny the claims of another who might be equally attractive and powerful. This position is existentialist or Nietzschean rather than Kantian: We are condemned to the often painful and even tragic choice between rival values, and we cannot slough off the burden of choice by claiming that it is not ourselves but the world as understood by science that dictates our conduct.

For politics, Weber favored an "ethic of responsibility" in preference to an "ethic of intention" (or of "absolute ends" as it has often—misleadingly, I think—been translated). An ethic of responsibility takes into account the consequences and further ramifications of realizing a particular end and also appraises an end in terms of the costs of attaining it. Empirical knowledge therefore enters into the consideration of ends to be pursued regardless of their status in some "ultimate" scheme of values. Here Weber places less of an existentialist emphasis on the autonomy and irreducibility of the choice of ends and gives weight to the interaction of ends and means and their frequent interchangeability, treating knowledge and values as complementary rather than as sealed off from one another.

It is impossible to confront Weber without a sense of the man behind the work. He is the only one of the classical sociologists who has been the subject of a psychobiography,[10] whose life and character have been made into a cultural symbol in a brilliant if tendentious study by a literary scholar,[11] and whose love letters, no less, are shortly to be published. Even Marx's life and personal history have not attracted comparable interest, largely because Marx's message was ultimately an affirmative one embraced by an entire movement whereas the tension and ambivalence of Weber's thought points in the direction of personal stoicism rather than collective commitment. The spell cast by the passion and the pathos Weber projects has been a source of irritation to his critics.

Donald MacRae, a proper Scotsman, who has written a little book deliberately intended to "demystify" Weber, remarks that "practically all that is written on Weber is written in awe," with the result that "when one is knocking one's forehead on the floor one's vision is certainly limited and probably blurred."[12]

Why then Weber's continuing spell? I write unashamedly from within the circle of the bewitched, also as one who in middle age feels historical nostalgia for the time of his parents' childhood, the years of Weber's manhood, and, moreover, as one with little inclination to apologize for his own "bourgeois values." Part of the answer lies in one remark of Donald MacRae's with which I can agree: "Our century has apparently dedicated itself, only half-knowingly, to acting out the ideas and dreams of [early twentieth-century Europe] in deadly earnest."[13] By the late 1970s we are perhaps entitled to conclude that the acting out has almost ended. This too is a source of Weber's relevance, for he anticipated the trajectories of our belief, disbelief and unbelief. A world of "specialists without vision and sensualists without heart" today sounds painfully more like a description of the way we live now than like the possible future described by Weber in 1905. And we have had a good deal of unsatisfactory experience with the "entirely new prophets" and "great rebirth of old ideas and ideals" that he expected to arise in reaction to the world of modernity. Although the imperatives facing us are scarcely the same, we are unable to improve upon his conclusion that "nothing is gained by yearning and tarrying alone" and that what remains is for us to "set to work and meet the 'demands of the day,' in human relations as well as in our vocation."

NOTES

1. Raymond Aaron, *Main Currents in Sociological Thought,* Volume 2 (New York: Basic Books, 1967), p. 250.

2. In 1918 or 1919, Weber met Joseph Schumpeter in a Vienna coffeehouse. Schumpeter observed that he was delighted by the occurrence of the Russian Revolution because it would provide a laboratory test of the viability of socialism. Weber responded angrily, insisting that the revolution would lead to unparalleled human misery and would prove to be "a laboratory filled with mounds of corpses." Infuriated by Schumpeter's detachment, he rushed out of the cafe leaving his hat behind. See Karl Jasper's account of this incident in *Three Essays: Leonardo, Descartes, Max Weber* (New York: Harcourt, Brace and World, 1964), p. 222.

3. Anthony Giddens, *Politics and Sociology in the Thought of Max Weber* (London: Macmillan, 1972), p. 46. The entire statement sounds like Weber, but Giddens gives only partial quotation marks, citing as his source Wolfgang J. Mommsen's 1959 untranslated book on Weber's politics.

4. H. H. Gerth and C. Wright Mills, eds. *From Max Weber: Essays in Sociology* (New York: Oxford University Press, 1946), p. 214.

5. Max Weber, *Economy and Society,* Volume 3, ed. Guenther Roth and Claus Wittich (New York: Bedminster Press, 1968), p. 1402.

6. Stephen Miller, "Bureaucracy Baiting," *American Scholar,* 47 (Spring, 1978), pp. 205-22. For a recent qualified defense of bureaucracy by a socialist, see Henry Pachter, "Freedom, Authority, Participation," *Dissent,* 25 (Summer, 1978), pp. 304-06.

7. Such as Randall Collins, *Conflict Sociology: Toward an Exploratory Science* (New York: Academic Press, 1975).

8. Wolfgang J. Mommsen, *The Age of Bureaucracy: Perspectives on the Political Sociology of Max Weber* (New York: Harper & Row, 1974), p. 3.

9. Jaspers, *Three Essays,* pp. 193, 257.

10. Arthur Mitzman, *The Iron Cage: An Historical Interpretation of Max Weber* (New York: Alfred A. Knopf, 1970).

11. Martin Green, *The von Richthofen Sisters* (New York: Basic Books, 1974).

12. Leo Strauss, "Natural Right and the Distinction Between Facts and Values," in Maurice Natanson, ed., *Philosophy of the Social Sciences: A Reader* (New York: Random House, 1963), pp. 430, 445-46.

13. Donald G. MacRae, *Weber* (London: Fontana, 1974), p. 92.

5

FROM POLITICAL ECONOMY TO POLITICAL SOCIOLOGY: MAX WEBER'S EARLY WRITINGS

Lawrence A. Scaff

Max Weber's work divides naturally into two parts: the early writings published prior to 1898, in the first decade of his career; and the essays and studies published after 1903. It is no secret that most of the attention bestowed upon Weber has been directed toward the commanding work of the later period: the studies of the "Protestant ethic," the methodological essays, the sociology of religion, the wartime political essays, and, of course, *Economy and Society,* with its endless complexities. This focus prevails not only in American sociology, where we have the best of excuses—viz., scarcely any of Weber's early publications have been translated— but also in German scholarship, where the early work has figured only sporadically, and then usually as evidence in the debate over Weber's politics. With few exceptions[2] the pre-1898 texts have been either completely ignored, dismissed as immature productions, or relegated to the esoteric marginalia of Weber's scientific corpus.

Neglect resulting from these difficulties should not be mistaken for complete ignorance, however, for we do possess what may be identified as three distinct views of the texts published before 1898: (1) In the interpretation of Bendix (1977, ch. 2) these texts announce Weber's scientific research program and lifelong intel-lectual orientation and thus appear important as a preparation for the later, major work on capitalism, social structure, and the sociology of domination. (2) For Mommsen (1974a, chs. 1-4) the early writings similarly anticipate Weber's later contributions, but now primarily as expressions of his most basic and persistent nationalist political values. These values are said to define the scheme within which his later studies take shape. (3) In Mitzman's psychobiographical portrait (1970, pt. 1) the work of the 1890s becomes a symbol of Weber's generational rebellion against "patriarchy" as well as a journey "from socialism to liberal nationalism" (!), whereas the work after 1903 is seen as a labor of recovery, marked by a "retreat from ascetic rationalism."

Five major claims appear most significant with respect to the early writings: (1) They contain an exposition of Weber's knowledge of economic theory and of his thinking as a "political economist." In fact, much of Weber's work was shaped by the language and perspectives of political economy, rather than by the professional "sociology" and "political science" of his day. (2) If the early writings show a line of development from "history" to "political economy," then they also demonstrate Weber's emergence as an original mind attempting to elaborate a complex network of economic, social, and political concepts for explaining (among other things) certain patterns of historical "development" and forms of "rationalization" peculiar to the West. What Weber devises in the 1890s can then be described as an innovative science of "political sociology."[3] (3) More broadly considered, these writings contain Weber's first and in some ways most explicit attempt to formulate an independent theoretical and political position in response to Marxism on the one hand and to the "liberal" historiography and social thought of his time on the other. It was in the period before 1900 that Weber took up the quarrel among the "schools" in the West, and it was also in this period that one finds the formative influences on Weber of major figures like Marx and Nietzsche. (4) The early writings exhibit a striking combination of scientific and political interests, a strong tendency to shuttle back and forth, as it were, between theoretical and practical knowledge. (With the possible exception of the years from 1916 to 1919, no other period in Weber's life displays this combination so impressively.) They can instruct us about Weberian "praxis," about the "unity" of the problems Weber chose to address, and about the "tension" between his roles as political sociologist and political educator. (5) A close examination of the early writings and a comparison of them with Weber's later thought reveals a single mind at work, not a writer who went through liberal, Marxist, historicist, or other phases, only to transcend them all in a new social science. Weber's early and late work exhibits specific minor differences, both practical and theoretical, but such differences are explained by Weber's continuing, unfinished, and only partially successful attempt to solve problems raised in the 1890s, not by any fundamental shift in emphasis or perspective.

In the following discussion I intend to clarify and interpret Weber's early writings, developing the main lines of argument and providing as many supporting details as possible. I propose to pay particular attention to the questions, Why are these writings important? What do they add to our understanding of Weber's thought? What do they contribute to our knowledge of theoretical problems in political sociology?

THE POLITICAL SETTING

Taking the 1870s as a starting point, it is important to note that Weber's earliest political consciousness was steeped in the politics of national liberalism, the politics of the generation that produced men like Bennigsen, whose parliamentary talents were recreated in Weber's later memory as a model to emulate. But in the 1880s Weber's own thinking and participation did not evolve for the most part within the legalistic tradition of the liberal *Rechsstaat*. Instead his political and scientific activities were guided by a search for a standpoint that would satisfactorily confront a new set of socioeconomic and political problems that became increasingly evident through the 1880s. Two influences are paramount for understanding this development: the effect on Weber of his uncle, Hermann Baumgarten, a liberal historian and iconoclastic critic; and Weber's increasing attraction to a group of younger political economists, many of whom were associated with the *Verein für Sozialpolitik*.

Baumgarten was important for Weber as a skillful critic of the growing complacency and confusion within liberalism's ranks in the 1880s and as a remarkably prescient (and isolated) analyst of the crippling effects of Bismarck's "ceasarist demagogy." As an "old liberal" from the days of the Frankfurt Parliament,

Baumgarten understood that the new Reich had transformed the political environment: not the earlier concern with ideal legal forms and postulated rights, but observation of the power position and political experience of classes, status groups, and their organized representatives had become the focus for an emerging national politics. Within this context Baumgarten advocated a new constitutional system incorporating principles of parliamentary rule. However, after the reversal of policy in 1878, his position grew sharply negative and pessimistic. The images of impending doom in Weber's early writings, the sarcastic jibes at his own generation's historical illiteracy, and the polemic directed against the "unpolitical" middle class and Bismarck's destructive "legacy" were modeled on Baumgarten's critique. For Weber, as for Baumgarten, it appeared incontestable that liberalism's future as a political movement and ideology was in peril, and both agreed that the decisive turning point had come in 1877-78.

A great deal is revealed in Weber's unconventional choice of this date, a choice that is reemphasized in his later political writings and correspondence with Michels. Unlike many contemporaries, who either viewed politics in the Reich as a continuous progression or interpreted 1890 (Bismarck's resignation) as the great divide, Weber insisted that all of the conditions for political paralysis, bureaucratic domination, and "feudalization" of the social order were present in 1878. His critical and gloomy assessment rested on three observations. First, in this year all possibility for the growth of parliamentary authority came to an abrupt end, following the collapse of negotiations between Bismarck and Bennigsen. Second, the new post-election strategy, appealing to a right-of-center majority, called for state intervention combined with repression of the left: the anti-socialist law, protectionism (including tariffs on grain and iron), civil service "reform" (actually a purge of liberal elements), and state-sponsored social security programs. Third and most important, the economic basis for the policy shift was secured by an alliance between industrial capitalism and the large agricultural interests, particularly the Junker estates in the East. This powerful bloc dominated foreign and domestic politics through World War I, and it aroused Weber's ire on countless occasions before and after 1900.

Weber's interest in political economy must be understood in the context of these troubling political developments. To be sure, representatives of the "liberal" school responded in different ways: Treitschke adopted a virulent nationalist and anti-Semitic stance; Brentano clung to free trade doctrine; Adolf Wagner fell back on social improvement through Christian humanism. For Weber, however, it was no longer a matter of making minor ideological adjustments or of relying upon well-worn slogans but of addressing a fundamental crisis in thought and action. The search for a theoretically grounded, critical, and constructive politics led Weber toward political economy.

THE TURN TO POLITICAL ECONOMY

As is well known, Weber began his university studies in history and law, with a minor interest in philosophy. But as early as 1883, he had begun to read Schmoller's major works, and eight years later he acknowledged to Baumgarten having "become approximately one-third political economist" (Weber, 1936:327, 3 January 1891). The letters to Baumgarten, covering these crucial years when Weber was in his twenties, record a growing attraction for political economy in the face of dissatisfaction with the older sciences. Explaining the progress of his studies, Weber noted arriving reluctantly at the conclusion that certain "practical" problems of the times "were not to be understood with the means of our science," a reference specifically to jurisprudence (30 September 1887). In order to understand the new post-1878 conditions, he identified with what he termed a new "school" of thought, composed of "political economists and *Sozialpolitiker*" (30 April 1888). This intellectual journey was completed in the 1890s with the appointment at Freiburg and the collaboration there with Schulze-Gaevernitz. Weber was highly conscious of the change brought about in his thinking, and he used the Freiburg inaugural address (1895) partly as a device for summarizing that change and identifying the new orientation.

Weber used the new orientation as a means for achieving a *modus vivendi* between theoretical work and practical activity at least to the extent that an operative compromise was ever achieved. In other words, the familiar tension between "politics" and "science," highly visible in this early period, was resolved not simply in favor of "science" as such, but in favor of a "practical science." This can be seen in Weber's work after the *Habilitation* (1891), all of which was organized around eminently practical-political topics, or guided by judgments of relevance to practical values. In addition, it is illustrated in Weber's numerous ventures into public and political education in this period, from courses on political economy for the *Evangelisch-Sozialer Kongress* to lectures before women's and workers' clubs. The former were especially significant for revealing Weber's purposes, since they were expressly intended to recruit a liberal audience for the new science, and since Weber always chose for himself the most controversial subject matter: labor relations, the power of the Junkers, and the goals of state policy (see 1893a). He made a point in this setting of attacking the natural inclinations of his liberal colleagues, men like Naumann and Göhre, believers in human progress and improvability, in order to remind them of the realities of power, especially in the East, and in order to warn them about the naiveté and ephemerality of an Enlightenment *Weltanschauung*. If Marx's earliest polemics were aimed against utopian socialism, then Weber's struck at "utopian liberalism," albeit as an expression of the "inconvenient" Nietzschean motif in the early writings.

Last of all, political economy (*Nationalökonomie*) had a strong national component for Weber, much as it had had earlier for Friedrich List.[4] In contrast to the classical theory of value and exchange, List's theory of the "national system" stressed development of national "productive forces" and acceptance in principle of protectionism and state intervention. Weber's analysis of *actual* foreign and domestic affairs stressed conflict and the clash of opposed material and ideal interests, from which the state itself was not excused. Weber was simply not a follower of the theorists of community, whether exemplified in Tönnies and the socialist commitment to *Gemeinschaft,* or in Gierke and the Germanic defense of *Genossenschaft.*

To state the case for political economy in this form is to suggest that Weber's "nationalism" was the logical political correlate of his economic theory. More precisely, Weber placed political economy in the service of "the permanent economic and political

power interests of the nation'' (1895:18), insisting that the popular
''economic point of view'' contained in itself no standards of
practical judgment. Such standards were external to economic
analysis, and Weber found them in two places: Machiavelli's
theory of ''*Staatsraison*'' (1893c:74; 1895:14) and the writings of
Friedrich Nietzsche.

THE CRISIS IN STATE AND SOCIETY

In the early writings, Weber employed the language and
symbolism of Machiavelli in order to repudiate both the ''idealist''
Hegelian view of the state and the Marxist ''theory of the
superstructure.'' On the one hand Weber wanted to demystify the
concepts of ''nation'' and ''state'' and replace them with a consideration of ''power organization'' and ''power interest'' which
could be used *critically* to evaluate the performance and prospects
of classes in modern society. On the other hand he deliberately
countered Marx with Machiavelli, rather than Treitschke or
Bismarck, in order to warn like-minded contemporaries of the
''modern overestimation of the 'economic' '' (1895:18) and the need
for a far more differentiated view of the state's functions. In fact, it
is important to notice that Weber's own brand of nationalism owes
much more to Machiavelli, whose works he encountered very early
(Weber, 1936:3, 21 August 1876), than to zealots like Treitschke,
whose invitation to ''mystical national fanaticism'' and philistine
Realpolitik Weber detested (Weber, 1936:232,298; 25 April 1887,
30 April 1888). Weber's sharply worded attacks on Treitschke,
Stöcker, Bismarck, and their youthful enthusiasts, appearing in
letters in the 1880s and restated in public later, cannot be
understood on any other terms.

The content of Weber's ''liberal nationalism'' was bound up
with his view that certain major ''asymmetries'' in the pattern of
economic development and social change in the 1890s—e.g., the
clash between finance capital and landed property, between the
capitalist mode of production and patriarchal domination, between
the fourth estate and other classes—were bringing about an
ominous political crisis. Contrary to what is often said about
Weber, here it is precisely the relationship between ''classes'' and
''state'' that attracted his attention. The main practical problem

could be summed up as a crisis in national political leadership *caused* by a crisis in social structure. What unsettled Weber most was the way in which the political consequences of increasing concentration of economic skill and power in the middle class were systematically frustrated by the "feudalization of capital" within an authoritarian political and normative order. The same prognosis could be made for the working-class movement and its prospects. The leadership and revolutionary potential of agrarian labor in the East, a matter Weber pursued with passionate interest, was in his judgment also virtually nil. Thus, a national policy that might have been secured by either of these classes was in practice left to dynastic and Junker interests fighting a desperate rear guard action against inevitable socioeconomic changes. For Weber it was a universal historical truth that a ruling class, having lost its material social and economic base of support, would next lose its political competence. No "cultural values" could compensate the loss of a foundation for authority in the state.

This understanding of the practical problem presupposes Weber's attachment to what might be called in more contemporary terminology a "conflict model" of society, a view of society as *necessarily* consisting of opposed interests, groups and classes. Even this phrasing, however, fails to do justice to the depth of Weber's critical perspective, to his Nietzschean "thoughts out of season."[5] Amid the fashionable reception of Nietzsche (the "Nietzsche cult" Tönnies called it [1897]), Weber sought to remind contemporaries of certain "inconvenient facts" or "hard truths" (Nietzsche, 1886: sec. 257). To take Nietzsche seriously was to explode what Weber identified as "the sentimental fiction of the harmony of interests between ruling and ruled classes" and the "belief in the unbounded future of technical progress" (1894a:473,477). It was to call into question the comfortable ideologies of "happiness" in a future world without domination and exploitation. Weber was prepared to insist on the challenge of Nietzsche's actual words against Marxists and liberals alike: "Everywhere people are now raving, even under scientific disguises, about coming conditions of society in which 'the exploitative aspect' will be removed. . . . 'Exploitation' does not belong to a corrupt or imperfect and primitive society; it belongs to the *essence* of what lives, as a basic organic function'' (Nietzsche, 1886: sec. 259).

POLITICAL SOCIOLOGY

The most general theoretical problem for Weber, one that unified his early studies of antiquity, medieval Europe, and nineteenth-century Germany, was, quite simply, the relationship between changes in economic structure (especially capital formation, the process of production, and organization of labor), changes in social structure, and changes in political authority and rule. The question should be stated in this form in order to emphasize Weber's interest in (1) identifying and explaining regularities within discrete processes of change, and (2) articulating a "theory" of social change. His analysis is structural, but not yet a universal history, or even a fully conceptualized typological scheme for analyzing *general* sociohistorical processes. In this sense it intentionally avoids those characteristics of generality and universality often stipulated as requisite for "theory." This is because Weber thought the quest for universal theoretical validity was misplaced, leading away from analysis of society to either metaphysics (Hegel) or vacuous historiography (Lamprecht). However, the early writings do not lack comprehensiveness, for the question raised above conceals in reality a highly complex, differentiated theoretical scheme, one in which history is depicted as a vast field of "ideal" and "material" forces that are impersonal, interactive, yet qualitatively distinct. In accounting for such forces Weber is able to employ factors that are not merely economic but also social, political, legal, technological, psychological, cultural, ideological, and even biological (e.g., nutrition, diet) and geographical. He is also prepared to insist that these are forces "against which the individual is powerless."[6]

The theoretical content in Weber's early work can only be understood by carefully dissecting the units of analysis and levels of analytic language and by addressing the problems of causality and explanation. In particular, clarity is enhanced initially if we note that the political sociology in *all* of Weber's texts is built around multiple units of analysis. An exhaustive ordering is presented in Table 1. Of course, thanks to the popular Gerth and Mills

Table 1
Units of Analysis in Weber's Early Writings

1. Individual	
2. Family	
3. Status Group	
4. Interest Group	
5. Estate, *Oikos*	
6. Class	
7. Party	
8. Region	
9. Political Community:	*Polis*
	Empire
	Nation-State
10. World Economy	

translation of one small section in *Economy and Society,* it is commonplace to credit Weber with having discovered "a trinity of units—class, status-group, and party" (Wallerstein, 1974:3)—for explaining sociopolitical processes. In fact the relevant "units" of Weber's scientific world are far more complex and differentiated.

Weber resists the veiw that any single unit is ultimately superior as an analytic tool for treating all relevant cases and answering all possible research questions. He does not reduce all discussion to "individuals" in the manner of utilitarian liberalism, nor does he insist on the opposite construction of an all-embracing "world-system." This was not an oversight but rather an expression of Weber's conviction that the choice of "units" will depend on the historical case, the theoretical point of view, and the explanatory questions.

In discussing the units of analysis selected by Weber as one part of a theory of social change we have already begun to use an analytic terminology—economic rationality, development, production—that must be present in order to relate one unit to another and in order to state adequate explanations of the patterns of change. Careful scrutiny of Weber's texts shows that this terminology, including the cause-effect language, can be separated into what I shall call five distinct "levels of language" (see Table 2). The actual historical and economic studies are filled with

Table 2
Levels of Language in Weber's Early Writings

I.	HISTORICAL-EMPIRICAL DATA	Antiquity Medieval trading companies Argentina East Elbia Stock exchanges	
II.	RELATIONAL CONCEPTS	Labor Capital Production Exchange Appropriation	Material interest Ideal interest Domination Division of labor Class-conflict
III.	DEVELOPMENTAL CONCEPTS	Developmental phase Developmental level Developmental tendency Cultural level Transitional stage Technical progress Rationalization	
IV.	CAUSAL FACTORS	Economic Social Political-legal Historical Technological	Cultural Psychological Ideological Biological Geographic
V.	TYPES	[See Table 3]	

second-level concepts like labor (free, unfree), labor power, capital, production, appropriation, exchange, interest (material, ideal), domination, division of labor, and class conflict, to cite the most prominent terminology. I designate these concepts "relational" since they identify social connections and since their characteristic properties must be identified essentially with reference to properties of other concepts. This is the case, for example, when Weber refers to "labor" as "rent of capital" (1894c:477). The relational concepts can be said to form the "core" of Weber's analysis in the sense that they do not vary a great deal from study to study, regardless of time, place, circumstance, and analytic problem. Thus, class conflict is found in antiquity as well as in nineteenth-century Europe, as are material and ideal interests, forms of domination, and so forth. The specific historical expressions of these relational concepts do change, of course, but never at random. They are always situated within a process of "development."

Weber's developmental language is the most intriguing aspect of the early writings. From his first scholarly publication (1889) to the essays of 1897-98 on antiquity, Weber employed concepts like "developmental phase" or "level" (*Entwicklungsstadium, Entwicklungsstufe*), "stage" or "level of culture" or "civilization" (*Kulturstufe*), "developmental tendency" and "transitional stage."[7] For Weber the developmental concepts should be understood not as historical laws or as an attempt to stake out an epistemological or metaphysical position, but rather as part of a terminology useful as a means for ordering the actual, significant explanatory questions. They illustrate what might be called the "Weberian heuristic," that is, the cautious nominalism of his scientific approach.

Reflecting later upon his own usage, Weber was to make this view quite explicit, arguing that concepts of "development" were at most "conceptual means of representation" for bringing forth "the historical *peculiarity* of each individual development in its causal dependency" (1904:517). Thus, the Marxist concept of "developmental law" with its universalist and realist connotations never appears in Weber's own terminology, nor does any precise classification of step-by-step progression from "inferior" to "superior" stages according to single, fixed criteria (e.g., "freedom," "class conflict," "adaptation"). The latter procedure, found in the Hegelians, the Marxists, the Social Darwinists, Comte and his followers, and historicists like Roscher and Lamprecht was rejected out of hand by Weber for its capacity to conceal political ideologies and to distort historical realities.

In a similar vein Weber treated causality as a problem of scientific observation and discovery in particular historical contexts, not as a logical dilemma or a problem in the philosophy of history. This view of causal factors and relationships, taking Marx's "shattered system" (1896b:26) as its immediate target, appears with great frequency. For example, in one representative passage reporting the results of his second inquiry into East Elbian agriculture, Weber proposed that it was neither the so-called "iron law of wages" (i.e., Lassalle's restatement of Ricardo's wage theory) nor the "intensity of cultivation," but rather the "historically evolving social stratification of the agricultural population" that was the "decisive factor" for explaining the workers' condition in the East:

The casual relationship is at least partially reversed here. With our modern scientific method we have become used to viewing technical-economic conditions and interests basically as primary, from which a people's social structure and political organization are derived . . . but here we see quite clearly that it is a matter of reciprocal effects in which the purely economic factor does not by any means play the leading role. Population distribution, division of trades, division of land, the legal forms of the organization of labor [*Arbeitsverfassung*] within individual districts have a much more decisive significance for the material and social-ethical condition of the agricultural worker, for his total standard of living, than do possible differences between favorable or unfavorable economic conditions for agricultural enterprise in certain areas, or than the relationship of profits from one form of production to profits from another form. It is those relations of social stratification [*soziale Schichtungsverhältnisse*] which almost entirely determine the workers' standard of living, and as a result of this standard of living—not the reverse—almost entirely determine their wages, their total economic condition" (1894d:66).

These remarks, written ten years before *The Protestant Ethic,* illustrate the typical Weberian procedure, one in which the explanatory power of economic factors is not dogmatically presupposed but is instead treated on a par with other factors. In this view the decisive influence of economic (or any other) factors is always a *possibility* to be checked against experience. Thus, in contrast to the above line of reasoning, Weber *does* insist on primary *economic* changes—disappearance of commerce, development of a rural natural economy—as the most basic causal factors explaining the *political* decline of the Roman Empire (1896a:308; 1976b:408). But whatever the case under discussion, it can be said that Weber's "sociological" perspective casts a much wider net of explanatory concepts and possibilities than do the alternatives in the various schools of political economy.

THE TYPOLOGY OF AGRARIAN ECONOMIES

Weber's differentiated view of "causal factors" and their "reciprocity" will come as no surprise. However, we may still wonder about his purpose in using developmental concepts. Is this a case of uncharacteristic concession to popular usage, an example of unbridled eclecticism, or a choice made for specific theoretical purposes? A clear answer emerges when we begin to consider the connections among Weber's various studies of the "social question." In general, Weber holds that this question must be understood not in terms of the "separation of the worker from the means of production," but in terms of the organization of labor, the *Arbeitsverfassung,* conceived as a function of the system of social stratification.

In the early writings Weber offers a sketch of four types of agrarian economies in the West that have organized labor, and therefore the entire social system, in radically different ways (see especially the summation in 1893b:24-26). The "slave state" sought to perpetuate a continuous supply of agricultural labor through conquest and strict control of social institutions (e.g., marriage, family, private property). At the other extreme some "colonial territories" have relied upon surplus (nomadic) labor, piece-wages, and surplus land to accomplish the tasks of production. The "patriarchal" system, characteristic of what Engels termed the "second serfdom,"[8] successfully bound labor to landed property by enforcing various forms of economic, social, and legal dependency. Finally, the solution most characteristic of the "modernizing state" has been based upon formally "free" labor, wage payments, intensive cultivation, technological innovation, and highly rationalized capital accumulation. All of this can be summarized, if somewhat more concisely than Weber's own account, as shown in Table 3. A complete discussion of this typology and its relationship to other parts of Weber's work would require more space than is available here; I shall restrict my comments to a few important points.

Weber's comparative studies of the *oikos* economy of antiquity, the colonial economy of contemporary Argentina (1894b), and the economic and social structure of Western Europe convinced him that neither the "slave" nor "colonial" nor "patriarchal" types were capable of sustained "technological" innovation and

Table 3
Typology of Agrarian Economies in Weber's Early Writings

	Economic Types			
	Slave	*Colonial*	*Patriarchal*	*Capitalist*
Factors of Production:				
Labor	unfree	free, nomadic, piece-wages	bondage, settled, share-rights, payment in kind	free, mobile, contractual relations, money-wages
Land	large estates	freeholding, surplus land	estates	commercial enterprise
Capital formation	irregular	irregular	virtually none	systematic, continuous
Social unit	community of slaves	nomadic band	monogamous family	monogamous family
Cultural level	low	low	medium	high
Technological innovation	low	medium	medium	high
Developmental tendency	autarchy, stagnation	wastefulness, exhaustion	autarchy, isolation	rational productivity, rising wages
Historical case	Roman Empire	Argentina (19th century)	Germany (16th to 19th centuries)	Germany (19th century)

economic "rationalization." All depended on the persistence of certain specific historical conditions—e.g., continual military conquest, uninterrupted access to surplus land, permanent isolation from market forces—that simply were not conducive to development of a "rational" system of production and exchange.

In other words, there could be no doubt that the fourth, "capitalist" type contained the most powerful forces of economic rationalization. Yet the full theoretical delineation of "developmental tendencies" *within* this type would point up socioeconomic and political conflicts, the opposition among classes and interests, from which possible consequences or "objective possibilities" could only be inferred.

The nature of the clash between patriarchal and capitalist orders is a more complicated issue for Weber, but a central argument can be reconstructed from the mass of details. The patriarchal system was a drag on economic rationalization due to the depressed condition of labor and the lack of dynamism characterizing it. In Weber's words, "lazy rentiers and an apathetic, traditionalistic mass" (1897b:109) were the hallmark of this type. From the viewpoint of national development and power, Germany (or any state) would be better off without patriarchalism; nevertheless, it persisted, but for all the "wrong" (i.e., political) reasons.

At this point in Weber's early writings we have encountered the seminal statement of the theory of rationalization and the methodology of the "ideal type." The definitive demonstration of this generalization comes in one key "transitional" text, "Agrarverhältnisse im Altertum" (1897a, trans. as *The Agrarian Sociology of Ancient Civilizations,* 1976a), the only one of Weber's writings that spans the early and later phase of his thought. It must be remembered that the "Agrarverhältnisse" essay dates from 1897-98 (first and second versions), not 1909 (the final, expanded version), and is in origin a companion piece for "Die sozialen Gründe des Untergangs der antiken Kultur" (The Social Causes of the Decline of Ancient Civilization, 1896a). A comparison of these versions shows the emergence in the last text of clearly identified "ideal types" of the "organizational stages" characteristic of agricultural societies in antiquity. Weber now defends the use of such types not only as means for classification and comparison but as rational reconstructions of particular "developmental stages." In fact, the language of "stages" and "types" is so closely associated in Weber's mind that the actual terms are used interchangeably. (As an illustration, the English translation even renders *"Stadien"* as "types" in one key passage [1909:44; 1976a:78]!) Furthermore, the 1909 text uses the terms *rationalization* and *rationalization process* (1909:38-39) in order to generalize about and explain structural relationships and changes both *internally* to a single type and *externally* among different types. Here rationalization is discussed by Weber in terms of functional specialization in the division of labor, structural differentiation of social and economic life, and (in one brief aside) secularization of culture. This is precisely the terminology and theoretical perspective of the earlier 1897-98 texts, only now the "ideal types" have become more sophisticated, the methodological underpinnings more precise, and the problem of "rationalization," subsequently clarified in Weber's later writings, much more explicit.

It should be noted, finally, that a fifth type is omitted from Weber's early writings: "agrarian communism" as either the earliest form of agricultural production or the final "fully rational" transcendence of the capitalist type. Weber was well aware of this proposed type, but he doubted its historicity, labeling it a political utopia of the intellectuals. The question was, would the hypothetical fifth type (in modern dress, of course) mark a further step along the path of economic rationalization, or would it instead sacrifice economic rationality to political goals (e.g., social justice, solidarity) and lead back toward forms of dependency imposed by the new "patriarch," the state? Weber suspected the latter outcome in practice. But it was a question best left to history, and it occupied Weber's thinking into his last lectures on economic development (1927: esp. ch. 1).

EARLY WEBER CONTRA LATE MARX

We are now in a better position to understand Weber's method in the early writings. Impressed by the apparently neo-Marxist concepts in these writings, including occasional references to "base" and "superstructure," some have maintained that Weber's approach was distinctive because he "took Marx seriously, and learned from Marx" (Dibble, 1968:99), while others have suggested that a text like "The Social Causes of the Decline of Ancient Civilization" was "based upon a free application of the method of historical materialism, in that it takes the contradiction between relations of production and forces of production as a guide for explanation" (Löwith, 1964:504). We must be careful about such judgments, however, emphasizing the phrase "*free* application" in Löwith's statement. No doubt Weber took Marx seriously, as did colleagues like Bücher and Sombart, and no doubt his method was broadly "materialist," if we mean by that using social conditions to explain human action (which is true for virtually all of modern social science). But these quickly become empty generalizations. I have tried to show specifically that Weber's scientific vocabulary came from political economy and historical sociology in general, not Marxism in particular. Weber did not use the terminology of "forces," "means," and "relations of production." His methodological principles were more differentiated, comprehensive, and flexible than those of the Marxism of his day; his use of different units of analysis, developmental concepts, causal factors, and ideal types was an attempt at scientific innovation, one that Weber thought of as a comprehensive, systematic alternative to the Marxist doctrines, among others. What we should beware of nowadays is not merely the denial of these far-reaching differences but also those contemporary reinterpretations in which Marx becomes Weber, and Weber becomes unrecognizable. The "Weberianized Marx" encountered so often in recent literature has much to do with the need to retain popular labels and precious little to do with the actual history and structure of social and political theory.

The problem of method is of course simply an aspect of the larger question suspended over these discussions: What can the early writings tell us about Weber's relationship to Marx, a relationship that is perhaps the most fateful of all for modern social theory? In answering this question we may attempt to distinguish among Weber's views toward (1) Marx himself, (2) other Marxist writers and academicians, and (3) the SPD and its programs (Giddens, 1977: ch. 5), but it will become quite apparent for the early writings that no precise separation can be maintained. Historical evidence knows little about such precise boundaries, and in order to say anything intelligible one view can only be adduced in relation to others.

Weber's few published, direct references to Marx and "materialism" (e.g., 1894a:473; 1895:8; 1896b:26) remain obscure until we see the precise points of contact between himself, Marx, and Marxism.[9] One of the most crucial points came in 1892, at the *Evangelisch-Sozialer Kongress* in Berlin, at which a two-and-a-half-hour speech, "The New Social-Democratic Program," was delivered by Adolf Wagner, Weber's former political science professor at Berlin. This was precisely the time at which Weber was conducting two surveys of labor relations in the East (one for the *Verein für Sozialpolitik*, the other for the *Kongress*), a task that led to a correspondence with Bebel (Weber, 1893c:63). Weber's interest in the social-democratic position could not have been greater. He attended the Berlin Convention and would have heard Wagner's speech, a surprisingly complete and balanced review of the nature and history of Marxist doctrine from the *Manifesto* onward and an explication and critique of the recently adopted Erfurt Program. Wagner characterized the latter as a scientific expression of "the Marxist theory of social and economic laws of development" and as a declaration of "the complete victory of the Marxist tendency, the victory of the radical international tendency" within the socialist movement (1892:23, 29). Behind this revolutionary program with its rejection of the Lassallean "iron law of wages" and its overtures to agrarian labor stood Marx's own "Critique of the Gotha Program" (1875), first published by Engels in 1891. Wagner scrutinized this "Critique" as well, citing its most striking phraseology—revolutionary dictatorship of the proletariat," "from each according to his ability, to each according to his needs" (1892:12,40,44)—and drawing out its theoretical and practical implications. Weber received quite specific knowledge about the relevant issues in these two texts—one from the SPD, the other from Marx himself.

The Marx with whom Weber duels through the 1890s is the Marx of the "Critique of the Gotha Program," the victorious later Marx of revolutionary (or Weber would have said "utopian") promise, economic equality, and "scientific" laws of development. It is little wonder then that Weber's early comparative studies of labor and social structure, both in the modern world and in antiquity, set out to parry these thrusts from Marx. The ensuing struggle proceeded on two levels: the scientific attempt to grasp agrarian labor's socioeconomic condition; and the practical-political attempt to win its loyalties for class, party, or nation. In the preceding two sections I have emphasized Weber's approach to the former, an approach that was not so much antithetic to Marx's science as it was synthetic. That is, it aimed at altering the terms of discourse, mastering Marx's categories by reconstituting them within a more comprehensive theoretical schema. Putting it differently, we can say that by siding with Nietzsche, by postulating the inexorability of those "inconvenient facts" and "prosaic laws" governing *real* social life, Weber thought it might be possible not only to blunt Marxian *praxis,* but also to recapture its hypotheses for a permanently skeptical science. In a sense Weber's project commenced just where Marx's ended. Or to paraphrase a well-known contrast, whereas Marx sought in his later work to discover the "law" of development of human history, Weber attempted in his early writings to discover the *form* of "development" and "rationalization" in the modern and ancient world. To accomplish this much would have been no mean feat for Weber; it was a scientific project that continued to occupy his thought.

CONCLUSION

Like social institutions, the nature of a body of thought is often revealed at its foundations. Max Weber's early writings are only a beginning, to be sure, but they do disclose above all a remarkably contemporary theoretical perspective and an impressive continuity with his later methodological, theoretical, and political concerns. Recently we have witnessed renewed interest in the type of analytic, comparative, and historical question raised by Weber in his earliest inquiries, an interest that will certainly persist as long as we are drawn to the problem of the world historical development of "capitalism" and its rationalization in relation to other socioeconomic systems. It is as if we have only now rediscovered the vast problem and literature out of which Weber's entire thought emerged, without, however, paying much attention to the advances contained in his early writings. To recover the origins of Weber's approach and the tools of analysis forged in his thought before 1900 is then to see the strong sense in which his "last analysis of capitalism" (Collins, 1980) was also his first. It is also to notice that *The Protestant Ethic and the Spirit of Capitalism* constituted only one episode within the larger course of his explanatory efforts and substantive work. "It is quite possible," Weber himself later remarked, not without irony, "once my investigations are finally completed, that having been provoked I will be accused for a change of capitulating to historical materialism, just as I am now accused of capitulating to ideology" (1908:56). Both possibilities were deliberately present from the start, as Weber criticized and reconstituted predecessors' categories. If we can discover even this much in the early writings, then we shall have gone some distance toward understanding their significance for the intellectual journey from political economy to a new political sociology.

NOTES

1. Only 3 out of some 54 texts (or about 60 pages out of nearly 2000!) have been translated: see Weber (1976b, 1978 [partial translation], 1979). In addition, *The Agrarian Sociology of Ancient Civilizations* (1976a) is a translation of a text that first appeared in 1897: see Weber (1897a, 1898). The third version (Weber, 1909), on which the translation is based, was considerably enlarged and revised.

2. To be precise, the exceptions are Bergstraesser (1957), Dibble (1968), Roth (1968:xxxiv-li), Mitzman (1970: pt. I), Mommsen (1974a: chs. 1-4), and Bendix (1977: ch. 2).

3. Following the lead of Bendix and his associates (1973: 10-12), I mean by "political sociology" the approach to the analysis of social life that emphasizes (1) the utility of employing multiple units of analysis instead of a single hypostatized "system," (2) the importance of "structural" variables for explaining human action, and (3) the significance of historical explanation and comparative historical development. In this conception the boundary between "political sociology" and "historical sociology" is amorphous.

4. For the historical developments in German political economy, see Winkel (1977). Although Weber himself said little about these developments, his Freiburg colleague and collaborator, von Schulze-Gaevernitz (1895), commented directly on List and the new political economy. We can assume that Weber shared Schulze-Gaevernitz's knowledge of the situation.

5. There can be no doubt that Weber knew Nietzsche's work quite well by the early 1890s. During the years (1892-95) in which Weber was publishing six articles in the *Christliche Welt,* no writers were more widely discussed in its pages than Nietzsche and Tolstoy. Essays covered Nietzsche's life work, his "new morality," and his philosophy in texts like *Beyond Good and Evil.* By 1895 this Protestant, reform-minded journal was noting that Nietzsche "is much discussed in Germany"; one of Weber's letters to his wife (26 July 1894; Nachlass Max Weber, Zentrales Staatsarchiv, Merseburg, Rep. 92 [NW], 30/1,50) confirms his own engagement in these debates.

6. Found in an undated letter to Naumann, probably from 1897; Nachlass Friedrich Naumann, No. 106, Zentrales Staatsarchiv Potsdam.

7. In his translation of Weber, *Roscher and Knies* (1975), Guy Oakes has chosen *evolution* rather than *development* for this terminology. I have used *development* because it has somewhat broader connotations in English,

suggesting the appropriate relationships between Weber's analysis, the "developmental" theories in the nineteenth century starting with Comte and Marx, and the most recent debates over "development" and "modernization." *Evolution* often has Darwinian or biological connotations that Weber wanted to avoid, *except* in those instances where he criticized the importation of biological metaphors into social analysis (e.g., 1895:9). In addition, Weber's German did permit the use of *evolution* when that was the intended meaning (e.g., 1894a.).

8. Engels to Marx, 15 December 1882, referring to Engels's own essay on the history of agrarian relations in the German "mark" (Marx and Engels, 1973, 35:128).

9. "If one hasn't read Marx, then one shouldn't judge him," Weber once wrote (letter to Alfred Weber, 30 January 1907; NW 30/7,6-7; he was referring specifically to Delbrück's negative review of Sombart's *Kapitalismus*,) Did this statement also apply to Weber's own earlier judgments about Marx, or was it intended as self-criticism? Mommsen argues that "at least up to 1906 Max Weber referred to Marxism in the vulgar versions of the day rather than to the original writings of Marx and Engels themselves" (1974b:49). But this dating and evaluation of the references appears excessively cautious. Roth (1971) has marshaled most (but not all) of the considerable indirect evidence for Weber's firm knowledge of Marx and Marxism in the 1890s. That no direct evidence exists on this matter is regrettable, but hardly surprising, given Weber's reluctance to pose as an interpreter of economic or political doctrines. Whether Weber's early understanding of Marx was "vulgar" or otherwise seems an academic question, for the lines of argument in this particular debate were clarified only much later, and the "humanized" or even "Weberianized" Marx is certainly a product of recent revisionism. Moreover, the question is likely to be answered differently, depending upon one's interpretation of *Marx*, not Weber. The relevant debate for Weber's contemporaries concerned Marxism as "science" versus Marxism as "ethics," a debate that engaged Weber's mind in a variety of ways throughout his life.

REFERENCES

Bendix, Reinhard
    1973   State and Society, A Reader in Comparative Political Sociology. Berkeley: California.
    1977   Max Weber, An Intellectual Portrait. Berkeley: California.
Bergstraesser, Arnold
    1957   "Max Webers Antrittsvorlesung in zeitgeschichtlicher Perspektive." Vierteljahrshefte für Zeitgeschichte 5:209-19.

Dibble, Vernon K.
1968   "Social Science and Political Commitment in the Young
          Max Weber." Archives Européennes de Sociologie
          9:92-110.
Löwith, Karl
1964   "Die Entzauberung der Welt durch Wissenschaft."
          Merkur 18:501-19.
Marx, Karl, and Friedrich Engels
1973   Werke. Berlin: Dietz.
Mitzman, Arthur
1970   The Iron Cage, An Historical Interpretation of Max
          Weber. New York: Knopf.
Mommsen, Wolfgang J.
1974a   Max Weber und die deutsche Politik, 1890-1920. Tübingen:
          Mohr.
1974b   The Age of Bureaucracy: Perspectives on the Political
          Sociology of Max Weber. Oxford: Blackwell.
Nietzsche, Friedrich
1886   (1964) Jenseits von Gut und Böse. Stuttgart: Kröner.
Roth, Guenther
1968   "Introduction." In Max Weber, Economy and Society.
          New York: Bedminster.
1971   "The Historical Relationship to Marxism." In Bendix and
          Roth, Scholarship and Partisanship: Essays on Max
          Weber. Berkeley: California.
von Schulze-Gaevernitz, Gerhard
1895   "Die gegenwärtigen Mittel zur Hebung der Arbeiterklasse
          in Deutschland." Ethische Kultur 3:137-39, 149-52.
Tönnies, Ferdinand
1897   Der Nietzsche-Kultus, Eine Kritik. Leipzig: Reisland.
Wagner, Adolf
1892   Das neue Sozialdemokratische Program: Rehtwisch.
Wallerstein, Immanuel
1974   The Modern World-System. New York: Academic.
Weber, Max
1889   (1924) Zur Geschichte der Handelsgesellschaften im
          Mittelalter. In Gesammelte Aufsätze zur Sozial- und
          Wirtschaftsgeschichte. Tübingen: Mohr.
1891   Die römische Agrargeschichte in ihrer Bedeutung für das
          Staats- und Privatrecht. Stuttgart: Enke.
1893a   "Die Evangelisch-Sozialen Kurse in Berlin im Herbst dieses
          Jahres." Die Christliche Welt 7:766-68.
1893b   "Die Erhebung des Vereins für Sozialpolitik über die Lage

der Landarbeiter." Das Land 1:8-9, 24-26, 43-45, 58-59, 129-30, 147-48.

1893c   "Referat [über 'Die ländliche Arbeitsverfassung']." In Schriften des Vereins für Sozialpolitik 58. Leipzig: Duncker.

1894a   "Was Heisst Christlich-Sozial?" Die Christliche Welt 8:472-7.

1894b   "Argentinische Kolonistenwirthschaften." Deutsches Wochenblatt 7:20-22, 57-59.

1894c   (1924) "Entwickelungstendenzen in der Lage der ostelbischen Landarbeiter." In Gesammelte Aufsätze zur Sozial- und Wirtschaftsgeschichte. Tübingen: Mohr. (Revision of 1894a.)

1894d   "Die deutschen Landarbeiter [Korreferat und Schlusswort]." In Bericht über die Verhandlungen des 5. Evangelisch-Sozialen Kongresses. Berlin: Rehtwisch.

1895   (1958) "Der Nationalstaat und die Volkswirtschaftspolitik, Akademische Antrittsrede." In Gesammelte Politische Schriften. Tübingen: Mohr.

1896a   (1924) "Die sozialen Gründe des Untergangs der antiken Kultur." In Gesammelte Aufsätze zur Sozial- und Wirtschaftsgeschichte. Tübingen: Mohr.

1896b   (1958) "Zur Grundung einer National-Sozialen Partei." In Gesammelte Politische Schriften. Tübingen: Mohr.

1896c   (1924) "Die Börse, II. Der Börsenverkehr." In Gesammelte Aufsätze zur Soziologie und Sozialpolitik. Tübingen: Mohr.

1897a   "Agrarverhältnisse im Altertum." In Handwörterbuch der Staatswissenschaften. Jena: Fischer.

1897b   "[Diskussionsbeiträge zum Vortrag Karl Oldengergs]. In Die Verhandlungen des 8. Evangelisch-Sozialen Kongresses. Göttingen: Vandenhoeck.

1898   "Agrarverhältnisse im Altertum." In Handwörterbuch der Staatswissenschaften, Jena: Fischer. [Revision of 1897a.]

1904   (1924) "Der Streit um den Charakter der altgermanischen Sozialforschung in der deutschen Literatur des letzten Jahrzehnts." In Gesammelte Aufsätze zur Sozial- und Wirtschaftsgeschichte. Tübingen: Mohr.

1909   (1924) "Agrarverhältnisse im Altertum." In Gesammelte Aufsätze zur Sozial- und Wirtschaftsgeschichte. Tübingen: Mohr. [Revision of 1897a, 1898.]

1927   General Economic History. Translated by Frank H. Knight. Glencoe: Free Press.

1936   Jugendbriefe. Edited by Marianne Weber. Tübingen:
            Mohr.
1975   Roscher and Knies: The Logical Problem of Historical
            Economics. Translated by Guy Oakes. New York: Free
            Press.
1976a   The Agrarian Sociology of Ancient Civilizations.
            Translated by R. I. Frank. Highlands, N.J.: Humanities
            Press. [Translation of Weber, 1909.]
1976b   "The Social Causes of the Decline of Ancient
            Civilization." In The Agrarian Sociology of Ancient
            Civilizations. Translated by R. I. Frank. London: New
            Left. [Translation of Weber, 1896c.]
1978   "Economic Policy and the National Interest in Imperial
            Germany." In Max Weber, Selections in Translation.
            Edited by W. G. Runciman. London: Cambridge. [Partial
            translation of Weber, 1895b.]
1979   "Developmental Tendencies in the Situation of East Elbian
            Rural Laborers." Economy and Society 8:177-205.
            [Translation of Weber, 1894c.]

Winkle, Harold
1977   Die deutsche Nationalökonomie im 19. Jahrhundert.
            Darmstadt: Wissenschaftliche Buchgesellschaft.

6

THE WEBER–LUKÁCS ENCOUNTER

Zoltan Tar and Judith Marcus

> The decision . . . on any truly important matter has to be an ethical one.
> —Georg Lukács, "Bolshevism as a Moral Problem"

> Ich bin der Ansicht, meine Entwicklung ist Schritt für Schritt vor sich gegangen und ich glaube, wenn man sich damit befasst, dann sollte man das am besten chronologisch tun, denn die Dinge hängen sehr stark in meinem Leben zusammen.
> —Georg Lukács, *Gelebtes Denken*

Albert Salomon, a pioneer in bringing Weber's legacy to this country, was of the opinion that Max Weber "became a sociologist in a long and intense dialogue with the ghost of Karl Marx".[1] In the same vein, I shall propose that Georg Lukács had had a lifelong dialogue with the ghost of Max Weber beginning in 1912 in Heidelberg, where next to Weber, Lukács was the most prominent member of the so-called Weber-*Kreis*. That dialogue at times took the form of a highly personal affair for Lukács.

To be sure, the Weber-Lukács relationship had had its share of ups and downs during its entire course. In this paper I will limit the discussion to the issues and themes that are important enough in their own right and that, beyond their topical relevance, are interesting from the viewpoint of the personal and/or intellectual history of the two men. I will have more to say on Lukács's relationship—or indebtedness—to Weber than the other way around, partly because Lukács was more obliging in giving us evidence and documentation to that effect. I will, moreover, cover only the Heidelberg period, that is, the years between 1912 and 1918.[2]

The Lukács-Weber encounter must be examined in the larger context of Lukács's relationship to German culture in general and to some leading members of the German intelligentsia of the Wilhelmian era in particular. Born in 1885 in Budapest as György Bernát Löwinger, the son of Joseph Löwinger, a self-made millionaire, György Lukács was, so to speak, *von Hause aus,* predestined to go beyond the geographical and intellectual boundaries of his native Hungary. His father changed his name to Lukács in 1890 and became ennobled (szegedi Lukács or von Lukács) in 1901. The son continued the assimilation process and converted to Protestantism in 1907, a year after he received his doctorate. The father, József von Lukács, provided all the necessary support—financial, emotional and intellectual—to motivate his son "to make it out in the world."[3] He cherished, encouraged and furthered his son's ambition to have a prestigious academic career; he presided over a home environment that welcomed the leading intellectuals, artists and public figures of the time, Hungarians and foreigners alike. Lukács *père* entertained the likes of Max Weber and Thomas Mann during their visits to Hungary; Béla Bartók, the eminent Hungarian composer, lived in the Lukács home for years. Georg's relationship with his mother, Adele Wertheimer, who was of Viennese birth, presents an entirely different, more complex picture, which could easily lend itself to psychohistorical treatment. Lukács himself had made veiled references to his contempt for his mother and to his projecting of his hatred for her upon the socioeconomic order of the Austro-Hungarian Empire. Be that as it may, this now proven antagonistic relationship provided another negative kind of motivation. It is more important for now to consider the effects of the home environment on Lukács's development: such factors as the bilingual—German and Hungarian—background and the opportunities to acquire a working knowledge of French and English and to travel widely that contributed to his widening horizon and experience. Upon Lukács's graduation from the Gymnasium, for example, his father presented him with a trip to Norway, to visit Henrik Ibsen, his then intellectual hero. Soaking up the new trends, such as naturalism, Lukács himself began experimenting with playwriting and later founded—together with a few like-minded friends and with a fatherly financial backing—the Thalia Theater, where avant-garde plays were to be staged along with the classical ones and shown to the workers at a very low price. Even before receiving his (first) doctorate degree in law in 1906 from the University of Kolozsvár (now in Romania), Lukács traveled to Berlin, attended the lectures of Wilhelm Dilthey and Georg Simmel, and became the latter's personal friend. As Lukács remarked in his 1918 obituary of Simmel, he was part of a "small group of philosophically inclined young thinkers who were attracted to Simmel, and who, for shorter or longer periods, were all touched by the magic of Simmel's thinking."[4] An older Lukács again credited Simmel with having contributed to his intellectual development: "Simmel posited questions about the sociological aspects of artistic creation," said Lukács during an interview, "thereby providing me with a perspective with the help of which, although going beyond Simmel but proceeding in the direction outlined by him, I studied literary works. The philosophy of my *History of the Development of Modern Drama* is truly a Simmelian philosophy."[5] Thus, Lukács encountered Dilthey, Simmel and then Marx before he met Weber; this seemed to be an excellent preparation for meeting Weber, who had already encountered the three thinkers. Lukács reflected later how the impact of Simmel and Dilthey was instrumental in the process of clarifying his ideas that by necessity "entailed the reading of historical and sociological works. This was the reason why my first acquaintance with the writings of Marx that was worthy of the name occurred precisely in this period." He added, "Naturally . . . this a Marx read through the eyes of Simmel."[6]

LUKÁCS'S ROAD TO HEIDELBERG—AND TO WEBER

Georg von Lukács was still a young, relatively unknown, aspiring scholar at the time he left the cultural confinement of his native Hungary and entered through personal and intellectual contacts the Central European—or more precisely, the German—cultural sphere. He spent the winter of 1911-12 in Florence working on a systematic philosophy of art; his friend at the time, the German-Jewish philosopher Ernst Bloch, persuaded him to move to the intellectually more conducive academic environment of Heidelberg. There existed another motivation: Lukács's request to have his *Habilitation* approved at Budapest University failed in May 1911, mainly because of the anti-Semitic sentiments of some of the leading professors there. The favorable reception of Lukács's writings such as the essay, "Metaphysics of Tragedy," published in the prestigious journal *Logos* (1911), and the essay collection *Soul and Form* (1911) provided an added incentive.

Lukács's entry into German intellectual circles was helped along by many friends, among them Emil Lederer and his wife in Heidelberg, the playwright Paul Ernst, Ernst Bloch and Franz Baumgarten.[7] Simmel's endorsement was especially helpful; he reported to Lukács in his letter of May 25, 1912,

I'll soon write to [Emil] Lask on your behalf. I do not recommend your looking up Windelband right away partly because he is a very busy man, but partly for other reasons. . . . Should you find it necessary, though, and important for some reason, please let me know at my Westend address and I will immediately send a few introductory lines.[8]

The decision to leave his "Italian period" behind and to commit himself entirely to the German sphere was not unambiguous for Lukács. As he reflected in 1969: "I always preferred the Italian everyday life to the German one, but the motivation to find understanding was irresistible. When I finally took off for Heidelberg it was without knowing for how long."[9] As it turned out, the stay stretched over five years with interruptions for travel and other commitments.

The Heidelberg Lukács and Bloch first saw in mid-May 1912 was populated by a galaxy of brilliant minds such as the philosophers Wilhelm Windelband, Emil Lask, Max and Alfred Weber, Ernst Troeltsch, Karl Jaspers, the poet Stefan George and his friend, the Goethe scholar Friedrich Gundolf and so on. We have today the reminiscences of some of the witnesses of the period and the impression that Lukács made. Marianne Weber, hostess at the best-known gathering of that period, the Weber-*Kreis,* reported:

From the opposite pole of the *Weltanschauung* the Webers also met some philosophers from Eastern Europe who were becoming known around that time, particularly the Hungarian Georg von Lukács, with whom the Webers struck up a close friendship. . . . These young philosophers were moved by eschatological hopes of a new emissary of the transcendent God, and they saw the basis of salvation in a socialist social order created by brotherhood.[10]

Paul Honigsheim also observed Lukács's impact on Weber, who told him: "Whenever I have spoken to Lukács, I have to think about it for days."[11] Another member of the Weber-*Kreis,* Karl Jaspers, commented some fifty-odd years later on the impression that Lukács (and Bloch) made on the gathering: "Lukács was regarded by some as a kind of 'Holy Man.' . . . The philospher Lask quipped: 'Do you know who the four apostles are? Mattheus, Marcus, Lukács and Bloch.' "[12] The gathering at the Weber home usually centered around the host; as he once remarked: "I simply weigh upon these people." Marianne adds: "Only a few of the guests like Gundolf or Lukács were able to express their ideas well enough to become independent points of interests."[15]

We can safely assume that the Heidelberg experience was a fruitful one for Lukács, in that his hopes for a "better understanding" materialized. As Lukács himself commented: "I found greater understanding than ever before. Of course, I soon had to realize that a Max Weber and an Emil Lask were rather exceptional phenomena within the German intellectual life."[14] Even in his old age, Lukács repeatedly spoke of his Heidelberg experience, especially of its congenial intellectual atmosphere:

It was in the winter of 1911-12 in Florence that I first contemplated the writing of an independent, systematic aesthetics, but I sat down to it in all seriousness only in Heidelberg, during the years 1912-1914. Even today, I remember with deep gratitude the interest—both sympathetic and critical—that Ernst Bloch, Emil Lask and Max Weber showed toward my work.[15]

As far as the Webers's perception of Lukács is concerned, it is interesting to note that they regarded the eschatologist Lukács as a typical product of the East European political sphere and cultural milieu. They shared this perception with others in Heidelberg, as the comments of contemporaries demonstrate. For example, it is not by accident that another illustrious German contemporary, the novelist Thomas Mann, perceived Lukács in a similar manner and gave some Lukácsian characteristics to his fictional character, Leo Naphta, the Jesuit-communist, in his novel *The Magic Mountain.*[16] I will have more to say on the specifics of this Lukácsian aspect later when discussing Lukács's interest in Dostoevskii and the Russian matters.

SHARED INTERESTS AND INTERACTION

Although Lukács and Weber stood at opposite poles of the *Weltanschauung,* as Marianne Weber put it, they shared many interests, had at times the same preoccupations and together developed some new concerns. The limited scope of this paper cannot even attempt to deal with a few of these themes in any detail or in true analytical fashion. I shall, therefore present in outline some of the concerns, themes and issues that constituted an intellectual bond between the two men. Any attempt to separate neatly and list these common interests either chronologically or in the order of importance is fraught with difficulties but should center around these issues: (1) their rejection of the vulgar Marxism of the Second International type and concurrently their adherence to (South-West) neo-Kantian epistemology; (2) their shared interest in problems of sociology of art and literature; (3) the reception of Dostoevskii and the "Russian experience"; and (4) their common interest in problems of ethics, especially with regard to politics or, more precisely, violent political action. There are problems with any such neat categorization. Lukács and Weber continuously and at times fervently discussed problems relating to art and literature, but their discussion has to be placed in the framework of Lukács's attempt to get his *Habilitation* through at the University of Heidelberg, a matter Weber was heavily involved in. Moreover, this problem area occupied both men during most of Lukács's sojourn in Heidelberg and cannot be pigeonholed chronologically. A similar difficulty occurs with the Dostoevskii reception and with the problems of ethics, which at times were juxtaposed and also touched upon by the controversy over Lukács's *Habilitation.* Thus, the present outline, which zeroes in on some of the above themes, may seem an arbitrary choice.

Weber's criticism of vulgar Marxism needs no elaboration since there exists an extensive literature on the subject.[17] As for Lukács, his *History and Class Consciousness* has been interpreted by many as *the* alternative to the unimaginative Marxism of the Second International after the turn of the century as well as to the dogmatism of post-Leninist Marxism in the Soviet Union. Regardless of his numerous disclaimers and self-critical comments about his *History and Class Consciousness,* Lukács emphatically stated in 1967: "I do not at all regret today that I took my first lessons in social science from Simmel and Max Weber, and not from Kautsky. Perhaps one can even say that this was a fortunate circumstance for my own development."[18] Without going into a detailed discussion of the most Weberian essay of *History and Class Consciousness,* the so-called reification essay, I wish to mention another, lesser-known reference to Weber, an essay from the same volume, "The Changing Function of Historical Materialism." In July 1919, at the height of the activities of the Hungarian Soviet Republic, Lukács as the deputy commissar of culture gave a speech on the occasion of the opening of the Institute for Historical Materialism in which he still emphasized the importance of the thought of the bourgeois Max Weber and contrasted it to that of the Marxist Karl Kautsky:

While historical materialism brought about a self-knowledge of nineteenth-century society, the research into earlier societies, e.g. early Christianity or the early history of the Orient conducted, for example, by Kautsky, has shown itself as not being sophisticated enough in comparison with more recent studies. . . . Consequently, we must utilize the work of those exceptional scholars . . . who understood the basic tenets of historical materialism and subjected them to detailed revision in the course of their own investigation into the history of the past. I am thinking of scholars such as Max Weber.[19]

Lukács's lecture was printed in the July 1919 issue of the *International.* Interestingly enough, the revised and expanded version of the essay in *History and Class Consciousness* omits the above passage. The omission may well have been for both personal and political reasons, such as Weber's extremely harsh and negative evaluation of the 1919 revolution and Lukács's role in it. Weber, namely, concluded that "these experiments can and will result in the discrediting of the cause of socialism for hundreds of years."[20]

As noted earlier, Lukács moved to Heidelberg in order to find a conducive intellectual environment and "understanding" and, even more importantly, to establish himself in his quest for an academic career. Soon after his arrival, his work on a systematic aesthetics continued, with the understanding that it was to serve as his *Habilitationsschrift.* To keep the historical record straight, it should be pointed out that Lukács attempted twice to have his *Habilitation* accepted: The first attempt was made in Freiburg, where the neo-Kantian philosopher Heinrich Rickert reigned supreme and was helped along by Lukács's friend, Franz Baumgarten, who wrote to Lukács in July 8, 1912: "The ground is prepared for you. It won't hurt that Simmel praised you and Lask also wrote enthusiastically about you."[21] In spite of such elaborate preparations, one of the things that worked against Lukács, and brought the Freiburg attempt to naught, was his reputation as exclusively an essayist incapable of sustained, systematic work. When Lukács arrived in Heidelberg in 1912, he was again confronted with the same problem. Although his first book published in Germany, *Soul and Form* (1911), impressed an array of his contemporaries, including Thomas Mann, Ernst Troeltsch, Martin Buber and Max Weber, it also put off the more conservative, that is, traditionally inclined academic circles in Heidelberg, whose backing Lukács needed if he was to succeed. His staunchest ally in the *Habilitation* affair was, besides Alfred Weber, Max Weber. Thus, the interest Lukács and Weber shared in problems of aesthetics and in sociology of art and literature is inseparable from the controversy over Lukács's *Habilitation,* that is, his entry into the exclusive club of German "Mandarins."

The proposition that Weber and Lukács shared these interests may come as a surprise in light of Weber's scant output in this area: he wrote only one monograph on music, *The Rational Foundations of Western Music*. As I will discuss later in relation to the Russian "experience," Weber planned to write a monograph on Tolstoy. But the key issue for both Weber and Lukács was the positing of the problem of aesthetics in Lukács's planned *Aesthetics* and/or *Habilitationschrift*. As Lukács recalled shortly before his death, the key issue in his relation to Weber, as he told Weber, was as follows:

According to Kant, the essence of aesthetics is the aesthetic judgment. In my opinion, there exists no such priority of aesthetic judgment, only the priority of *Sein*. I put the question to Weber "Es gibt Kunstwerke—wie sind sie möglich"[Works of art exist; how are they possible?], and that made a deep impression on him.[22]

Indeed, Weber was impressed enough to reflect on the Lukácsian positing of the problem and refers to it in his "Science as a

Vocation" (1917). He discusses the meaning of science and draws
the parallel between Kant's and Lukács's positing of the problematic treatment of meaning: "Every theology . . . presupposed
that the world must have a *meaning,* and the question is how to
interpret this meaning so that it is intellectually conceivable. It is
the same with Kant's epistemology. He took for his point of
departure the presupposition, "Scientific truth exists and it is
valid," and then asked, "Under which presupposition of thought is
truth possible and meaningful? The modern aestheticians (actually
or expressly, as for instance, G. v. Lukács) proceed from the
presupposition that 'works of art exist' and then ask: 'How is their
existence meaningful and possible?' "[23]

As is shown by the recently recovered Lukács treatise, originally
intended as *Habilitationschrift* for Heidelberg University and
published in both German and Hungarian,[24] Weber quoted the
opening sentence. Through his interest in Lukács's progress and his
"solving" of the problem of the meaning and possibility of works
of art, Weber received impetus for his own reflections. However,
there was an additional significance to any progress that Lukács
made in his work toward a systematic aesthetic: it was intended to
prove to Weber, and through him to his colleagues at the
University, that Lukács was, after all, "the systematic type and
beyond his essayist period." Weber thus urges Lukács: "I have to
express my view over and over again that only a completed work
would give the optimal possibility for a positive solution of your
Habilitation."[25]

As the surviving correspondence between Weber and Lukács
shows, their frequent intellectual and also social relationship
continued with Weber steadily following and commenting on
Lukács's progress on his aesthetics, which later bore the title
Heidelberger Philosophie der Kunst (The Heidelberg Philosophy of
Art). As early as March 1913, Weber could read chapter 1 with
approval and asked: "I wonder how you will do when you come to
the concept of form?"[26] On March 22, Weber had already received
chapter 2, and although he could not spend too much time on it
before his impending travel, he wrote enthusiastically: "My
impression is a very strong one, and I am quite convinced that the
statement of the problem is definitely the correct one—at last."
He also encouraged Lukács to continue full speed ahead because

"the more material you have to hand in, the better your chances for success in a situation fraught with difficulties."[27]

The situation became more difficult as events of the year 1913-14 did not further Lukács's progress: Lukács met and married his first wife, the Russian anarchist refugee, Yelena Grabenko, and was thinking about *Habilitation* with Alfred Weber when World War I broke out. As a result, Lukács's interest and activities were turned around. In the "age of complete sinfulness," as Lukács called the war period using Fichte's phrase, he felt that to work on an aesthetics would be "barbaric"—to paraphrase Adorno's post-Auschwitz expression. Lukács then turned to ethics and reported to his friend, the playwright Paul Ernst, in March 1915, "At last I will begin my new book on Dostoevskii. *I put aside the aesthetics.*"[28]

In September 1915 Lukács returned to Budapest and served in the Army's "auxiliary service" in a censor's office. Very soon his old friends and new disciples, about two dozen intellectuals, gathered around him and formed the so-called Sunday Circle, modeled after the Weber-*Kreis,* under his undisputed leadership. Other participants of the evening discussions included Béla Balázs, Karl Mannheim, Frederick Antal, Arnold Hauser, to name but a few of the people who achieved fame later on. The discussions revolved around problems of ethics, aesthetics, Kierkegaard and Dostoevskii. In the spring of 1917 the Free School of Humanities (*Szellemtudományok Iskolája*) grew out of the Circle, which gave a series of public lectures with speakers added such as Béla Bartók and Zoltán Kodály.[29]

In spite of his service in the Army and involvement with the Sunday Circle, Lukács did not give up the attempt for a *Habilitation*; he based his hopes on rumors that Simmel and Rickert would be appointed in Heidelberg and thus approached Weber:

I would like to propose the following. Since it is unpredictable how long the war and my military confinement will go on, compounded by the fact that I cannot do any concentrated work on such a project as the *Aesthetics,* the possibilities of a *Habilitation* would be postponed indefinitely in spite of the present favorable personal conditions [the appointment of Rickert and Simmel]. Therefore, it would mean so much to me if we could still arrange something during the war. What I mean is: could Simmel or maybe Rickert take care of my *Habilitation* on the basis of the already completed part of my *Aesthetics*?[30]

Although we do not possess Weber's answer it must have been positive, judging from Lukács's letter of thanks:

I am very thankful for the information concerning the Heidelberg matter. Had you not assured me specifically, I would never have had any doubts about your taking a great interest in my case. I am proud of what I have achieved in Heidelberg objectively, meaning that my case *as a case* has become important for you.[31]

After Lukács's "escape" from his military service in Budapest, he returned to Heidelberg in 1916 and resumed working on his *Aesthetics.*[32] Weber followed the renewed efforts closely, and in a truly Weberian manner he discussed the alternatives, means and ends for possible action in the matter of Lukács's *Habilitation.* In his letter of August 14, 1916, as an addendum to their conversation on the previous day, he outlined the following three alternatives. First, a *Habilitation* with Alfred Weber in sociology and political economy because of the close relationship of the two; as it turned out, Alfred Weber became one of the staunchest supporters of Lukács in the long battle for a *Habilitation.* Weber's own preference was for the second alternative, both for Lukács's own sake and for the sake of his intellectual development: a *Habilitation* with Rickert in philosophy, although the relationship of the two was at times somewhat strained. After all, wrote Weber, "the most direct road leads to the man whose field really encompasses your interest." The third alternative reiterated the old problematic of "the essayistic nature of Lukács intellectual work." Weber was quite blunt when he told Lukács:

I have to be honest with you. I know that R[ickert] wants to get acquainted with you. It would help if you could force yourself to cut grass on a sheep meadow in order to quiet your nerves and *then* to get yourself again into the work you quit. A *very* good friend of yours, Lask, is of the opinion: ". . . he is a born essayist and will not stay with systematic work, therefore should not be habilitated." Of course, the essayist is not less than the systematic scholar, perhaps even on the contrary! But he does *not* belong to the university, and it would not do any good for the university and what is even more important for himself. On the basis of what you read for us from the brilliant fragment of your *Aesthetics* I sharply disagreed with this opinion. And because your sudden turn to Dostoevskii seemed to prove Lask's view as correct, *I hated* that work and I still hate it. . . .

If it is really painful and prohibitive for you to complete a systematic work and you begin another in the meantime, then, with heavy heart I advise you to forget about *Habilitation*. Not because you are not worthy of it, but because it does not help you and ultimately does not help the students either in the deepest sense. Then your vocation is something else. But you do what *you* deem as correct.[33]

The problem Lukács's essayistic tendencies versus the desirability of a systematic body of work is one that I cannot go into here. However, it is not a sufficient explanation and/or interpretation to separate his early, pre-Marxist period as the "essayistic" one and the latter as the systematic, Marxist period and explain the former period with Lukács being a "traveler" both in a literary and a figurative sense. As all Lukács scholars well know, Lukács found time between travels for the conception and writing of a systematic massive two-volume work, *The History of the Development of the Modern Drama*. It was paralleled by purely essayistic ventures collected in the volume *Soul and Form*. During Lukács's Moscow sojourn (1933-1945), he produced both a purely essayistic body of work and a systematic one, *The Young Hegel*. There existed another massive study on *Goethe* which Lukács—and some of those who knew it in Moscow—regarded as his best work and which was lost in manuscript in the course of the evacuation from Moscow at the time of the German advance. Toward the end of his life, Lukács attempted to finish up the writing of a systematic Marxist aesthetics, ontology and ethics; he finished the first, part of the second and none of the third. Any interpretation of Lukács the essayist has to start not with his traveling schedule but with his description of the essay as an "intellectual poem" and a form which enables the modern intellectual to "go radically" to the roots of the problems of the age.[34]

As it turned out, what Weber started out to question was Lukács's Dostoevskii project, a fragment of which has been published as *The Theory of the Novel*. Although deeply resenting this work, Weber nevertheless mediated between Lukács and the would-be publisher of the study, Max Dessoir, and advised Lukács of necessary changes, especially regarding style. Weber also supported—although halfheartedly—Lukács's efforts to gain recognition through this study, and wrote to him in August 23,

1916: "There is nothing else I'd like better than to have you as a colleague of mine here. The question, however, is how to achieve this goal?"[35] Many who received a copy of the monograph reacted enthusiastically, among them Karl Jaspers, Alfred Weber, Ernst Troeltsch, Ernst Bloch and Karl Mannheim. Others—important to Lukács's *Habilitation* quest—like Rickert remained unenthusiastic. It can only be assumed that this circumstance must have contributed to Lukács's change of mind and return to the original project, the *Aesthetics*. Preoccupied anew with matters of aesthetics, Lukács appeared at a meeting of the Heidelberg Sociological Society and in January 1917 presented the "Form Problems of Painting." The lecture was well received, and Weber immediately sent a note to Lukács to that effect: "I am very happy about the continuation of your lecture, which was very convincing and of great interest to me."[36]

Lukács sounded a very optimistic note on his progress in a letter to Gustav Radbruch in the spring of 1917: "I am working away on my *Aesthetics,* and I do hope to finish the first volume— approximately 900 pages—by the summer."[37] Instead, Lukács went into a deep depression as "never before" in his life and had to admit: "I am absolutely unable to work."[38] The reasons for this were certainly personal, intellectual and complex and can only be surmised. Some clues are provided in a letter written to Paul Ernst in September 1917 in which Lukács reported on his wife's move to Munich (complete with her young lover, a German pianist, whom she had been living with, along with Lukács, for some time) and on his plans to return to Budapest to "live only for my work" and to "exclude life entirely."[39] Now Budapest beckoned to him: in the spring of 1917, the informal gathering of young intellectuals, the Sunday Circle, mentioned earlier, developed a Free School of Humanities with a lecture series and stepped-up intellectual activities. As far as can be ascertained from their correspondence and Lukács's reports of it, there was some looser contact during 1917 with the Webers, who seemed to travel a lot.[40] The manuscript of the *Heidelberg Aesthetics* and many of the letters to Lukács were preserved by a quirk of fate: On November 7, 1917, before leaving for Budapest, Lukács deposited a suitcase full of manuscripts, his diary and some 1,600 letters in a safe of the Deutsche Bank in Heidelberg, which survived the wars and everything else only to be discovered some 56 years later and finally deposited at the Georg Lukács Archives in Budapest. After 1945 Lukács either forgot or did not care enough to recover his suitcase.

Although Lukács returned to Budapest in the fall of 1917, he did not give up his hopes or attempts to have his *Habilitation* accepted at Heidelberg. During 1918, there seemed to have been more activities on his behalf by Alfred Weber and Eberhard Gothein, both on the faculty of the University, than by Max Weber. In May 1918, Lukács inquired from Eberhard Gothein about practical details as he assembled the topics of his *Habilitation* presentation. He then submitted his formal application on May 18, 1918, along with a curriculum vitae and topics of the colloquium to be presented. The Heidelberg University files show that Rickert, Alfred Weber and Gothein campaigned heavily on his behalf but met with strong opposition that only grew more vicious as time went by. According to Max Weber's letter of January 9, 1920, sent to Lukács's father, "Professor Gothein has been handling this matter not the right way formally."[41] Lukács reminisces in 1971 about his being in Heidelberg in July 1918 and sounded an optimistic note: "I went back to Budapest in August with the idea that I would be back in Heidelberg next spring."[42] It did not turn out that way. Lukács was informed in a letter by Dean Domaszevsky, dated December 7, 1918, that his application for *Habilitation* had been rejected. The reason given: He was of "foreign nationality," a Hungarian (and certainly, Hungarian-Jewish, although this remained unstated). Lukács answered this rejection on December 16, 1918, stating that he was withdrawing his request "with pleasure" since he "intended to embark on a political career."[43] Although this external circumstance alone would not account for Lukács's "conversion," the fact remains that in the middle of December he joined the Hungarian Communist Party, which he rejected as late as early December in an essay entitled "Bolshevism as a Moral Problem."[44]

THE WAR YEARS: "THE AGE OF SINFULNESS" AND EMERGING NEW CONCERNS

A large segment of the European intelligentsia prior to World War I was caught up in the Dostoevskii fever without regard to differences in political/ideological stance and the ultimate conclusions from that experience. Spengler held that Tolstoy and Dostoevskii pointed to the future of humanity. Rainer Maria Rilke exclaimed: "Other countries are bordered by mountains, rivers and oceans, but Russia is bordered by God." Heidelberg and the Weber-*Kreis* were no exception. As Paul Honigsheim reminisced: "I do not remember a single Sunday conversation in which the name of Dostoevskii did not occur." He may have stretched the point a little, but he also quotes Weber as agreeing with Bloch "that the wife of every professor keeps a cup of tea ready in her salon every day at five in anticipation of the Messiah whom she expects to come straight to her."[45] Karl Mannheim, eight years Lukács's junior, just starting out under the benevolent guidance of Lukács, also planned to write a book on Dostoevskii and justified the project to Lukács in a letter in 1912: "I wish to write on Dostoevskii. Not only because I feel that I shall best be able to pose my problems and questions through a study of his work, but also because I feel that his life and world are most akin to our own in all of its vicissitudes, lack of fulfillment and distortions."[46]

Lukács's Dostoevskii reception was different from that of his intellectual peers in Germany and Heidelberg. Although he and Weber shared an interest in Dostoevskii, their reception was by no means identical. To state it summarily, Weber's (Western) individualism contrasted sharply to Lukács's belief in collectivism. It was Honigsheim again who remembered their differences:

With regard to . . . Max Weber's position on Lukács, one should not forget one thing: Weber's ability to empathize with, and to interpret, the meaning of human action was . . . unlimited: he was therefore able to understand Lukács's position, or, more exactly, his turning from modern occidental individualism to a notion of collectivism. Weber explained it to me this way: "One thing became evident to Lukács when he looked at the paintings of Cimabue [who painted at the beginning of the Italian Renaissance, but who had a closer relation to the Middle Ages than to the Renaissance], and this was that culture can exist only in conjunction with collectivist values.[47]

Lukács's Dostoevskii reception had already taken on a collectivist coloration in 1913, when he first personally encountered Dostoevskii's Russian spirit: Lukács was vacationing in an Italian coastal resort in August 1913 with his friends, Béla Balázs and wife, when he met Yelena Grabenko, a Russian SR anarchist and painter who had to flee Russia and had moved around from Paris to Italy and Heidelberg. Balázs, the poet, described Yelena as "a wonderful example of a Dostoevskii figure. Every single one of her stories, experiences, ideas and feelings could have come from some of Dostoevskii's most fantastic passages. . . . She was a terrorist. She spent years in prison. She destroyed her nerves, stomach and lungs by working so hard."[48] Interestingly enough, Yelena must have held the same kind of fascination for Weber, who mediated between Lukács's father and Lukács himself, thus becoming instrumental in the former's agreement to the marriage. Since Lukács's parents opposed the marriage, Max Weber suggested that Lukács "tell them that she is a relative of his in order to help overcome their objections."[49] Lukács then married Yelena in Heidelberg in May 1914. According to his friend at the time Ernst Bloch, "Through her, Lukács married Dostoevskii, so to speak; he married his Russia, his Dostoevskiian Russia."[50] The marriage turned out to be a complete failure but was not formally dissolved until 1919. (Parenthetically, it might be noted that Bloch's first wife was of Russian extraction.[51])

We may ask what this Dostoevskii and/or Russian experience may have meant for both Lukács and Weber, what the similarities were—besides the difference already noted—and how it influenced either Lukács's career or his relationship to Weber. Weber's interest in Russian matters dates back to the turn of the century and to the abortive 1905 Russian Revolution. As reported in Marianne Weber's book,

His political interests were again powerfully stirred when the first Russian revolution broke out in 1905. He quickly mastered the Russian language, avidly followed the events of the day in several Russian newspapers. . . . Weber fully *empathized* with the *psyche and civilization* of the Russian people, and for months he followed the Russian drama with bated breath.[52]

It is appropriate to recall that Weber concluded his *Protestant Ethic* (part two published in 1905) with the most severe indictment of Western capitalist civilization: "Specialists without spirit, sensualists without heart; this nullity imagines that it has attained a level of civilization never before achieved."[53] This indictment was coupled with a vaguely expressed hope that perhaps "at the end of this tremendous development entirely new prophets will arise," and that there would be a "great rebirth of old ideas and ideals."[54] It is legitimate to ask whether Weber was expecting the rebirth from the Eastern "psyche and civilization." Be that as it may, we have to remember Marianne Weber's report of the role of the young "philosophers from Eastern Europe . . . from the opposite pole of the *Weltanschauung*," who were stimulating Weber's interest in the Eastern European ideas and culture. It is a fact that this "intellectual atmosphere provided by these men [among them Lukács] stimulated Weber's already strong interest in the Russians. For a long time he had been planning a book about Tolstoy that was to contain the results of his innermost experiences."[55] It is alleged that during his prolonged illness Weber once remarked: "If someday I am well again and can hold a seminar, I shall accept only Russians, Poles and Jews."[56]

Weber was not alone in his vague hopes for the "great rebirth" and "new prophets." One of the most fervent and articulate expression of those hopes came from Thomas Mann; the feeling of *ennui*, the spiritual and intellectual malaise that many intellectuals felt, permeated Central European culture and produced these sentiments, which almost culminated in a yearning for a "catastrophe." This partly explains the enthusiastic greetings of the outbreak of World War I in German intellectual circles. Weber also exclaimed: "It is a great and wonderful war."[57] The outbreak of the war also brought a change in Lukács's relationship to German intellectuals, his then spiritual home, and, to a lesser degree, to that to the Webers.

Lukács recalled his immediate reaction, his negative evaluation, almost half a century later:

My own deeply personal attitude was one of vehement, global and especially at the beginning, scarcely articulate rejection of the war and especially of enthusiasm for the war. I recall a conversation with Frau Marianne Weber in the late autumn of 1914. She wanted to challenge my attitude by telling me of individual, concrete acts of heroism. My only reply was: "The better the worse."[58]

Lukács's personal attitude was so shocking to the Webers and their friends that they discussed it repeatedly. Simmel, for example, complained in a letter to the Webers regarding Lukács's lack of understanding of and enthusiasm for the war: "The experience has to be at a practical and personal level, so to speak, in an 'intuitive' way. If Lukács is unable to share this experience, we cannot explain and demonstrate it to him."[59] There were a few friends of Lukács who shared his rejection of the war or lack of enthusiasm for it: Ernst Bloch, for example, left Germany immediately and settled in Switzerland. Lukács himself made every effort to escape being drafted or, as he put it, not to become a "victim of the war Moloch." He enlisted the help of Karl Jaspers, a licensed medical doctor, and received a medical excuse. Beyond this practical reaction, Lukács also reacted to the events and feelings about the war in an article entitled "The German Intellectuals and the War." The article was written for the *Archiv für Sozialwissenschaft und Sozialpolitik* but was never published.

Thus, it is safe to say that, after the outbreak of the war, Lukács became somewhat of an "outsider," in Heidelberg circles, as Lukács described himself using the English term.[60] It is also true that in spite of a certain distance that emerged because of their differing reception of the war, the relationship between Lukács and the Webers was never broken off. This must be partly ascribed to Weber's gradual sobering from the initial feverish enthusiasm for the war. Lukács's state of mind was epitomized in his outcry, "Who was to save us from Western civilization?" in light of the barbarous events of the war. Thus it is no wonder that he soon gave up laboring on the *Aesthetics* and turned to problems of ethics and a philosophy of history deeply imbued with ethical considerations. His ethical position then centered around the problem of guilt; in turn, the ideas of the Dostoevskiian world began to occupy a certain position in Lukács's thinking and reflections. In this connection Lukács's letter of March 1915 is of great significance. First, Lukács tells about his breaking of the work on the aesthetics, at least temporarily. Second, Lukács reports that he started his book on Dostoevskii which, however, "will contain much more than mere Dostoevskii: it will contain a greater part of my metaphysical ethic and history of philosophy, among others." Finally, Lukács asked for a copy of a book—or its serial publication in the *Berliner Tageblatt*—by Ropshin (pen name for Boris Savinkov, a Russian SR terrorist) entitled *The Pale Horse*. All of these new themes mentioned in the single letter were harbingers of Lukács's thinking,

work and action for years to come. As Lukács explained to Paul
Ernst in a follow-up letter: "I am not interested in the book as a
work of art. It is *the ethical problem of terrorism* that matters most
to me, and the book is an important document in this respect."[62]
Indeed, we have another theme and issue that preoccupied German
intellectuals both in the war periods before and after World War I.
At the Sunday gatherings at the Weber home, for example, Lukács,
Bloch, Jaspers and others participated in lengthy debates during
the war about the problem of justifying the use of force at decisive
historical times.[63]

As stated at the beginning of my essay, among the interests that
Weber and Lukács shared the problem of ethics loomed large. At
times the use of force, that is, violence, in order to bring forth a
just society was at the heart of the discussions. If we accept
Lukács's numerous autobiographical utterances backed up with
correspondence and his life work, we can safely state that in
Lukács's case we can talk of the "primacy of ethics." Only extremely insensitive intellectuals with a superficial acquaintance with
Lukács's life and work, like Martin Jay, can deny this.[64] As late as
1968, in his new "Introduction" to the reissue of his *History and
Class Consciousness,* Lukács asserted: "My decision to take an
active part in the Communist movement was influenced profoundly
by ethical considerations."[65] Moreover, in one of his rare bits of
autobiography, Lukács spoke of his "greatest childhood
experience," which was reading the Hungarian translation of the
Iliad at the age of nine, and specifically, "the fate of Hector, i.e.,
the fact that the man who suffered defeat was in the right and was
the better hero, was determinant for my entire later development."[66]
Even if we take such a statement with a grain of salt, we cannot
disregard the evidence in Lukács's life work and the fact that
Lukács's contemporaries, among them Max Weber, were already
in 1912 deeply impressed by his "profound artistic essay" about
the "Poverty of the Spirit."[67] In this essay, Lukács had already
gone beyond the Kantian, formal ethic and opted for one of a
"higher order." Here means and ends are discussed and the
possibility of giving up of conventional ethical norms for the sake
of an ultimate end are contemplated, thus pointing the way to
Lukács's later development. This ethical essay and the Dostoevskii
experience must have influenced Weber's thinking when in the
spring of 1914 he came to the help of a jailed anarchist and his

female friend. Reflecting on the "meaning of goodness" (Lukács's preoccupation in the "Poverty of the Spirit") and the problematic of means and ends, Weber wrote his wife:

The facts that the *result* of good action is often wholly irrational and that "good" behavior has bad consequences have made him doubt that one *ought* to act well—an evaluation of moral action on the basis of *results* rather than intrinsic value. For the time being he does not see that there is a fallacy here. I shall try to obtain *The Brothers Karamazov* for him and at some later time Lukács's dialogue about the poor in spirit [*sic*!], which deals with the problem.[68]

It is obvious that, while Weber could still approve Lukács's ethical position in the "Poverty of the Spirit," he would not draw the same conclusion as Lukács when contemplating the "political realist's" violation of the absolute commandment. Lukács put in a nutshell his ethical statement that took new directions after the war experience and his immersion into the Dostoevskii-Russian-anarchist themes:

I discover in [Ropshin] a new form of the old conflict between the first morality (i.e., duty toward the established social order) and the second one (duty toward one's soul). The order of priorities is always dialectical in the case of politicians and revolutionaries whose souls are not directed toward the self but toward humanity. In that case, the soul has to be sacrified in order to save the soul; on the basis of a mystical morality one must become a cruel political realist and thus violate the absolute commandment: "Thou shall not kill!" In its inner depth it is and remains an ancient problem expressed maybe most succinctly in Hebbel's *Judith* as she says: "And if God has placed sin between myself and the action I am ordered to do,—who am I to be able to escape from it."[69]

Lukács never succeeded in working out his "metaphysical ethic" in the Dostoevskii book; soon he went beyond the "metaphysical ethic" and on August 2, 1915, reported to Paul Ernst that he had "abandoned the Dostoevskii book." It was too long. A larger essay has been finished taken from the book; it was going to be called "The Aesthetic of the Novel" (which turned into the *Theory of the Novel*).

In conclusion it should be mentioned that in his last pre-Marxist writing, "Bolshevism as a Moral Problem" (December 1918), Lukács was still wrestling with the problem. He had already accepted Marxism as a research method for historical sociology but refrained from the practical consequences and rejected Bolshevism as an alternative for himself. As has been noted before, hardly two weeks went by before Lukács joined the Communist Party and embraced *praxis* and the ethics of ultimate ends justifying the means. As he remembered 50 years later:

I have to admit that I joined the CP after a certain wavering. . . . Although the positive role of violence in history was always clear to me and I never had anything against the Jacobins, when the problem of violence arose and the decision had to be made that I should promote violence by my own activity, it turned out that one's theory does not exactly jibe with practice.[70]

Lukács's is a classic case of the Marxian proposition that

in times when the class struggle nears the decisive hour, the process of dissolution going on within the ruling class, . . . assumes such a violent, glaring character, that a small section of the ruling class cuts itself adrift and joins the revolutionary class, . . . a portion of the bourgeoise goes over to the proletariat, . . . a portion of the bourgeois ideologists, who have raised themselves to the level of comprehending theoretically the historical movement as a whole.[71]

Thus the coincidence of structural-historical (objective) factors with those of psychological (subjective) ones is the necessary and sufficient condition. Lukács stated the predisposition for the latter as follows: "With me, everything is the continuation of something. I believe there is no nonorganic element in my development."[72]

Lukács and Weber finally parted ways. Weber wrote in his probably last letter to Lukács: "Dear friend, certainly political views separate us, I am absolutely convinced that these experiments can and will lead only to the discrediting of socialism for a hundred years."[73]

NOTES

I am indebted to the American Philosophical Society (Philadelphia) for the generous grant that made my research possible.

Unless otherwise indicated all letters from and to Lukács quoted in this paper refer to the originals or copies housed in the Georg Lukács Archive of the Hungarian Academy of Sciences, Budapest. I am grateful to Dr. László Sziklai, director of the Archive, and to Dr. Ferenc Jánossy, the literary executor of György Lukács, for generous assistance.

1. Albert Salomon, "German Sociology," in *Twentieth Century Sociology,* Georges Gurvitch and Wilbert E. Moore, Eds. (New York: Philosophical Library, 1945), p. 596.

2. The reconstruction of the "Weber-Lukács Encounter" is to be sought in four kinds of sources: (1) letters to and from Lukács, (2) Lukács's writings from that period, (3) Marianne Weber's biography of her husband, (4) reminiscences of the old Lukács in prefaces to his German- and Hungarian-language *Collected Works,* in numerous interviews, and *Gelebtes Denken,* the intellectual autobiographical interviews conducted by his student István Eörsi and the literary scholar Erzsébet Vezér and published in German. Of the earlier literature dealing with the Weber-Lukács relationship, see N. M. de Feo, *Weber e Lukács* (Bari: De Donato, 1971); Arthur Mitzman, *The Iron Cage* (New York: Grosset & Dunlap, 1969), pp. 271-76; Maurice Weimbergh, "M. Weber et G. Lukács," and Irving Fetscher, "Zum Begriff der 'objektiven Möglichkeit' bei Max Weber und Georg Lukács," both in *Revue Internationale de Philosophie,* No. 106 (1973), pp. 474-500 and 501-25, respectively. See also the perceptive and reflective essay by Daniel Bell, "First Love and Early Sorrows," *Partisan Review,* 48, 4 (1981), pp. 532-51, esp. pp. 541-47. Factual errors in this article are based on false information supplied by Ms. Agnes Heller to Professor Bell: (1) Heller was certainly *not* the last student of Lukács; and (2) she is *not* the literary executor of Lukács; Dr. Ferenc Jánossy is.

The secondary literature on Lukács has become an industry and ranges from scholarly works to hatchet jobs. For the former, three standard works in English should be listed: István Mészáros, *Lukács' Concept of Dialectic* (London: The Merlin Press, 1972); Ehrhard Bahr and Ruth Goldschmidt Kunzer, *Georg Lukács* (New York: Ungar, 1972); and Michael Löwy, *Georg Lukács: From Romanticism to Bolshevism* (London: NLB, 1979). For the latter, examples from the right and left: Victor Zitta, *Georg Lukács' Marxism: Alienation, Dialectics, Revolution* (The Hague: Martinus Nijhoff, 1964); and Andrew Arato and Paul Breines, *The Young Lukács and the Origins of Western Marxism* (New York: The Seabury Press, 1979). See also my review of recent Lukács literature in *Slavic Review* (Summer 1981).

3. Lukács, *père,* wrote to his son on August 23, 1909:

As you will admit, I have always, and liberally so, given free scope to your development and to your choosing your own way in this. I have done this consciously, for I have unlimited confidence in you and love you immeasurably—and I would sacrifice everything to see you great, appreciated and famous; I'll feel boundlessly happy to be pointed out as György Lukács's father.

These were not just words. Very generous financial support was behind them, enabling Lukács to live an existence as a member of the *"freischwebende Intelligenz."* Thus, on June 1, 1911, Lukács, *père,* wrote: "The consideration of several circumstances led to my conclusion that . . . within a year I will be in the situation that I can give you a minimum of 5000 korona yearly allowance." A few months later the father wrote to the son:

I was very happy to learn that your book [*Die Seele und die Formen*] was published. I am equally happy to hear that you received a 500 mark honorarium, but I want to ask you to consider this money as your own and not to spend it on things that are my duty to provide for you. You have to get used to the idea of accumulating capital, and first of all your royalty should serve this purpose.

In his May 25, 1914, letter the father assures Lukács of a raise in his allowance to the yearly sum of 10,000 German marks. The late Lukács, reflecting on pre-World War I intelligentsia said: "At that time there was a large section of intellectuals, university intellectuals in particular, who belonged to the rentier stratum by virtue of their private incomes, which gave them a material autonomy. This was the economic basis of Mannheim's free-floating intelligentsia." In Theo Pinkus, Ed., *Conversations with Lukács* (Cambridge, Mass.: MIT Press, 1975), p. 88.

4. Georg Lukács, "Georg Simmel," in Kurt Gassen and Michael Landmann, Eds., *Buch des Dankes an Georg Simmel* (Berlin: Duncker & Humblot, 1958), pp. 171-76.

5. Georg Lukács, *Gelebtes Denken. Eine Autobiographie im Dialog,* István Eörsi, Ed. (Frankfurt am Main: Suhrkamp Verlag, 1981), p. 58.

6. György Lukács, *Utam Marxhoz,* v. 1 (Budapest: Magvetö, 1971), p. 10.

7. Lukács's friend, the Hungarian literary scholar Franz Baumgarten wrote to him on May 27, 1909: "My dear friend, the fact is that you may look forward with hope to your future in Germany! In vain do they protest to me that you are 5 '3 " (or is it more?); I see you standing on the pedestal of your book, getting taller and taller. So, hope and self-assurance, please."

8. Georg Simmel to Lukács, May 25, 1912.

9. György Lukács, *Magyar irodalom, magyar kultúra* (Budapest: Gondolat, 1970), p. 13. Lukács wrote to his friend Leo Popper, "Florence

is a fairy-tale city where the streets sing." (September 1910 letter).

10. Marianne Weber, *Max Weber: A Biography,* trans. Harry Zohn (New York: Wiley Interscience, 1975), pp. 465-66.

11. Paul Honigsheim, *On Max Weber* (New York: The Free Press, 1968), p. 28.

12. Quoted in Judith Marcus-Tar, *Thomas Mann and Georg Lukács* (Cologne-Vienna: Böhlau Verlag, 1982), p. 150.

13. Weber, *Max Weber,* p. 468.

14. Lukács, *Magyar irodalom,* p. 13.

15. Georg Lukács, *Die Eigenart des Ästhetischen* (Neuwied: Luchterhand, 1963), p. 31.

16. See Judith Marcus, *Georg Lukács and Thomas Mann: A Study in the Sociology of Literature* (Amherst: University of Massachusetts Press, 1983).

17. See Guenther Roth, "The Historical Relationship to Marxism," in Reinhard Bendix and Guenther Roth, *Scholarship and Partisanship* (Berkeley: University of California Press, 1971). See also Lukács's "Stalinist" (1954) assessment of Weber, now available in English in *The Destruction of Reason,* trans. Peter Palmer (London: Merlin Press, 1980), pp. 601-19, and of more recent literature, Franco Ferrarotti, *Max Weber and the Destiny of Reason* (Armonk, N.Y.: M. E. Sharpe, 1982), pp. 66-86, and Johannes Weiss, *Das Werk Max Webers in der marxistischen Rezeption und Kritik* (Opladen: Westdeutscher Verlag, 1981). I am grateful to Professor Roth for calling my attention to this book.

18. Pinkus, *Conversations with Lukács,* p. 100. *Conversations* is a remarkable document of the working of a great mind. See my review in *Slavic Review* (September 1976).

19. György Lukács, "A történelmi materializmus funkcióváltozása," in *Mindenki újakra készül,* 4 (Budapest: Akadémiai Kiadó, 1967), p. 659.

20. Quoted in Wolfgang J. Mommsen, *Max Weber und die deutsche Politik,* 2nd ed. (Tübingen: J.C.B. Mohr/Paul Siebeck, 1974), p. 332.

21. Franz Baumgarten to Lukács on July 8, 1912.

22. Lukács, *Gelebtes Denken,* p. 58.

23. Hans Gerth and C. Wright Mills, Eds., *From Max Weber: Essays in Sociology* (New York: Oxford University Press, 1958), p. 154.

24. Lukács left behind fragments of two works written in Heidelberg under the guidance of Max Weber, available now in German and Hungarian: *Heidelberger Philosophie der Kunst (1912-1914)* (Darmstadt und Neuwied: Luchterhand, 1974), and *Heidelberger Ästhetik (1916-1918)* (Darmstadt und Neuwied: Luchterhand, 1974). Lukács tried to clarify the story of "the old *Aesthetics*" in a letter to István Mészáros on February 2, 1969, which reads in part as follows:

As to the old *Aesthetics*, it would be very difficult to reconstruct the original plan exactly. "Die ästhetische Setzung" should have constituted Part One. The essays published in *Logos* ["Die Subjekt-Objekt Beziehung in der Ästhetick"] was planned as the Introduction to Part Two, and it should have been followed by "Geschichtlichkeit und Zeitlosigkeit des Kunstwerks." Part Two should have contained the chapters on "Individualität und Überpersönlichkeit des Kunstwerks" and on "Das erreichte Werk als Formkomplex." Part Three was to analyze the various types of receptivity.

Credit is due to György Márkus, who reconstructed the two works for publication, see his "Nachwort" in the *Heidelberger Ästhetik (1916-1918)*.

25. Max Weber to Lukács, July 22, 1912.
26. Max Weber to Lukács, March 10, 1913.
27. Max Weber to Lukács, March 22, 1913.
28. Lukács to Paul Ernst, March 1915.
29. On the Sunday Circle, see two recent Hungarian monographs, Zoltán Novák, *A Vasárnapi Társaság* (Budapest: Kossuth Könyvkiadó, 1979), and *A Vasárnapi Kör,* Éva Karádi and Erzsébet Vezér, Eds. (Budapest: Gondolat, 1980).
30. Lukács to Max Weber, December 30, 1915.
31. Lukács to Max Weber, January 17, 1916.
32. Lukács truly suffered during his military service, as he wrote to Paul Ernst: "I can write only during breaks between my office hours. . . . It is a sad life. . . . I have only three free afternoons per week and I could work fourteen hours a day if I were free. It is a desperate situation" (July 1916). He was lucky enough to get out of the service by the end of July, and he tells how:

I worked in the auxiliary service. . . . When my one-time schoolmate Ivan Rakovszky, who later became Minister of the Interior, visited my father to see if he might become a member of the board of directors of the Credit Bank the question came up as to what Gyuri [Lukács] was doing. My father complained that I was fed up with working in the auxiliary services. Rakowszky then said: "Look, Uncle Joe, this is a mere trifle: tell Gyuri to come to see me in the Parliament and we will talk it over." And we did talk it over, and I was exempted in four weeks' time. . . . By the same token, Rakovszky became a member of the board of directors of the Credit Bank.

In Lukács, *Gelebtes Denken,* p. 72.
33. Max Weber to Lukács, August 14, 1916.
34. Georg Lukács, "On the Nature and Form of the Essay," in *Soul and Form,* trans. Anna Bostock (Cambridge, Mass.: MIT Press, 1971).
35. Max Weber to Lukács, August 23, 1916.
36. Max Weber to Lukács, January 1917.

37. Lukács to Gustav Radbruch, March 11, 1917.

38. Lukács to Paul Ernst, July 1917.

39. Lukács to Paul Ernst, September 5, 1917.

40. In a July 1917 letter, Lukács asks Paul Ernst about the Webers' whereabouts: "They both left for the Rhineland, but I don't know exactly where."

41. Max Weber to József von Lukács, January 9, 1920.

42. Lukács, *Gelebtes Denken,* p. 71.

43. See, *Text + Kritik,* no. 39/40 (October 1973). I am also grateful to Professor Elaine Spitz for allowing the study of "Lukács's Heidelberg Habilitations Documents" in the Morris Watnick Lukács Collection.

44. Georg Lukács, "Bolshevism as a Moral Problem," *Social Research,* V. 44, no. 3 (Autumn 1977), pp. 416-24.

45. Honigsheim, *On Max Weber,* pp. 81, 109.

46. Karl Mannheim to Lukács, January 5, 1912.

47. Honigsheim, *On Max Weber*, p. 27. Béla Balázs reports about Lukács's plan to set up a commune in Heidelberg after the war: "We envisaged all kind of wonderful things about the commune. It was to have been the final solution to all of our problems." In *Kritika,* V. 11, (1975), p. 20.

48. "The Diary of Béla Balázs," *Valóság,* V. 2 (1973), p. 83.

49. Mészáros, *Lukács's Concept of Dialectic,* p. 123.

50. Michael Löwy, "Interview with Ernst Bloch," *New German Critique,* no. 9 (Fall 1976), pp. 43-44.

51. Cf. the Löwy interview; ibid.: "Karola Bloch: Ernst Bloch's first wife, Else von Stritzky, was very rich. . . . In the Revolution of 1917, they lost everything. . . . Bloch: I used to say to my friends that I paid 30 million marks for the Russian Revolution, but that it was worth the price to me."

52. Weber, *Max Weber,* p. 327. Wolfgang Mommsen writes, "Weber greeted the Russian revolution with great hopes." In Mommsen, *Max Weber,* p. 60. See also Paul Honigsheim, "Max Weber: His Religious and Ethical Background and Development," in *Church History,* V. 19, no. 4 (1950), esp. pp. 237-39; and Richard Pipes, "Max Weber and Russia," in *World Politics,* V. 7 (1955-56), pp. 371-401.

53. Max Weber, *The Protestant Ethic and the Spirit of Capitalism,* trans. Talcott Parsons (New York: Charles Scribner's Sons, 1958), p. 182.

54. Ibid.

55. Weber, *Max Weber,* p. 466.

56. Honigsheim, *On Max Weber,* p. 13.

57. Weber, *Max Weber,* pp. 521-22.

58. Georg Lukács, *The Theory of the Novel* (Cambridge, Mass.: MIT Press, 1971), p. 11.

59. Gassen-Landmann, *Buch des Dankes,* p. 133.

60. Lukács, *Magyar irodalom,* p. 13.

61. Lukács to Paul Ernst, March 1915.

62. Lukács to Paul Ernst, April 14, 1915.

63. For a perceptive discussion of Weber's solution to the problem of *Wertfreiheit* and *Verantwortungsethik,* see Wolfgang Schluchter, *Wertfreiheit und Verantwortungsethik. Zum Verhältnis von Wissenschaft und Politik bei Max Weber* (Tübingen: Mohr, 1971). On the problem of violence, see Zoltán Tar, *The Frankfurt School: The Critical Theories of Max Horkheimer and Theodor W. Adorno* (New York: Wiley Interscience, 1977), pp. 43-51.

64. Martin Jay asserts that "to make Lukács into an ethical Marxist is to misunderstand the depth of his repudiation of Bernstein and the Revisionists, who were the true moralists of the socialist movement." In *Central European History* (March 1979), p. 93. Interestingly enough, the more sensitive Susan Sontag perceives Lukács as one who "does treat literature as a branch of moral argument"; she even complains about his "chronic moralizing" in "The Literary Criticism of Georg Lukács," in *Against Interpretation and Other Essays* (New York: Farrar, Straus & Giroux, 1969), pp. 87-89.

65. Georg Lukács, *History and Class Consciousness,* trans. Rodney Livingstone (London: Merlin Press, 1971), p. xxxi.

66. Pinkus, *Conversations,* p. 33.

67. Weber, *Max Weber,* p. 466.

68. Ibid., p. 490.

69. Lukács to Paul Ernst, May 14, 1915. It is interesting to note that Lukács concluded his first essay after his conversion, entitled "Tactics and Ethics," justifying revolutionary praxis, using the same Hebbel quotation.

70. Lukács, *Gelebtes Denken,* pp. 86-87.

71. Karl Marx and Frederick Engels, *The Communist Manifesto* (New York: International Publishers, 1948), p. 19.

72. Lukács, *Gelebtes Denken,* p. 39.

73. Mommsen, *Max Weber,* p. 332.

PART II

Theory

Rationalization as a Central Concept in Max Weber's Political Sociology

7

INTERPRETATIONS AND MISINTERPRETATIONS OF MAX WEBER: THE PROBLEM OF RATIONALIZATION

Jose V. Casanova

PROBLEMS IN THE INTERPRETATIONS OF MAX WEBER

In 1975 Friedrich Tenbruck, a well-known Weberian scholar, wrote an essay asking the question, "How well do we know Max Weber?" His answer followed in another essay, "The Work of Max Weber," in which he argued that by assuming generally that *Economy and Society* (*EaS*) was Weber's *major* work, we have blocked for ourselves the possibility of answering what is also generally assumed to be Weber's major question, i.e., What is the process of rationalization? Therefore we cannot find a coherent and unifying interpretation of the whole of Weber's work.

I am of the opinion with Tenbruck that as long as *EaS* is considered to be Weber's "major" work and the one that gives unity and meaning to his whole work, Weber's work is condemned to remain an "impressive," "gigantic," but "fragmentary," "unhomogeneous" and "unfinished" "Torso," as has been often expressed. The anti-systemic feelings of Weber and his untimely death are usually presented as tranquilizing justifications for Weber's unclear aims. The unfortunate end result is, as Mommsen has put it, "that Weber has sometimes become little more than a useful quarry for concepts and ideal types" (Mommsen, 1974:18). Ideal types like charisma and bureaucracy are picked up without prior thought to their context in Weber's work and to their function in his methodology. No wonder they are rejected once "reality" is found to be different from what the ideal type "seemed" to indicate.

Parsons and Bendix

This confusing situation is aggravated by the conflict between the two main interpretations of Weber in America and their respective schools (Harvard and Berkeley). While for Parsons Weber absolutely intended to set down a universal general theory of social action, for Bendix Weber was primarily a historical sociologist eager to understand definitive historical institutions and structures in different societies and spheres; accordingly, sociology remained for Weber an auxiliary discipline to historical studies.

PARSONS

In addition to Weber's methodological writings and to part 1 of *EaS,* Parsons emphasizes the importance of *The Protestant Ethic* as a "refutation" of historical materialism at the methodological as well as at the empirical level and as a prime example of scientific causal explanation in the social sciences. The *Collected Essays* are also emphasized, but they are interpreted mainly as a "negative proof" of the functional relationship between Protestantism and capitalism and as a further elaboration of the "anti-Marxian interpretation." Parsons contributed to the misinterpretation of Weber's work and to the neglect of the *Collected Essays* by presenting the sociology of religion of *EaS,* which was written at the latest in 1914, as "the most important single segment of his work" and as the last statement of Weber on the sociology of religion (Weber, 1964b:xix-xx, lxi).

In addition Parsons distorted Weber's intention by presenting *The Sociology of Religion* as "the strategically central part of a general evolutionary view of the development of human society"(lx). According to Parsons, Weber viewed the modern Western world "as standing in the vanguard of the most important general evolutionary trend"(lx).

However, in Tubingen, at the sociology meeting in honor of Max Weber, Parsons stated that "the core of Weber's substantive sociology lies neither in his treatment of economic and political problems nor in his sociology of religion, *but in his sociology of law* (Stammer, 1972:40). Apparently since Weber's views of the historical roles of religions could put into question Parsons' functionalist view of religion, it was in "law" that Parsons found now the foundation for a "normative" and legitimate order. In this sense Cohen-Hazelrigg-Pope's "de-Parsonization of Weber" is correct in seeing "the crux of Parsons' misinterpretation in the overweening emphasis on the category of the 'normative'" and in a "confusion of 'factual regularities' with 'normative validity'" (1975:229). Understandably, Parsons has forgotten Weber's critique of Stammler. Weber's phenomenological position in the essay could hardly serve as a foundation for structural functionalism since Weber's argument was that such a perspective would confuse the normative with the empirical validity of any order and would be tempted to deduce the second from the first (Weber, 1968a:303-58).

BENDIX

Bendix's, as well as Roth's, interpretations of Weber have to be seen in some respects as a reaction to what they rightly see as Parsons' misinterpretations of Weber's intentions. From the beginning Bendix emphasized the historical elements in Weber's work to counter Parsons' general-theoretical interpretation, while later on Bendix and Roth have emphasized the "typological" to counter Parsons' "evolutionist" interpretation (Parsons, 1971:4).

On the substantive level, both Bendix and Roth show a strong preference for *EaS* and a heavy emphasis upon Weber's "Sociology of Domination" (Weber, 1968c) to counter, no doubt, Parsons' neglect. Roth thinks justly that the crucial importance of the sociology of domination has for the most part passed unnoticed due to its piecemeal translation (Weber, 1968b:xxvii).

Bendix is then able to offer not just an additive interpretation of all of Weber's empirical writings but also a comprehensive interpretation because he organizes his study around what he sees as the two main foci of Weber's life work: (1) *The problematic focus:* as Bendix says, "Weber was preoccupied throughout his career with the development of rationalism in Western civilization" and dedicated his life to the study of this development (Bendix, 1962:9). Bendix identifies therefore the process of rationalization as the central theme in Weber's comparative historical sociology. (2) *The thematic focus:* Bendix is able to find already in a rudimentary form in Weber's early studies of farm laborers in eastern Germany and of the stock exchange "the basic concepts and central problems" which occupied Weber's life (xxiii). Bendix points out that the analysis of the tensions and intercrosses between class and status, and between ideas and interests, forms the uniting link which overcomes the differences between Weber's sociology of religion and his political sociology (85-87).

Bendix attempts also to correct the imbalances of Parsons' interpretation of Weber's sociology of religion by placing *The Protestant Ethic* in its proper perspective, both with respect to Weber's sociology of religion as a whole and with respect to the place it has in Weber's genetic explanation of modern Western rationalism.

Bendix points out first that *The Protestant Ethic,* rather than being the culmination of Weber's sociology of religion, is only his point of departure and that it is misleading to understand the comparative studies in the world religions from the perspective of *The Protestant Ethic* as if they were only or even mainly a negative proof of his earlier causal explanation. Bendix thinks that it is rather the later contrast between Oriental and Occidental civilization which puts *The Protestant Ethic* in proper perspective (79). In this way he is able to overcome the usual methodological interpretation of Weber's studies on *The Economic Ethics of the World Religions* as a series of comparative studies where, according to Parsons, "Weber attempted to hold the factor of 'economic organization' constant and to treat religious orientation as his independent variable" (Weber, 1964:xxi-xxii).

From the wider perspective of Weber's later work it was the study of *Ancient Judaism* which for Bendix formed "the cornerstone of his attempt to explain the distinguishing characteristics of Western civilization" (Bendix, 1962:199). For it was only during his research on ancient Judaism in 1916 that Weber came across the idea that it was in ancient Jewish prophecy that one could find the origins of the ethical rationalism which he had first analyzed in *The Protestant Ethic.*

It is misleading, however, to argue that the study was complete once he had explained the origin of ethical rationalism because, as

Bendix himself says, *Ancient Judaism* (1917) was only the starting point of the explanation which occupied Weber until his death three years later. We know that at the time of his death Weber had already started to work on early Christianity, Islam, and Talmudic Judaism and planned a similar work also on medieval Catholicism, which, as Bendix himself points out, were "intended to provide this 'missing link'" (70, 285). Only then could it be said that the comparative study was complete.

Although in part 3 of his book Bendix offers an excellent analysis of the major parts of *EaS*, he does not offer any answer, as he promised, to the meaning of the process of rationalization in Weber's work. In fact the only reference in this section is a disappointing footnote in which, in the context of analyzing the process of legal rationalization, Bendix states: "The term 'rationalization' in the sense of 'increasing rationality' is perhaps still subject to misunderstanding, and I have therefore either avoided the term or put it in quotation marks as above" (1962:391).

To sum up, Bendix's intellectual portrait of Weber can certainly be seen as the definitive interpretation of most of Weber's empirical writings. It offers, in addition, a lucid interpretation of some of the dominant themes and problems in Weber's work; but it can hardly be the interpretation of Weber's work as a "comprehensive whole." After reading Bendix, Weber's work still remains relatively unknown.

Nelson and Tenbruck

While proceeding through different ways and being moved by different interests, Nelson and Tenbruck in around 1973-74 came to very similar conclusions with respect to the problems of interpreting Weber's work. Both came to the conclusion that *EaS* could not be considered Weber's major work because it offers no answer to the problematic which dominated the last years of Weber's life.

Both agree also that, although questions about the meanings of rationalism, rationality and rationalization were present from the beginning in Weber's work, it was in around 1915, in the midst of his comparative studies on *The Economic Ethics of the World Religions,* that Weber achieved a crucial breakthrough in thinking about these matters.

Both think that "The Social Psychology of the World Religions" (1915), "Religious Rejections of the World and their Directions" (1916) and the "Author's Introduction" are the three most systematic statements of Weber's new way of thinking about the processes of rationalization.

TOWARD A COMPREHENSIVE INTERPRETATION OF WEBER

I am of the opinion with Burger that (1) Weber's methodological position remained basically unchanged, although one can find multiple emphases and focuses across Weber's life history; and (2) his position forms a well-rounded, coherent and logical statement once one accepts Weber's epistemological point of departure. I also think that there is no contradiction, as it has been often said, between his methodological and his empirical writings. In fact, his methodological writings can help us greatly in the interpretative understanding of his empirical writings and in locating them within Weber's whole work. In addition, it is my thesis that the "primary historical fact"—in Weber's sense of the term, which he took from Rickert (Weber, 1949:155f.)—of Weber's life work was the "total modern culture" in which he and his contemporaries moved.

There were, however, changes of focus and of emphasis in Weber, and these are closely related to the different perspectives or points of view from which he saw the "primary historical fact." Although Weber himself did not use this unifying term, for analytical purposes I will call Weber's ideal-typical construction of the present *modern-Western-rational-capitalism*. Selecting the focus of sociological significance from 1903 on, one can construct three major phases in Weber's work.

1903-1909

Weber views the present as modern-Western-*rational-capitalism*; the "iron cage" image of bureaucracy and of the fateful economic cosmos forms the unifying link for the three major works of this period: *The Protestant Ethic and the Spirit of Capitalism* (1904-1905), the two main essays on the *Russian Revolution* (1905-1906) and *The Agrarian Sociology of Ancient Civilizations* (1908). This last work already offers the methodological and substantive link with the second phase.

1910-1914

Economy and Society is the great work of this period. In this phase Weber views the present primarily as Western-*modern-rational*-capitalism. The modern rational character of political, economic and legal structures is constructed and defined in contrast to the traditional past. Weber's analysis is already comparative historical and differential, and one already finds crucial elements of the later civilizational analytic. *The Religion of China,* which was originally written in 1913, although later revised in 1915 and again in 1919, forms the link between the second and the third phases.

1915-1920

The Collected Essays in the Sociology of Religion are the main works of this phase. The civilizational aspect becomes the predominant one, creating a shift of emphasis. The present is now viewed by Weber as modern-*Western-rational*-capitalism. It is the great merit of Nelson's interpretation to have insisted on the crucial importance of the civilizational perspective in Weber's later work and to have attempted to articulate systematically Weber's comparative historical and differential method.

RATIONALIZATION AS THE UNIFYING THEME IN WEBER'S WORK

Looking now at the perspectives of the three phases, one can see that the term *rational* is the unifying concept common to all three phases and that therefore it is the problematic from which the whole of Weber's work can comprehensively be interpreted. However the type of *rationality* involved in each of the phases changes, respectively, from "capitalist," to "modern," to "Western." It is in this sense that the three main lines of interpretation of Weber, namely, the "Neo-Marxist," the "sociological" and the "civilizational," are only emphasizing three different moments of Weber's work.

If my argument is correct, the question, What is rationality? and the different meanings of rationalism and rationalization remains the undeciphered interpretative clue to Weber's work.

Tentatively, I see the possibility, following a somewhat modified classification by Gittleman (1977:1, 7, 10), of distinguishing three levels in Weber's analysis of the process of rationalization: (1) rationalization of the organization of life-conduct; (2) institutional rationalization; and (3) cultural-intellectual rationalization. One can see that these three levels correspond roughly to the three dominant problematics in the three phases: (1) vocational asceticism; (2) bureaucracy; and (3) sciences, theodicies and world views.

It seems to me that the decisive breakthrough came when Weber realized that the crucial element in this general rationalization was not the rationalization of technique, of organization, of conduct, i.e., of the external world, but the rationalization of the way of looking into the world, of the mind. Gittleman is, I think, correct when he calls this "the rationalization of rationality" (1970:21). The end result was not only the disenchantment of the world but the disenchantment of Reason itself.

The problem of rationality thus forms the link among his methodological position, his existential cognitive interest and his sociological work. Only an interpretation which is able to connect the three in a unifying whole will be able to offer a comprehensive interpretation of Weber.

INTEGRATING SOCIOLOGY AND HISTORY

In following Tenbruck it has been one of the major themes of my presentation that a prime obstacle in the comprehensive interpretation of Weber has been to consider EaS as Weber's last major work. I see, moreover, that another obstacle has to be solved if my four theses are to hold together, namely, the problem of integrating sociology and history in Weber's work. I think that this problem cannot be solved as long as we hold on to extremely narrow definitions of both history and sociology, which unfortunately Weber himself imposed, i.e., "history" as the causal explanation of particular events and "sociology" as the formation of generalizations (Weber, 1964a:121, 109). It should be clear that Weber's "sociology" (the label is irrelevant) does not fit either definition.

As long as we oppose history and sociology we will not be able to find a comprehensive interpretation. Only a clarification of what is meant by comparative, historical and differential sociology can help in solving the problem. Weber himself gives in several places very clear indications of what he means by it.

We find the first systematic comment on what would later become Weber's typical method in his "Critical Studies in the Logic of the Cultural Sciences" (1906). Weber states one of the main reasons for the critique of the historian E. Meyer:

Meyer's arguments confuse two quite different conceptions of "historical facts": (1) those elements of reality which are "valued" "for their own sake" in their concrete uniqueness as objects of our interest; (2) those components of reality to which attention is necessarily drawn by our need to understand the causal determination of those "valued" components, as a "cause" in the causal regress. One may designate the former as historical individuals, the latter as historical (real) causes, and, with Rickert, distinguish them as "primary" and "secondary" historical facts. (Weber, 1949:155)

As "primary historical fact" one could choose, according to Weber, *any* historical phenomenon or event which receives "significance" for us through our "value-relatedness" (*Wert-beziehung*). Weber gives a clue to what he chose as the primary historical fact of his investigations when he continues: "It might be, for example, the total 'modern culture,' i.e. our present-day Christian capitalistic constitutional culture which 'radiates' from Europe and which is a fantastic tangle of 'cultural values' which may be considered from the most diverse standpoints" (1949:155).

It is in this sense that I have called "the total modern culture" Weber's primary historical fact. I have argued also that the perspective from which he analyzed this fact changed, however, during his life work. The Protestan ethic, moreover, was of interest as a "secondary historical fact," that is, as a causal determination of one of the elements of the total modern culture, namely, of vocational asceticism. The study of these two different historical facts corresponds to what Roth has called the "situational" and the "developmental" levels of analysis in Weber's work (Roth, 1976:309).

Had Weber remained at this level, he would not have been a sociologist. Weber continues, however:

other cultural developments like the ones of the Incas and Aztecs . . . become relevant to us neither as a "historical object" nor as a "historical cause," but rather as an "heuristic instrument" for the formation of theoretical concepts appropriate to the study of culture. This knowledge may function positively to supply an illustration, individualized and specific, in the formation of the concept of feudalism, or negatively, to delimit certain concepts with which we operate in the study of European cultural history from the quite different cultural traits of the Incas and the Aztecs; *this latter function enables us to make a clearer genetic comparison of the historical uniqueness* of European cultural development. (1949:155-56, emphasis added)

A correct understanding of this paragraph may help to put into question the common assertion that there are different methodologies in Weber. It seems more appropriate to talk like Roth of different levels of analysis in his work. In this sense, Roth is correct when, in following Bendix's earlier interpretation, he says, "The sociology of *Economy and Society* is "Clio's handmaiden," the purpose of comparative study is the explanation of a given historical problem" (Weber, 1968b:xxxi). The fact that the two foremost interpreters of *Economy and Society* insist that it is a means to something else should have made people reflect more seriously about the assumed central position of *EaS* and about the opposition of history and sociology in Weber's work.

In *The Agrarian Sociology of Ancient Civilizations* (1908) one can already find two methodological comments which can help one to understand further Weber's comparative historical and differential sociology:

So one might take these anomalies and exceptions as yet another demonstration that "there is nothing new under the sun," and that all or nearly all distinctions are simply matters of degree. The latter is true enough, of course; but the former notion annuls any historical study. One must instead focus upon what is of central importance in a society, despite all analogies, and *use the similarities of two societies to highlight the specific individuality of each.* (1976:341, emphasis added)

This done, one can then determine the causes which led to these differences. (1976: 385-86)

PHENOMENOLOGY AND STRUCTURAL ELEMENTS IN WEBER'S WORK

There remain, of course, many serious problems for clarification in the interpretation of Weber. The most important being, in addition to the already mentioned analysis of the meanings of rationalizations, the clear definition of the meanings and the relationship among understanding (*Verstehen*), interpretation (*Deutung*) and explanation (*Erklaerung*).

This definition would help to clarify some of the differences between the various phenomenological schools, as well as the differences between the phenomenological and structural interpretations of Weber. Again, rather than opposing phenomenon and structure, I think that it is necessary to try to interpret and integrate them as they are found in Weber's work, especially in his *Collected Essays*. I follow here an interpretation started by A. von Schelting (1934: 360ff) and which was continued by J. Winckelmann when he called Weber's "interpretive sociology" a "structural phenomenology of world history" (Nelson, 1974: 270,n.5). I think this is also what Nelson means by "civilizational analysis of the structure of consciousness."

Although I cannot elaborate further on this point here, it seems to me that Weber has both a "proto-hermeneutic" and a "proto-phenomenological" position. Both can be found in his 1906 essay "On the Logic of the Cultural Sciences" and in his 1907 "Critique of Stammler," respectively. Weber did not differentiate clearly enough, however, between the phenomenological understanding of the subjective meaning of the actor (*Sinnverstaendnis*) and the hermeneutic interpretation of the cultural significance (*Kulturbedeutung*) of certain phenomena and of their contexts of meaning (*Sinnzusammenhaenge*). Both, as Weber himself seems to indicate, are integral components of sociological interpretation, and his own empirical work corroborates this. Both are also logical results of Weber's epistemological and existential point of departure. Once the real world has become disenchanted and devoid of meaning, it is only "we," "man," "the creators of culture" (*Kulturschaffende Menschen*) who can infuse some meaning into certain phenomena, which then become "culture."

This "we" however, includes both the author and the actor, and therefore the meaning will differ depending upon whether it is the meaning that a phenomenon has from the author's historical standpoint (hermeneutic meaning) or the meaning that the actor infuses into the phenomenon (subjective or motivational meaning). Both are mutually, necessarily and irremediably interrelated because both are two main moments of the "hermeneutic circle." This becomes clearest when one attempts to understand the actual experiences of people of other cultures. Weber's interpretative understanding of social action requires the knowledge of the actors' intentions and intended ends. The fact that by this intention Weber did not only mean the subjectively conscious intention of the actor should be clear from the following quotation from *The Religion of India:*

The fact that the devout individual Hindu usually did not realize the grandiose presuppositions of "karma" doctrine as a whole is irrelevant for their practical effect, which is our concern.

"Karma" doctrine transformed the world into a strictly rational, ethically determined cosmos; it represents the most consistent theodicy ever produced by history. The devout Hindu was accursed to remain in a structure which makes sense only in this intellectual context; its consequences burdened his conduct. (Weber; 1967b: 121)

(Note: in the original, the word for "structure" is an unusual German term, *Gehäuse,* the same term translated as "cage" in *The Protestant Ethic.*)

REFERENCES

Bendix, Reinhard
   1962   Max Weber: An Intellectual Portrait. New York: Anchor Books.
Cohen, Jere; Hazelrigg Lawrence E.; and Pope, Whitney
   1975   "Di-Parsonizing Weber: A Critique of Parsons' Interpretation of Weber's Sociology." *A.S.R.* 40: 229-41.
Gittleman, Jerome
   1970   "Tentative Notes on the Paradoxical Form of 'Rationalization.'" Ms., New School Reserve Library.
   1977   "Max Weber's Concept of Rationalization Porcess in History and the Crisis of Modern Culture." Dissertation Proposal.
Mommsen, Wolfgang
   1974   The Age of Bureaucracy. New York: Harper and Row.
Nelson, Benjamin
   1974   "Max Weber's Author's Introduction (1920): A Master Clue to His Main Aims." *Sociological Inquiry* 44: 269-78.
Parsons, Talcott
   1971   The System of Modern Societies. Englewood Cliffs, N.J.: Prentice-Hall.

Roth, Gunther
    1976   "History and Sociology in the Work of Max Weber."
                British Journal of Sociology 27: 306-18.
Schelting, A. von
    1934   Max Weber's Wissenschaftslehre. Tubingen: J.C.B. Mohr.
Stammer, Otto (ed.)
    1972   Max Weber and Sociology Today. Oxford: Basil Blackwell.
Weber, Max
    1949   The Methodology of the Social Sciences. New York: Free
                Press.
    1958   The Protestant Ethic and the Spirit of Capitalism. New
                York: Scribners.
    1964a   The Theory of Social and Economic Organization. New
                York: Free Press.
    1964b   The Sociology of Religion. Boston: Beacon.
    1967a   Ancient Judaism. New York: Free Press.
    1967b   The Religion of India. New York: Free Press.
    1968a   Gesammelte Aufsätze zur Wissenschaftslehre. 3d ed.
                Tubingen: J.C.B. Mohr.
    1968b   Die Protestantische Ethik II. Munich: Siebenstern.
    1968c   Economy and Society. New York: Bedminster Press.
    1976   The Agrarian Sociology of Ancient Civilizations. Trans.
                R. I. Frank. Highlands, N.J.: Humanities Press.

8

WEBER VS. PARSONS: DOMINATION OR TECHNOCRATIC MODELS OF SOCIAL ORGANIZATION

Robert J. Antonio

Talcott Parsons's translations and exegeses were instrumental both in introducing Weberian social theory to English speaking scholars and in fashioning the dominant interpretation of Weber in American sociology.[1] In recent years, as interest in Weber has intensified and several new English translations of his work have appeared,[2] Parsons's interpretation has become the subject of increasing debate. For example, there has been considerable disagreement over the concept of *Herrschaft*.[3] In his important translation, *The Theory of Social and Economic Organization,* Parsons, borrowing from Timasheff (see Parsons's note 83 in Weber, 1964:152), interprets the term as "imperative control." He (Parsons 1960a:752; see also 1960b:150) asserts, elsewhere, that "in its most general meaning" *Herrschaft* should be translated as "leadership" or "authority." Parsons criticizes other Weber scholars who interpret the concept as "domination" because, in his view, this translation implies arbitrary, coercive force, "rather than the integration of the collectivity, in the interest of effective functioning." Parsons believes that the latter is the crucial factor in Weber's thought.

The translation of *Herrschaft* is mentioned because it is central to a much broader issue concerning Weber's analysis of modern social organization and the roles of power and coercion within it. This wider topic will be the primary concern of the essay. I will clarify Weber's approach to modern society by contrasting his organizational theory to Parsons's. In short, an attempt will be made to demonstrate that the theories constitute different and almost contradictory portrayals of modern social organization. Furthermore, it will be shown that Parsons himself recognizes most of these crucial differences explicitly. However, in appropriating certain elements of Weber's approach for his own theory, Parsons creates the misleading impression, at certain important junctures (as in his interpretation of *Herrschaft*), that he and Weber are in general agreement. As a result, Parsons implies mistakenly that Weber emphasizes integration more than power and coercion. This contradicts his correct claims, at other points, that Weber gives strong emphasis to these two elements. Unfortunately, organizational sociologists have often gained an integrationist understanding of Weber from their reading of Parsons, which misrepresents the Weberian analysis of bureaucracy. They have not grasped the ambiguities in Parsons's translations and interpretive essays. Thus, one sometimes finds the incorrect conclusion that Weber's organizational theory constitutes a functionalist approach (e.g. Blau and Meyer, 1971:22; Blau, 1970:143).

This essay will not be a litany of Parsons's alleged errors. Instead, emphasis is upon the fact that Parsons and Weber, despite limited agreement, have fundamentally different conceptions of modern society. Both scholars begin with the centrality of rationalization.[4] However, Weber's use of the concept gives primary emphasis to formal rationality, as opposed to Parsons's emphasis on substantive rationality. In other words, Weber's analysis focuses on the development of rational means of administration that increase the effectiveness of the leadership's ("master's") regulation of large organizations. On the other hand, Parsons's perspective suggests that modernization produces organizations with increasingly rational ends more effectively coordinated with societal values and community needs. In short, Weber argues that rationalization enhances the power of the "master," (although not necessarily in opposition to the interests of the masses), but Parsons implies that it advances a more pluralist pattern of power, serving the general interests of the society. These differences are significant because both theorists present carefully articulated, systematic analyses of the organizational foundations of modern society. More importantly, these approaches, properly understood, will help clarify two broader perspectives with contrasting concepts of power—domination theory and technocratic theory—which underlie some of the fundamental debates in both classical and contemporary social theory.[5]

WEBER'S THEORY OF MODERN BUREAUCRACY

Weber argues that, "from a purely technical point of view," bureaucracy is "capable of attaining the highest degree of efficiency" (1968:223). He states further that the "primary source of the superiority of bureaucratic administration lies in the role of technical knowledge which, through the development of modern technology and business methods in the production of goods, has become completely indispensible." Weber's description of modern bureaucracy stresses characteristics that promote the efficient completion of tasks requiring collective coordination (1968:956-58). Moreover, he implies that this organizational rationalization contributed significantly to the productive advances that accompanied capitalist development. In Weber's view, modern bureaucracy's emphasis upon specialized training, technical competence, merit and exact calculation undermines patrimonialism and nurtures social relations based on rational discipline. This highly standardized and impersonal type of obedience is a primary facet of the technical efficiency of modern bureaucracy and is the basis for Weber's claim that capitalist bureaucratization improved the administration of production.

Weber stresses the technical advantages of modern bureaucracy, but he does *not* suggest that these elements have displaced hierarchical domination, *nor* does he imply that modern bureaucratic efficiency necessarily serves general community needs. Weber stipulates carefully,

Formal and substantive rationality, no matter by what standard the latter is measured, are always in principle separate things, no matter that in many . . . cases they may coincide empirically. For the formal rationality of money accounting does not reveal anything about the actual distribution of goods. This must always be considered separately. Yet, if the standard used is that of the provision of a certain minimum of subsistence for the maximum size of population, the experience of the last few decades would seem to show that formal and substantive rationality coincide to a relatively high degree. The reasons lie in the nature of the incentives which are set into motion by the type of economically oriented social action which alone is adequate to money calculations. But it nevertheless holds true under all circumstances that formal rationality itself does not tell us anything about real want satisfaction unless it is combined with an analysis of the distribution of income. (1968:108-09)

My point is that Weber describes bureaucracy as a system based on formal rationality with no inherent connection to specific substantive ends. Bureaucracy can serve the interests of social and economic elites, the general needs of a community or some combination of the two. Most importantly, Weber defines modern bureaucracy as a *structure of domination*[6] characterized by a sharply defined, rationally regulated administrative hierarchy controlled by a nonbureaucratic head[7] whose substantive decisions (commands) are transformed into bureaucratic rules and routines. The master's place in the societal stratification system influences these decisions, shaping the organization's productive ends. When Weber speaks historically he implies that bureaucracies have tended to centralize societal power rather than disperse it, and that by doing so they have usually served the interests of elites who use the organizations to control people and resources. Weber also recognizes that bureaucratization can improve the provisioning of community subsistence needs, but he does not imply that reductions in economic, social and political inequalities need accompany it.

Under domination, the ruler's command becomes the objective of the social action of the ruled (Weber, 1968:946). Weber equates domination with the ruler's "authoritarian power of command" and "obedience" from the perspective of the ruled. On the other hand, he does not treat domination as *pure* coercion, because "it refers to a meaningful interrelationship between those giving orders and those obeying, to the effect that the expectations toward which action is oriented on both sides can be reckoned upon" (1968:1378). Weber implies that domination requires "self-justification through appealing to the principles of its legitimation"[8] (1968:954). Accordingly, he argues that there are three ultimate principles of legitimation (rational rules, tradition, charisma) accompanying the three broad modes of domination (bureaucratic, patrimonial,[9] and charismatic). However, the fact that Weber connects legitimacy and domination in no way contradicts his emphasis on hierarchy and obedience. Rather, it stresses that hierarchical social systems do not rely exclusively on force (although force and material sanctions exist as threats if obedience breaks down) for their maintenance. Weber asserts that *"rationally regulated* association within a structure of domination finds its typical expression in *bureaucracy"* (1968:954, emphasis added).

Though Weber lists many important "rational" attributes of bureaucracy, including jurisdictions, files, training, career, monetary wages, impersonal rules and technical capacity (1968:217-26, 956-1005), he emphasizes strongly "compliance," "obedience," "rule" and "authoritarian power of command" throughout the analysis (see 1968:211-15, 941-47). He asserts,

Bureaucracy is *the* means of transforming social action into rationally organized action. Therefore, as an instrument of rationally organizing authority relations, bureaucracy was and is a power instrument of the first order for one who controls the bureaucratic apparatus. . . . Where administration has been completely bureaucratized, the resulting system of domination is practically indestructable. (1968:987)

Weber's portrayal of bureaucracy (see 1968:1394) is quite clear; the technical capacities of the expert are chained to the domination interests of the master (the nonbureaucratic head). In fact, expert training, functional specialization, promotion on merit, differential reward and professionalism all contribute to the official's dutiful obedience to the master's commands:

The individual bureaucrat cannot squirm out of the apparatus into which he has been harnessed . . . the professional bureaucrat is chained to his activity in his entire economic and ideological existence. In the great majority of cases he is only a small cog in a ceaselessly moving mechanism which prescribes to him an essentially fixed route of march. The official is entrusted with specialized tasks, and normally the mechanism cannot be put into motion or arrested by him, but only from the very top. The individual bureaucrat is, above all, forged to the common interest of all the functionaries in the perpetuation of the apparatus and the persistence of its rationally organized domination. (Weber, 1968:987-88)

Weber states explicilty that bureaucratization routinizes the work of technical specialists such that they are forced to obey a master just as the factory operative or soldier does (1968:1394). Finally,

Weber sees knowledge control as a tool of power (see 1968:992-93). Bureaucratic elites keep certain aspects of their knowledge and intentions secret to insure that the flow of knowledge is regulated by the "power interests of the given structure of domination *toward the outside*." Knowledge control may occur not only through direct concealment of potentially damaging information, but also through obfuscation built into specialized, technical jargons. In short, the growth of technical vocabularies limits the general public from access to information formally available.

Weber does associate "leveling" with bureaucratization (1968:983-87). However, this concept definitely does not imply a trend toward pluralist democracy, because Weber also suggests that "bureaucratic structure goes hand in hand with the concentration of the material means of management in the hands of the master" (1968:908), that "caesarism" often develops from democracy (1968:961), that a "crypto-plutocratic distribution of power" often results from bureaucratization (1968:989) and that *mass* democracy accompanies bureaucracy (1968:983). Weber explains that "mass democracy" should *not* be confused with "minimization of the civil servants' power in favor of the greatest possible 'direct' rule of the *demos*" (1968:983). Instead, he asserts emphatically that the "decisive" and exclusive fact "is the *leveling of the governed* in the face of the governing and bureaucratically articulated group, which in its turn may occupy a quite autocratic position, both in fact and form" (1968:985). Thus, despite his differences with the left, and his rejection of state socialism, Weber stresses that modern social organization promotes, rather than diminishes, inequalities in the societal distribution of power.

Weber attributes to bureaucracy a "dehumanized nature" reflected in its "discharge of business according to *calculable rules* and 'without regard for persons'" (Weber, 1968:975). This implies that bureaucracy is a pure system of formal rationality. Production for general need is never guaranteed by organizational structure, no matter how great its productive potential. Weber warns explicitly that "the mere fact of bureaucratic organization does not unambiguously tell us about the concrete direction of its *economic* effects" (1968:990) (because it can be put "at the disposal of quite varied interests"). His argument implies that the productivity of modern bureaucracy does not derive merely from its formal rationality, but from the conjunction of this property with economic, social and political factors in capitalist development. Most importantly, Weber's awareness of improved productivity does not contradict his contention that bureaucratization has contributed to the rationalization of domination by elites. In his view, this domination is so effective that modern bureaucratic elites can only be overthrown by other elites who continue to operate the same bureaucratic apparatus. Thus, *coups d'état* take the place of revolutions (Weber, 1968:988-89).

There are three dimensions implicit in Weber's approach to bureaucracy which need to be drawn out more clearly. First, the linkage of bureaucracy to production can never be deduced a priori, nor can it from the achieved level of rationalization of organizational structure. Instead, it can be explained only by historical/empirical inquiry considering the development of the organization in the context of the larger system of social, political and economic relations. Second, bureaucracies stress discipline because their functioning both as means of domination and as means of production depends upon it. However, the actual and optimal levels of discipline varies with the empirical bureaucracy. Third, Weber's discussion of "secrecy" emphasizes the tendency of bureaucracies to control information according to their (and the masters') power interests. Aspects of this process implied by Weber, but not directly discussed, are that bureaucracies propagandize the quality, quantity and value of the goods and services they claim to produce, while also attempting to conceal waste, destructiveness, coercion and impropriety. Thus, bureaucracies tend to substitute a service ideology (often expressed in official organizational goals) for actual production.

PARSONS'S THEORY OF MODERN SOCIAL ORGANIZATION

According to Parsons, the early modern development of bureaucracy has been followed by a late modern (American) move away from it to an even higher form of complex organization (1971:122).[10] Parsons's analysis of modern society emphasizes a sharp divergence between nineteenth- and twentieth-century capitalism (1960b:113). Parsons's perspective emphasizes a managed, rational economy no longer characterized by the anarchical, nonrational tendencies of laissez-faire capitalism. He believes that the differentiation[11] of ownership and management and the development of a highly trained, specialized labor force ("occupationalized") cause the modern firm to be mobilized more effectively for production. Parsons states explicitly that the value of market profit is secondary to production in the modern firm (1960b:47). This alleged fundamental transformation of the capitalist firm (and division of labor) is an important facet of Parsons's theory of modern complex organization.

Parsons asserts that analysis of the modern organization must proceed, like other social system inquiries, from the reference point of its "value pattern." He claims that the characteristic feature of an organization, from an analytic perspective, is the *"primacy of orientation to the attainment of a specific goal"* (1960b:17, emphasis added). In his view, the goal is defined by group values. Output is linked to the broader social system through legitimation processes which insure the connection of production to societal value patterns. Parsons concludes that a formal organization is a mechanism to implement "goals somehow important to society, or to various subsystems of it" (1960b:63).

Parsons classifies organizations according to four action-system prerequisites: *adaptation*/economic goals (e.g., business firms); *goal attainment*/political goals (e.g., offices of state); *integration*/integrative goals (e.g., interest groups); and *pattern maintenance*/symbolic meaning goals (e.g., churches and schools) (1960b:44-77). The different types of organization produce outputs governed by their central functional goals: respectively, the production of economic utilities; effective collective action; consensus; and commitment to societal value patterns (see Parsons, 1971:4-12; Parsons and Smelser, 1965:46-51; Hills, 1976:808-19).

Parsons conceptualizes complex organization as a *means of production* guided by societal functional requirements. Furthermore, his functionalist terminology, emphasizing legitimation, societal goals, shared values and consensus, implies that production benefits the whole of society. He does not discuss the meaning and impact of production and distribution for the various sectors of a class-stratified population.

Parsons conceives of political power as "the *generalized capacity of a social system to get things done in the interest of collective goals*" (1906:180, emphasis added). This power reflects consensus rather than coercion because it is guided by institutionalized system goals that legitimate both organizational means and ends.

Parsons explains that modern complex organization has three levels: *management,* with "special responsibility" for "policy formation"; a line *formation* of "operative groups" controlled by management; and a *staff* "of experts who stand in an advisory capacity to the decision makers" (1960b:22). He believes that persons in positions of "legal authority, the higher the more so, generally are in some important sense and degree 'superior' to those under them in respect to ability and achievement" (1961:59).

Parsons asserts that large organizations are purportedly moving away from line authority because "it is essential to secure the cooperation of specialists without asserting sheer authority" (1971:105). He believes that the trend is toward an increasing number of "collegial associations" organized like academic departments, where collegial relations are "most fully institutionalized" (1971:98, 105).[12] He asserts that the "basic equality of 'colleagues' in a faculty or department is in particularly sharp and persistent contrast with bureaucratic (line) hierarchy" (1971:105).

Parsons envisions modern organization as a complex network of functionally interdependent technical roles. It requires a hierarchy of authority and power to achieve its goals, but its technical nature diminishes the verticality of authority relations. In such organizations, administrative hierarchy is transformed into a "facilitating agency" for managing resources, the physical plant and relations with the public (Parsons, 1960b:54). Managerial activity is limited to loose regulation, rather than strict control. The institution's professional workforce is largely self-coordinated by internalized technical norms and a spirit of interdependence.

Parsons admits a strain between the "egalitarian component" and the "achievement complex" of modern values (1971:111), but asserts that it is counterbalanced by "the institutionalization of accountability" of officials and "equality of opportunity" among the masses (1971:119-20). Furthermore, political authority is "limited to the legally defined powers of office, so that private prerogatives, property interests, and the like are strictly separated from those of office" (Parsons, 1971:91). The "nonbureaucratic top," which achieves its position by election, is regulated by the possibility of electoral defeat, recall, and judicial restraints (Parsons, 1971:103). The differentiation of the polity from the societal community and the legal subsystem from the executive and legislative branches of the polity produce a trend toward "representative democracy" (Parsons, 1971:91).

In the private sector, separation of ownership and management is crucial. Parsons claims that "management is organized predominantly in occupational roles, which depend little or not at all upon personal property rights or lineage structures in which property rights are institutionalized" (1971:104). He rejects the thesis that the "corporate rich" control the activities of large organizations (1960b:203), arguing that "fiduciary boards" make crucial decisions about income, dividends, expenses and investment (Parsons, 1960b:88). Board members do not act out of individual interest, as nineteenth-century owner-managers did, but instead arrive at balanced decisions reflecting both *organizational* interests and broad social responsibility (Parsons, 1960b:90).

Parsons claims that managerial organization is subjected to numerous societal controls. First, it acts within limits set from above by fiduciary boards. This involves loose regulation, rather than strict control, because the boards must allow managers sufficient freedom to use their professional competencies (Parsons, 1960b:68). Second, they are regulated from below by their dependence upon professional staffs requiring similar freedom. Third, managers are regulated from within by the internalized norms of their professional roles. Fourth, they are limited by reciprocities that develop between their organizations and other groups (e.g., outside experts, consumers, resource people). Fifth, managers are motivated by values (of fairness) and required by union safeguards to act responsibly toward their nonprofessional employees. Finally, free laborers can seek new positions outside the organization.

All these controls contribute to management's role as a means of coordinating organizational processes with societal goals.

In Parsons's view, modern society makes a significant move away from "hereditary ascriptive" relations toward "totally nonascriptive stratification" (1971:96). Representative democracy and human rights guarded by law result in "equality of citizenship," while the "educational revolution" brings about "equality of opportunity" (Parsons, 1971:96-97). Parsons recognizes that ascriptive inequality is still a problem and will remain so for years to come, but he claims that modern systems are moving toward "substantive" or "functional" inequality (differential rewards based on competence and the socioeconomic importance of the skill) (1971:114-21). Increasingly, inequalities reflect "the competitive educational process," native ability and motivation, rather than arbitrary ascription. The emerging mode of inequality is unavoidable, being necessary for worker motivation and distributive justice.

Parsons implies that modern organization has a *metarational* structure; it is both formally and substantively rational. This unfolds from his argument that production (regulated by societal values) is its governing principle. He not only suggests that complex organization manages production efficiently, but he also implies that production fulfills system, collective and even individual needs more rationally. In Parsons's organizational theory, productivity eclipses coercion and domination, thereby qualitatively breaking with the past. The "lead society" (the United States) is portrayed as a historical approximation of the heretofore imagined "rational society."[13]

PARSONS'S AMBIGUOUS PORTRAYAL OF WEBER'S VIEW OF POWER AND ORGANIZATION

Parsons says he agrees with "Weber's broad model of bureaucratic structure," but asserts that it must be modified to take account of "technical competence" at the professional level (1960b:113). Parsons asserts that "instead of a rigid hierarchy of status and authority [as described by Weber] there tends to be what is roughly, in formal status, a 'company of equals,' an equalization of status which ignores the inevitable gradation of distinction and achievement to be found in any considerable group of technically competent persons" (1964a:60). Here, Parsons pinpoints the crucial difference between his collegial form of organization and Weber's hierarchical line bureaucracy.

Parsons believes that Weber's "neglect" of professional authority "is associated with a tendency to overemphasize the coercive aspect of authority and hierarchy in human relations"

(1964a:60). (Parsons even in his early work—*The Structure of Social Action*—comments on Weber's strong emphasis on coercion [1968:658].) This theme in Parson's critical commentary on Weber reflects a most significant difference between the two theorists' concepts of power. Parsons argues that Weber, like Marx and C. Wright Mills, adopts a "zero-sum" concept of power, emphasizing "the capacity of one unit in a system to gain its ends *over the opposition* of other units" (1960b:182). Parsons explains, in a critique of C. Wright Mills, that according to the "zero-sum" perspective "power is not a facility for the performance of function in, and on behalf of, the society as a system, but is interpreted exclusively as a facility for getting what one group, the holders of power, wants by preventing another group, the 'outs,' from getting what it wants" (1960b:219-20). In short, Weber and other "zero-sum" theorists stress *power over others* (Parsons, 1960b:182). On the other hand, Parsons views power as a *means of collective goal attainment* (1960b:41-44, 182, 220-21; 1971:116-21).

Parsons's concepts of leadership and authority contradict the so-called zero-sum power model that he attributes to Weber. Since Parsons criticizes Weber's alleged overemphasis on coercion, his functionalist interpretation of *Herrschaft* seems misplaced. The concept of *Herrschaft* should be seen against the background of Weber's broader approach. It is necessary to understand the concept in light of Weber's pervasive concerns about how social organization and particularly modern bureaucracy regulates peoples' behavior in accordance with a master's commands.[14] This is the appropriate context for interpreting the term because Weber applied it frequently and systematically in this part of his work. Weber precedes his analysis of bureaucracy with a discussion linking domination and legitimacy to organizational structure, the power of command and the master (1968:212-15, 941-55).

CONCLUSION: THE DOMINATION AND TECHNOCRATIC MODELS

Weber's approach to modern bureaucratic social organization takes account of productivity but gives analytic priority to hierarchy, control and obedience. Therefore, I refer to it as the *domination model*. Weber believes that modern organization ties the various occupations firmly to the power interests of the master. He states that "the secretary, the engineer, or the worker in the office or plant . . . is subject to a discipline no longer different in its nature from that of the civil service or the army'' (1968:944).

Weber's analysis of bureaucracy stresses hierarchy in wider society as well as within the organization. He does not suggest that technical development erodes hierarchy. On the contrary, he implies that technology and organizational rationalization promote the centralization and refinement of power by societal elites.

Parsons's approach can be considered a *technocratic model* of complex organization because it gives analytic (though by no means causal) priority to production. This model suggests that organizational rationalization in modern society is accompanied by technical advances in the division of labor that promote the democratization of both the organization and the broader social order. Parsons implies that modern organizations are so dependent upon knowledge, training and merit that greater autonomy has to be given to professional personnel and workers. Finally, at the policy-making level, fiduciary boards replace the master, coordinating the organization's long-term interests with those of other organizations as well as with broader social values.

The main point of this paper is that the social theories of Max Weber and Talcott Parsons suggest very different views of rationalization, modernization and bureaucratization. In American sociology these two approaches have often been treated erroneously as almost synonymous frameworks. Parsonsian functionalist interpretations of Weberian theory imply that Weber's concepts of bureaucracy and rationalization collapse formal rationality and substantive rationality into a unity. This creates a strawman theory that can be knocked down easily by organizational sociologists who, after having absorbed a "Parsonized" Weber, criticize Weber for having an overly rational model of modern organization.[15] At least partial responsibility for this confusion comes from Parsons's ambiguous and sometimes contradictory commentary on the relations of organization, coercion, power and domination in Weberian theory. However, a careful reading of Parsons's own work provides ample evidence that the two theories must be seen as separate and even contradictory models.

The differences between Weber's and Parsons's models derive largely from a disagreement about the balance between domination and production in modern organization, and whether the trend in modern society is toward democracy or plutocracy. The positions encompass very important (and ideologically charged) historical/ empirical issues that are central to both classical and contemporary sociology. However, the controversy has been obscured somewhat by the fact that many sociologists have subtle ideological commitments to either technocratic theory or domination theory that remain implicit and hidden in the designs of their empirical studies or in the assumptions of their theoretic discourses. This situation discourages direct confrontation with the issues that need to be clarified, investigated and debated. It is my contention that Weber's and Parsons's organizational theories, properly interpreted, provide explicit and detailed models of domination theory and technocratic theory. These models could be used to promote a sharpened sociological dialogue about the nature of modern social organization[16] that deals specifically on the analytic level with the relations of formal rationality and substantive rationality and on the historical level with the relations of production and domination.

NOTES

David Willer's excellent criticism has contributed strongly to this project. Also, I want to thank Michael Lacy for his careful reading and criticism of several drafts of this essay. This investigation was supported by the University of Kansas, General Research allocation #3485-x0-0038.

1. Probably the most influential works by Parsons involving Weber are the translations of Weber's *The Protestant Ethic and the Spirit of Capitalism* [1930] (1958b) (The bracketed date refers to first date of publication while the one in parenthesis refers to the edition used in this paper) and *The Theory of Social and Economic Organization* (translated with A. M. Henderson) [1947] (1964). Parsons's interpretations of Weber's work in *The Structure of Social Action* [1937] (1968) and in *Essays in Sociological Theory Pure and Applied* (1949) have also been extremely important to American sociologists. Of course, there are other essays devoted explicitly to Weber, as well as relevant discussions and asides in still others of Parsons's papers and books not addressed specifically to Weberian theory. Certainly, commentary on Weber's thought can be found throughout Parsons's works.

2. Among the most significant (other than Parsons's) English translations of Weber are *General Economic History* (Knight, 1927), *From Max*

Weber (Gerth and Mills, [1946] 1958a), and *The Methodology of the Social Sciences* (Shils and Finch, 1949). Important interpretive works are *Max Weber and German Politics* (Mayer, 1956), and *Max Weber: An Intellectual Portrait* (Bendix, 1960; 2d ed. 1977). Indicative of the more recent wave of interest in Weber are the following translations: *Economy and Society* (Roth and Wittich, 1968; 2d ed. 1978), *Roscher and Knies* (Oales, 1975), *The Agrarian Sociology of Ancient Civilizations* (Frank, 1976), *Critique of Stammler* (Oakes, 1977), and *Max Weber: Selections in Translation* (Matthews, 1978). Some recent interpretive essays (and collections of essays) are Honigsheim (1968), Freund (1968), Mitzman (1969), Wrong (1970), Lachmann (1970), Bendix and Roth (1971), Dronberger (1971), Sahay (1971), Bruun (1972), Giddens (1972), Runciman (1972), Beetham (1974), MacRae (1974), Mommsen (1974), Burger (1976), Roth and Schluchter (1979).

3. The reader should see Roth and Wittich (Weber, 1968:61-62), Bendix (1977:481-82), Bruun (1972:287-88), Cohen, Hazelrigg, and Pope (1975a; 1975b), Hättich (1967), and Parsons (1960a; 1960b:149-56; 1964a:59-60; 1972; 1975).

4. "Rationalization" must be placed in the context of Weber's broader concept of reason. The term is most often associated with social action and structures emphasizing demystification, exact calculation, prediction and quantification concerning the *means* of action. This meaning is reflected in his use of "instrumentally rational action" (1968:24-26), "technical rationality" (1968:63-68), "rational economic action" (1968:71-74) and "formal rationality" (1968:85-86). Weber contrasts these to "value rational action" (1968:24-26) and "substantive rationality" (1968:85-86), which involve reflection about ultimate ends. Weber's concept of rationalization refers to the "disenchantment" of the world; the displacement of "magical elements of thought" (see Gerth and Mills, 1958:51). Horkheimer captures the sense of this process: "Today . . . it is not only the business but the essential work of reason to find means for goals one adopts at any time" (1974:vii). Rationalization means the intensification of formal reason in social organization and technical routines as well as in action/thought. In this paper, formal rationality refers to means-oriented action stressing calculation (particularly economic and quantitative), prediction and accounting. Substantive rationality refers to action (guided by a set of ultimate values) aimed at provisioning a community.

5. These terms are *not* substitutes for *conflict theory* and *functionalism*. Although this paper has some implications for the "conflict-functionalism debate," the differences between domination theory and technocratic theory should not be reduced to a dimension of this debate.

6. In this section, I am using the Roth and Wittich translation of *Wirtschaft and Gesellschaft* (Economy and Society) (1968), in which *Herrschaft* is interpreted as domination. This work is appropriate because it involves "Weber's major comparative treatment of forms of domination" (Roth, 1965:213). The term *structure of domination* refers to a network of social roles involving systematic, interrelated patterns of obedience.

7. Weber has been criticized recently for portraying bureaucracy as a mere organ of power transmission for the master. Some theorists, using modern states and particularly state-socialist systems as examples, argue that the ultimate power holder can be the upper rank of bureaucratic personnel (see Lefort, 1974/75). Weber (1968:1401-02) implies some sensitivity to this issue in his discussion of the possible effects of the destruction of "private capitalism."

8. Legitimation involves beliefs that justify compliance with commands (Weber, 1968:212-15).

9. Weber (1968:1006-10) also discusses patriarchal domination. The differentiation of patriarchal power in a communal household (*oikos*) results in the development of patrimonial domination.

10. In this section, I rely heavily upon Parsons's essays on social organization and modernization. Effrat (1973:800, 804) states that the theory of organization is one of the less developed aspects of Parsons's general theory. However, Parsons has written several seminal essays on the topic that are the basis of this section. Furthermore, the nature of social organization is a central issue in Parsons's general theoretical works, such as *The Social System* (1964b). Finally, his concept of modernization, which has a prominent role in his general theory (especially the later work focusing on the evolution of society), gives strong and central emphasis to organizational change. The scope of this essay is limited to a few of Parsons's works, which address these issues most directly and clearly. These works tend to be descriptive and/or historical (roughly so) and for the most part avoid the inevitable problems of interpretation that flow from the abstruse terminology in Parsons's more abstract theoretical works.

11. Parsons defines "differentiation" as "the division of a unit or structure in a social system into two or more units or structures that differ in their characteristics and functional significance for the system" (1971:26). Differentiation increases the system's adaptive capacity because ensuing specialization promotes rationalization of role tasks, thereby improving productive efficiency.

12. Parsons does not assert that all complex organizations are already collegial. Instead, he implies that the nature of the modern division of labor produces a trend toward collegialism (Parsons, 1971:101-14).

13. Parsons's claims seem extreme to this author, but they should not be interpreted as meaning that premodern societal elements have been completely eradicated in the United States. Instead, Parsons's point is that great strides have been made in this direction and that the path of structural development has been revolutionalized and will probably continue to unfold in this direction in the future.

14. While I disagree strongly with Parsons, my criticism should not be taken as a dogmatic rejection of his interpretation. I am well aware that Weber's concept of *Herrschaft* (and the broader theory of which it is a part) is a debatable topic. There are Weber scholars (e.g., Bruun, 1972:287-88) who concur with Parsons's interpretation, stressing Weber's concern for legitimate authority. However, as is clear in this paper, I concur with those who consider Weber's concept of authority a subordinate part of his power theory (e.g., Hättich, 1967).

15. I am not suggesting that Weber's theory of bureaucracy is completely invulnerable to this type of critique. However, if one takes account of his emphasis on the strain between the two types of rationality, Weber's model can be viewed as being sensitive to both rationality and irrationality. For example, organizational action based on formal rationality (e.g., exact calculation, technical mastery and careful coordination) may be designed explicitly for substantively irrational ends (e.g., expropriation, waste and destruction). The obverse is also true, because concern for substantively rational ends may contradict formal rationality (e.g., safety standards in the work area may slow production and reduce profit).

16. I do not imply that these are the only two approaches that could contribute to the clarification of this debate. For example, Marx and the Marxists have had much to say about domination theory and confront many of Parsons's claims directly. Critical theorists have attempted a synthesis of Weberian theory and Marxian theory that focuses on the critique of technocratic approaches. System theorists have developed models that take into account some of the issues stressed by Parsons, but without his sweeping historical claims. Despite these other models, Weber's and Parsons's theories are particularly useful for orienting debate about the structure and functioning of complex organization.

REFERENCES

Beetham, David
    1974   *Max Weber and the Theory of Modern Politics.* London: Allen and Unwin.
Bendix, Reinhard
    1977   *Max Weber: An Intellectual Portrait.* 2d ed. Berkeley: University of California Press.

172   Max Weber's Political Sociology

Bendix, Reinhard, and Guenther Roth
1971   *Scholarship and Partisanship: Essays on Max Weber.*
          Berkeley: University of California Press.
Blau, Peter M.
1970   "Weber's Theory of Bureaucracy," pp. 141-45, in Dennis
          Wrong (ed.), *Max Weber.* Englewood Cliffs, N.J.:
          Prentice-Hall.
Blau, Peter M., and Marshall W. Meyer
1971   *Bureaucracy in Modern Society.* New York: Random
          House.
Bruun, H. H.
1972   *Science, Values and Politics in Max Weber's Methodology.*
          Copenhagen: Munksgaard.
Burger, Thomas
1976   *Max Weber's Theory of Concept Formation: History,
          Laws, Ideal Types.* Durham, N.C.: Duke University Press.
Cohen, Jere, Lawrence E. Hazelrigg, and Whitney Pope
1975a   "De-Parsonizing Weber: A Critique of Parsons's
          Interpretation of Weber's Sociology." *American
          Sociological Review* 40:229-41.
1975b   "Reply to Parsons." *American Sociological Review*
          40:670-74.
Dronberger, Illse
1971   "Introduction," pp. 800-4, in J. J. Loubser, Rainer C.
          Baum, Andrew Effrat, and Victor Meyer Lidz (eds.)
          Explorations in General Theory in Social Science (Vol. 2).
          New York: Macmillan.
Effrat, Andrew (ed.)
1973   *Perspectives in Political Sociology.* Indianapolis: Bobbs-
          Merrill.
Freund, Julien
1968   *The Sociology of Max Weber* (translated by Mary Ilford).
          New York: Vintage Books.
Gerth, H. H., and C. Wright Mills
1958   "Introduction: The Man and His Work," pp. 3-74, in Max
          Weber, *From Max Weber.* New York: Oxford University
          Press.
Giddens, Anthony
1972   *Politics and Sociology in the Thought of Max Weber.*
          London: Macmillan.
Hättich, Manfred
1967   "Der bergriff des politischen bei Max Weber." Politische
          Vierteljahresschrift 8:40-50.

Hills, R. Jean
    1976   "The Organization as a Component in the Structure of Society," pp. 805-28, in Jan J. Loubser, Rainer C. Baum, Andrew Effrat, and Victory Meyer Lidz (eds.), *Explorations in General Theory in Social Science* (Vol. 2). New York: Macmillan.

Honigsheim, Paul
    1968   *On Max Weber*. New York: Free Press.

Horkheimer, Max
    1974   *Critique of Instrumental Reason* (translated by Matthew J. O'Connell and others). New York: Seabury.

Lachmann, L. M.
    1970   *The Legacy of Max Weber: Three Essays*. London: Heinemann.

Lefort, Claude
    1974/75   "What Is Bureaucracy?" *Telos* 22:31-65.

MacRae, Donald G.
    1974   *Weber*. London: Fontana.

Mayer, J. P.
    1956   *Max Weber and German Politics*. London: Faber and Faber.

Mitzman, Arthur
    1969   *The Iron Cage: An Historical Interpretation of Max Weber*. New York: Knopf.

Mommsen, Wolfgang
    1974   *The Age of Bureaucracy: Perspectives on the Political Sociology of Max Weber*. New York: Harper & Row.

Parsons, Talcott
    1949   *Essays in Sociological Theory Pure and Applied*. Glencoe, Ill.: Free Press.
    1960a   "Review Article: 'Max Weber.'" *American Sociological Review* 25:750-52.
    1960b   *Structure and Process in Modern Societies*. Glencoe, Ill.: Free Press.
    1964a   "Introduction," pp. 1-86, in Max Weber, *The Theory of Social and Economic Organization*. New York: Free Press.
    1964b   *The Social System*. New York: Free Press.
    1968   *The Structure of Social Action* (2 Vols.). New York: Free Press.
    1971   *The System of Modern Societies*. Englewood Cliffs, N.J.: Prentice-Hall.
    1972   "Review of 'Scholarship and Partisanship: Essays on Max Weber.'" *Contemporary Sociology* 1:200-3.

1975   "Response to De-Parsonizing Weber." *American Sociological Review* 40:666-69.

Parsons, Talcott, and Neil H. Smelser
1965   *Economy and Society*. New York: Free Press.

Roth, Guenther
1965   "Political Critiques of Max Weber." *American Sociological Review* 30:213-23.

Roth, Guenther, and Wolfgang Schluchter
1979   *Max Weber's Vision of History: Ethics and Methods*. Berkeley: University of California Press.

Runciman, W. G.
1972   *A Critique of Max Weber's Philosophy of Social Science*. Cambridge: Cambridge University Press.

Sahay, A.
1971   *Max Weber and Modern Society*. London: Routlege & Kegan Paul.

Weber, Max
1927   *General Economic History* (translated by Frank H. Knight). London: Allen and Unwin.
1949   *The Methodology of the Social Sciences* (translated by Edward Shils and Henry Finch). New York: Free Press.
1958a   *From Max Weber* (translated by H. H. Gerth and C. Wright Mills). New York: Oxford University Press.
1958b   *The Protestant Ethic and the Spirit of Capitalism* (translated by Talcott Parsons). New York: Charles Scribner's Sons.
1964   *The Theory of Social and Economic Organization* (translated by Talcott Parsons and A. M. Henderson). New York: Free Press.
1968   *Economy and Society* (3 Vols.) (edited by Guenther Roth and Claus Wittich). New York: Bedminister Press (2d ed. Berkeley: University of California Press, 1978).
1975   *Roscher and Knies: The Logical Problems of Historical Economics* (translated by Guy Oakes). New York: Free Press.
1976   *The Agrarian Sociology of Ancient Civilizations* (translated by R. I. Frank). New York: Free Press.
1977   *Critique of Stammler* (translated by Guy Oakes). New York: Free Press.
1978   *Max Weber: Selections in Translation* (edited by W. G. Runciman and translated by Eric Matthews). New York: Cambridge University Press.

Wrong, Dennis (ed.)
1970   *Max Weber*. Englewood Cliffs, N.J.: Prentice-Hall.

9

MAX WEBER AND THE DILEMMA OF RATIONALITY

Roslyn Wallach Bologh

Max Weber has been accused of identifying the formal rationality of capitalism with rationality in general. Critics such as Herbert Marcuse[1] have denounced Weber's treatment of formal rationality as an apology for the domination and irrationality of the capitalist system. Jurgen Habermas[2] replied to Marcuse by pointing out that although technical rationality, a derivative of Weber's formal rationality, may justify domination, it is impossible to eliminate technical rationality and maintain modern industrial production. However, as Wolfgang Mommsen[3] points out, Weber himself although appreciative was also passionately critical of formal rationality, and none of the scholars at the Heidelberg conference (where Marcuse raised the issue) who spoke up in defense of Weber seemed to realize this.

Although Weber supported capitalism precisely because of its formal, economic rationality, he also distinguished between formal rationality and substantive rationality and recognized an inherent tension and conflict between the two. Despite his analysis of the separate and oppositional character of the two types of rationality, Weber steadfastly retained his dualistic conception of rationality and championed the "reality" that grounds that conception.[4] Nevertheless, the conflict between formal and substantive rationality and the dilemma occasioned by that conflict was the source of Weber's pessimism and even anguish. Weber saw this conflict as the dilemma of modern life. The following analysis will make clear the nature of that dilemma and Weber's attempt to come to terms with it.

It is important to examine Weber's analysis of this dilemma and the depth of his understanding because Weber's work remains one of the most thoroughgoing and brutally "realistic" assessments of modern social life and its possibilities for rationality. Because Weber accepted the unpleasant "reality" that he analyzed and saw through, he is considered one of the most "realistic," tough-minded, and self-conscious social theorists we have had. Before we, as social scientists, can be critical of Max Weber and question his "realism" and its limits, we must first appreciate the extent of his analysis.

According to Weber,[5] from the perspective of instrumental or formal[6] rationality, value or substantive rationality is always irrational. For there is no rational method for determining values as there is for choosing among alternative means. The choice of one value over another remains ultimately a value decision; ultimate values are always irrational in this sense. On the other side, formally rational, instrumental action uncontaminated by the irrationality of values would be what we call expedience. This would be taking formal rationality to its limits. Weber reminds us that from the perspective of value rationality, pure instrumental rationality is substantively irrational. The most rational choice of means would have no ultimate value, purpose, or reason. Thus, whereas value rationality is instrumentally irrational, formal rationality is substantively irrational.

This analysis of the conflict between the two types of rationality, and the irrationality of each from the perspective of the other, is abstract, however. It remains to be shown how this dual and contradictory conception of rationality expresses real contradictions or dilemmas in the world. By tracing the path of this conception and its attendant dilemma as it makes its appearance in Weber's analysis of bureaucracy, capitalism, socialism, law, and democracy, we can begin to see how the dual conception of rationality implicates all of social life, including the sphere of politics which was Weber's major concern.

DILEMMA OF BUREAUCRACY

1. "The monocratic variety of bureaucracy [which has a single head] is, from a purely technical point of view, capable of attaining

the highest degree of efficiency and is in this sense formally the most rational known means of carrying out imperative control over human beings. It is superior to any other form in precision, in stability, in the stringency of its discipline, and in its reliability."[7] However, the ends to which such control over human beings is put may not be substantively rational. In addition, we may question whether the imperative control over human beings is the most rational or desirable in terms of values. This represents a conflict between formal and substantive rationality.

2. Despite the greater rationality of the monocratic form, the operations of the bureaucracy tend to undermine its own rationality as officials concerned with their own security and self-interest struggle against monocratic power and attempt to establish a collegial form.

3. While it replaces domination on the basis of property and other external considerations with domination on the basis of technical qualifications, hence providing opportunity for the nonpropertied classes, bureaucracy nevertheless also produces "the tendency to plutocracy growing out of the interest in the greatest possible length of technical training."[8]

4. Bureaucracy requires a technically trained population from which to recruit officials. On the one hand it favors the expansion of the educated population in order to develop a broad base for recruitment; on the other hand it is also responsible, according to Weber, for "the tendency to leveling"[9] and therefore the destruction of high culture.

5. Although it eliminates domination through personal relations and ties of loyalty as in patrimonialism, thus promoting personal freedom, it substitutes "dominance of a spirit of formalistic impersonality, without hatred or passion, and hence without affection or enthusiasm."[10] Thus personal freedom is gained at the cost of dehumanization and the absence of inspired leadership.

6. Bureaucratic government develops along with democracy, breaking down traditional privilege and patrimonial domination. Yet bureaucracy tends to obstruct democracy due to the power of experts to obstruct the power of the head of the bureaucracy. "The question is always who controls the existing bureaucratic machinery. And such control is possible only in a very limited degree to persons who are not technical specialists. Generally

speaking, the trained permanent official is more likely to get his way in the long run than his nominal superior, the cabinet minister who is not a specialist."[11]

7. Instead of producing individuals who feel free to act out of conviction and commitment to values, "rational calculation reduces every worker to a cog in this (bureaucratic) machine, and seeing himself in this light, he will merely ask how to transform himself from a little into a somewhat bigger cog."[12]

The source of Weber's despair is the tendency of bureaucratic government to eliminate the possibility of the type of political leadership that he values and feels is necessary, the political leader who acts rationally but with passion and conviction.

DILEMMA OF ECONOMIC ACTION (CAPITALISM)

The term *formal rationality of economic action* refers to the extent of quantitative calculation or accounting. "Expression in money terms yields the highest degree of formal rationality."[13] On the other hand, substantive rationality in the economy means "the application of certain criteria of ultimate ends, whether they be ethical, political, utilitarian, hedonistic, feudal, egalitarian, or whatever."[14]

1. Formally rational economic action is based on money calculation. This means that needs, such as of the poor, that are not backed up by money will not be met through production and the marketplace.

2. The formal rationality of money calculation depends on certain quite specific substantive conditions such as market freedom (the absence of monopolies) and "shop discipline" together with the appropriation of the means of production. This means the existence of a "system of domination,"[15] another example of conflict between substantive and formal rationality.

3. Conflict between formal and substantive rationality also occurs when economic interests become tied to the continuation of the organization "even though its primary ideological basis [its substantive rationality] may in the meantime have ceased to exist. . . . Organizations of all kinds which even in the eyes of the participants have become 'meaningless,' continue to exist because . . . some official makes his 'living' in this manner and otherwise would have no means of support."[16] Hence it may be

formally rational or instrumentally rational in its structure yet substantively irrational.

4. Through the striving for profits, production becomes instrumentally rationalized and revolutionized. However, the most rational form of capitalistic enterprise is the bureaucratic, which despite its formal rationality tends to cause "a paralysis of private economic initiative,"[17] thereby restricting the rationalizing of the economy—another example of substantive irrationality stemming from formal rationality.

5. On the one hand, the market community of capitalism opposes coercion based on personal authority; on the other hand, it continues and even increases authoritarian constraint. The formally rational laws of the market end up giving tremendous power to capitalist commercial establishments—power over employment and unemployment, for example—while inducing them to exercise authoritarian coercion relentlessly,[18] a form of substantive irrationality.

6. Another type of irrationality occurs with the development of outside control over an economic enterprise. Such outside control over management may develop from power over credit or financing, as in the case of bankers or financiers who finance the enterprise or from stock acquisition by speculators seeking gain only through resale. These outside business interests, such as banks or financiers, may pursue their own economic interests often foreign to those of the organization as such.

Speculative interests acting on the basis of instrumental rationality in the market situation are one source of the crises of modern market economy—its substantive irrationality.

DILEMMA OF SOCIALISM OR A PLANNED ECONOMY

Whereas the formal rationality of capitalism may involve a conflict with substantive rationality, the substantive rationality of socialism may involve a conflict with formal rationality. Weber offers the following examples:

1. A planned economy oriented to want satisfaction must weaken the incentive to labor if there is no risk of lack of support.

2. Where a planned economy is radically carried out, it must further accept the inevitable reduction in formal, calculatory

rationality which would result from the elimination of money and capital accounting.

3. With a substantively rational planned economy, individuals would be administered dictatorially, that is, by autocratic determination from above in which they had no voice. "But once any right of codetermination were granted to the population, this would immediately make possible, also in a formal sense, the fighting out of interest conflicts centering on the manner of decision making, and on how much should be saved. What is decisive is that in socialism, violent power struggles would be the normal result: struggles over the alteration of rations, struggles over particular jobs, work cessations as in strikes, boycotts, in short, appropriation processes of all kinds and interest struggles would also then be the normal phenomena of life."[19]

4. Furthermore, socialism would require a still higher degree of formal bureaucratization than capitalism.

DILEMMA OF LAW, SOCIAL JUSTICE, AND DEMOCRACY

Formal justice guarantees maximum freedom for the interested parties to represent their formal legal interests. But all interested parties may not be able to realize this formal freedom in practice. In other words, those without economic power will find it difficult if not impossible to represent their cause legally and hence will suffer accordingly. Organizations with economic power, on the other hand, will be "free" to represent their formal, legal interests regardless of their substantive merit. "Because of the unequal distribution of economic power . . . this very freedom must time and again produce consequences which are contrary to the substantive postulates of religious ethics or of political expediency."[20]

Democracy, too, suffers from the conflict between substantive and formal rationality. Weber distinguishes four types of democracy: collegiality, immediate democracy, and two types of representative democracy. There are two sources for democracy, and they influence the form it takes. One is the aim of legitimizing positions of authority by means of plebiscite. The other is the aim of reducing to a minimum the control of some people over others.[21]

Collegiality divides personal responsibility; in large bodies, personal responsibility disappears almost entirely. In monocratic organizations, on the other hand, it is perfectly clear where responsibility lies. Also collegiality almost inevitably involves obstacles to precise, clear, and above all, rapid decision.[22] Hence, it is technically irrational. For the above criteria of instrumental rationality, it is better to have a single head. However, collegiality is technically rational in one respect: It favors greater thoroughness in the weighing of administrative decisions.[23] Because collegiality unavoidably obstructs the promptness of decision, the consistency of policy, the clear responsibility of the individual, bureaucratic authority in the modern world has led to a weakening of the role of collegiality in effective control.[24]

Immediate democracy requires the following necessary conditions: (1) short term of office; (2) liability to recall at any time; (3) principle of rotation or of selection by lot in filling offices so that every member takes a turn at some time; (4) a strictly defined mandate such that the sphere of competence is delimited and not of a general character; (5) a strict obligation to render an accounting to the general assembly; (6) the obligation to submit every unusual question that has not been foreseen to the assembly of members or to a committee representing them; (7) the distribution of powers among a large number of offices, each with its own particular function; (8) the treatment of office as an avocation and not a full-time occupation.[25]

In addition to the above conditions, Weber adds that there must be no functions which require professional specialists. "If permanent technical officials are appointed alongside of shifting heads, actual power will normally tend to fall into the hands of the former, who do the real work, while the latter remain essentially dilettantes."[26]

These conditions for immediate democracy he believes are not compatible with administering a large, complex society. While substantively rational as an ideal, it would be technically irrational in practice. Therefore, he considers representative democracy.

Representative democracy may take one of two forms: instructed representation or free representation. In the former case, the representative's power is strictly limited by an imperative mandate, and the exercise of power is subject to the consent of those represented. The representative is, in effect, an agent of those he represents. A free representative, in contrast, is not bound by instruction but is in a position to make his own decisions. He is obligated only to express his own genuine conviction and not to promote the interests of those who have elected him.[27]

With respect to the instructed type, we find a dilemma due to the fact that situations are always unstable and unanticipated problems always arise. Hence, for purely technical reasons, "it is not feasible to tie the mandate of the representative completely to the voters' will."[28] This leaves free representation as the only possibility—that is, a plebiscite form of democracy. But the latter brings the danger of demagoguery or sponsorship by a party that owes favors to its supporters.

Furthermore, groups governed by representative bodies are by no means necessarily democratic in the sense that all their members have equal rights.[29] With every development of economic differentiation arises the probability that administration will fall into the hands of the wealthy because they can afford the time to engage in it. "Hence, direct democratic administration will tend to turn into rule by notables."[30] Either that or people who "live off politics."[31]

On the basis of technical rationality, democracy promotes bureaucratization by breaking down the appropriation of positions of power by propertied or privileged groups who are not technical experts. Yet "once fully established, bureaucracy is among those social structures which are the hardest to destroy. . . . Where administration has been completely bureaucratized, the resulting system of domination is practically indestructible.[32]

Thus we have the dilemma that democracy promotes bureaucracy as a means of breaking down the domination by propertied or privileged groups, but bureaucracy produces its own domination and leveling of the governed. Weber states, "Democracy as such is opposed to the 'rule' of bureaucracy."[33]

CONCLUSION

The distinction between the two types of rationality gives rise to two related political dilemmas, one which Weber accepts and even celebrates as the challenge of a rational life, and one which he deplores and despairs of. He accepts the "inevitable" conflict between the ethic of love or brotherhood and the formal rationality of the economy and politics. This dilemma can be resolved by an ethic of responsibility according to which one acts not on the basis of an absolute value but by considering consequences as well as values. The conflict may mean having to use violence, and it certainly means employing some system of domination. But he reconciles himself to these as part of a "manly" life, the former as occasionally necessary, the latter as a fact of social life.

The other dilemma, and the one that is the source of his pessimism, is the *exclusion* of substantive value rationality from spheres of life in which instrumental rationality has become formalized, particularly the bureaucratization of politics and political administration. Despite the conflicts between formal and substantive rationality in the economy, he feels that on the whole the consequences of formal rationality tend in the direction of the economic well-being of large numbers of people, one version of substantive economic rationality. However, the formalization of rationality (bureaucratization) in politics and political administration opposes the development of politicians imbued with an ethic of responsibility, capable of bringing both value rationality and instrumental rationality to bear in decision making. Hence, the political sphere will lack good and effective leadership. It would become a culture of functionaries and masses: a bureaucratic, mass culture incapable of greatness.

We see that despite his critics' accusations Weber was painfully aware of the irrationality of formal rationality. He saw this as the great dilemma of modern life. His greatest concern and the source of his despair was the reduction of German political life to that of a formally rationalized, bureaucratic, mass culture incapable of determining action on the basis of strongly held individual values and convictions. His own ultimate value was for a political state that would devote itself to preserving and furthering the greatness and integrity of a nation and its culture.[34] This concern took precedence over all other issues. In fact, he accepted the domination of formal rationality in all other spheres of life as necessary and desirable for the development of culture.[35] He saw substantive rationality as tending to repress and stifle the development of culture because substantive rationality forces all cultural forms to serve some ultimate value. In this way the cultural form is prevented from being treated as itself an ultimate value worth serving and developing for its own sake. Treating the cultural form, rather than the substance, as a value in its own right constitutes formal as opposed to substantive rationality.

Because political action should aim at protecting and expanding the greatness of a nation's culture, all decision making ought to consider and determine modes of action and their consequences in terms of that ultimate value. If not that particular value, then some ultimate value ought to guide political action.[36] Yet Weber realized that the formal rationality of modern political organization works against the emergence of politicians who can infuse value rationality into political action. Formal rationality reduces all actors to "cogs" in a machine, each desiring only to become a larger cog. Weber, therefore, turned to the possibility of charismatic leadership by means of plebiscitarian democracy. That possibility represented his hope for a leadership that could emerge alongside the formal rationality of political bureaucracies and that could bring to political life an orientation and commitment to some ultimate values.

Weber saw plebiscitarian democracy as the only hope of bringing together the substantive rationality of charismatic leadership with the formal rationality of modern organization. He therefore supported this form of government despite his awareness of the dangers of demagoguery and machine politics.

Weber was concerned throughout his sociological work with the dualistic conception of rationality and the dilemma to which that conception, and the reality in which it is grounded, gives rise. However, he saw no alternative holistic or dialectical version of rationality and no alternative reality that could overcome the dilemma.[37] Only charismatic leadership tied to a formally rational organization could provide a possible resolution.

NOTES

1. Herbert Marcuse, "Industrialization and Capitalism," *New Left Review* 30, 1965, pp. 2ff.

2. Jürgen Habermas, *Technik und Wissenschaft als Ideologie,* Frankfurt, 1970, pp. 48ff, cited in Wolfgang J. Mommsen, *The Age of Bureaucracy* (New York: Harper & Row, 1974).

3. Mommsen, *The Age of Bureaucracy,* p. 68.

4. On the critical necessity of treating concepts as historically specific, which means grounded in a historically specific form of life, see Roslyn Wallach Bologh, *Dialectical Phenomenology: Marx's Method* (Boston: Routledge & Kegan Paul, 1979).

5. Max Weber, *Economy and Society,* Guenther Roth and Claus Wittich, Eds., (Berkeley: University of California Press, 1978), Vol. 1, p. 26.

6. Stephen Kalberg notes that formal and substantive rationality are not identical with but based on instrumental and value rationality. Stephen Kalberg, "Max Weber's Types of Rationality: Cornerstones for the Analysis of Rationalization Processes in History," *American Journal of Sociology* 85 (5), 1980, p. 1158.

7. Weber, *Economy and Society*, p. 223.

8. Ibid., p. 225.

9. Ibid.

10. Ibid.

11. Ibid., p. 224.

12. "Introduction," by Guenther Ross, in ibid., p. lix.

13. Ibid., p. 85.

14. Ibid., p. 202.

15. Ibid.

16. Ibid., p. 202.

17. Ibid., p. lviii.

18. Ibid., Vol. 2, p. 731.

19. Ibid., Vol. 1, pp. 202-03.

20. Ibid., Vol. 2, p. 812.

21. Ibid., Vol. 1, pp. 268-69.

22. Ibid., p. 277.

23. Ibid., pp. 277-78.

24. Ibid., p. 280.

25. Ibid., p. 289.

26. Ibid., p. 291.

27. Ibid., p. 293.

28. Ibid., Vol. 2, p. 1128.

29. Ibid., Vol. 1, p. 296.

30. Ibid., Vol. 2, pp. 949-50.

31. Max Weber, "Politics as a Vocation," in H. H. Gerth and C. W. Mills, Eds., *From Max Weber* (New York: Oxford University Press, 1946), pp. 84-85.

32. Weber, *Economy and Society,* Vol. 2, p. 987.

33. Ibid., p. 991.

34. Mommsen, *The Age of Bureaucracy*, pp. 38-40.

35. Max Weber, "Religious Rejections of the World and Their Directions," in Gerth and Mills, Eds., *From Max Weber,* p. 330.

36. Weber, "Politics as a Vocation," p. 117.

37. Roslyn Wallach Bologh, "A Feminist Dialogue with Max Weber: Rationality, Ethics and Erotic Love," manuscript in progress, addresses this issue.

History, Charisma, and Social Change

10

THE SCIENCE OF HISTORY AND THE THEORY OF SOCIAL CHANGE

Stanford M. Lyman

Much confusion is generated when theorists fail to distinguish between a science of history and a theory of social change. Such confusion has been prevalent in recent years in numerous publications. The particular error that occurs involves a synecdoche; thus certain sociologists have supposed that establishing a theory of social change will also perforce establish a science of history. In fact, however, any theory of social change is and must be only a part of any science of history. To equate a theory of social change with the whole of a science of history is to foreshorten the scope of the latter. Moreover, there is another type of error entailed here: equating changes with history, assuming that all of history is change and that history can embrace no topic other than change. History, however, can and does include stasis, the cake of custom, formed and maintained over a long period of time.

Among the great scholars of both history and social change this error of conflation was not committed. Here, I will mention two major figures: Frederick J. Teggart and Max Weber. Both Teggart and Weber developed sciences of history, and each also contributed a theory of social change. In the cases of both Teggart and Weber their distinctive sciences of history are distinguishable from their respective theories of social change. However, in the years that followed their productive periods, a tendency to perceive sciences of history within theories of social change has led to a certain confusion in the understanding of each of these men's works and in the relation of history to social change. The confusion finds its most representative form in the assertion that a theory of social change is of itself a complete science of history. By reviewing both Teggart's and Weber's sciences of history and theories of social change, I hope to contribute to ending this confusion and also, by elaborating Weber's theory of social change, to provide a basis for a theory of change appropriate to a sociology of the absurd, i.e., that sociology developed a decade ago by Marvin B. Scott and myself in order to elaborate an existential-phenomenological perspective.

TEGGART'S SCIENCE OF HISTORY

Teggart's science of history may be designated as a variant of positivism. According to its essential principles history is to be conceived of as a plurality of happenings whose relationship to one another may be obtained by the processes of hypothesis and "experiment." The hypothesis for Teggart must always take the form of a statement of causal or correlational probability that links happenings or sets of happenings to one another in a patterned geo-temporal manner. The "experiment" consists not of a laboratory reproduction of the happenings—which would be impossible in the nature of the case—but rather of a careful investigation and classification of the occurrences recorded in the historical record, respecifying these happenings in an array such that time and space phenomena can be shown to have the hypothesized relationship to one another, and filling in the explanatory links.[1] Teggart's best-known study employing this method is *Rome and China*.[2] That work, published in 1939, constituted the single most significant case of what I have elsewhere designated as neopositivist historicism.[3]

TEGGART'S THEORY OF SOCIAL CHANGE

It is sometimes supposed that Teggart's science of history is the same as his theory of social change. Such is suggested, for example, in Robert Nisbet's work, *Social Change and History*.[4] In fact, however, Teggart's theory of social change is separate from his science of history and, I would argue, given the nature of the case would have to be since, as Teggart himself insisted, history includes long periods of time in which no social change occurs.[5] For Teggart, then, as for ourselves as well, a science of history would embrace far more kinds of phenomena and far more varied periods of duration than would a theory of social change. A theory of social change is but one aspect of a science of history.

Teggart's theory of social change is built around the central significance of a phenomenological process that he calls release.[6] According to Teggart, what goes on most of the time in most places, past or present, is conduct oriented by habit and tradition. People carry on their daily lives in accordance with customs and ways that are deeply ingrained in their culture and in their consciousness. These customs and ways constitute the taken-for-granted features of their culture—or, in the words of Alfred Schutz, the "recipes for living" that every member of the society and culture knows.[7] Elaborating the tacit phenomenology entailed in Teggart's position, I would like to add that knowledge of these customs and ways resides at the subliminal level of consciousness, finding its expression in conduct rather than cognition. Further, let me suggest that the way to obtain an actor's knowledge of these habits, customs, and deeply ingrained ways of living is to carry out an ethnomethodological experiment wherein the effect of the strange behavior of the experimenter forces the content of that subliminal consciousness to rise to either cognitive or emotional awareness.[8]

Of course Teggart—who died twenty years before Garfinkel enunciated the principles of ethnomethodology—was aware that no direct experiment on the peoples, cultures, societies, and civilizations that historians wished to study could be performed. However, Teggart noticed, history itself provided the kind of occurrences that lead to a general breakdown of the habits and customs of a people and would, thence, give rise to a naturalistic ethnomethodological experiment, i.e., a liberation from habitual ways of thinking. Such events in history, Teggart reasoned, were rare and occasional. When they did occur, however, a fundamental social change could be brought about by and through the innovative outlooks that arose to replace the moribund folkways. But, Teggart reasoned, the character and content of that change could not be predicted in advance. Teggart's nonteleological theory of social change stands in sharp contrast to those that claim to see a definite and unmistakable trajectory of change in history.

For Teggart the principal phenomenon triggering social change was "release" from the slavery of habit. Such a "release" could only occur when a major crisis intruded on the ordinary lives of people. The effect of a major intrusion was to make the "recipes-for-living" that "everyone knew" inoperative or inefficacious. At such moments of terrible intrusion people would be released from their unconscious commitment to these habits, ways, and customs and in this state of liberation placed in a position to engage in innovative conduct, entering into new roles and new relationships with others. For Teggart the most significant example of a major social change was the foundation of the state. The state, as Teggart conceived of it, was a particular kind of organization that had been invented several times in the past. Central to the formation of the state was the release of individuals from their commitment to ascriptive solidarities such as families, clans, ethnic groups, and racial aggregations. The state, by embracing peoples in relationships that transcended their ascriptive associations, constituted a fundamental social change, bringing into existence new roles, new role relationships, new sources of authority, and new conditions for status.

Teggart reasoned that the ascriptive solidarities with their powerful commitment based on blood could not be broken down easily. The kinds of conduct, the patterns of everyday life, the developments of economy and polity and other forms of sociality that were occasioned by membership in clans, races, or tribes are buttressed by mystery and tradition.[9] These could only be undermined and broken through by an especially powerful or especially long-term intrusion that would render these awesome associations powerless or ineffective. As Teggart saw it, certain migration patterns led in turn to certain forms of settlements at borderlands and hinterlands. The borderland settlers were placed in the unenviable position of having to defend entrance to the land behind them when it had filled up. The invaders—would-be settlers being held back by the borderland forces—would hammer away for decades or even centuries at the borderland settlements. In turn, the modes of social, political and economic organization at the borderlands would be battered down by these successive assaults, and their principal mode of association—ascriptive solidarity— would be weakened if not destroyed. Out of this weakening or destruction would emerge the individual released from his identification with and commitment to family clan or race and open to the formation of new commitments, new identities and new social relations based on something other than principles of birth. New associations formed voluntarily constituted the beginnings of the political state. Conquerors or adventurers who left the borderland society would in turn politicize the interior.

WEBER'S CONTRIBUTION TO A SCIENCE OF HISTORY

Like Teggart, Weber recognizes that history consists of a concatenation of happenings or events, but unlike Teggart, Weber's approach to history stresses the consequences of one type of happening or event for another. What is significant about Weber's attitude toward history is the emphasis he places on the unintended consequences of happenings or events. Perhaps the best-known effort of Weber in this respect is *The Protestant Ethic and the Spirit of Capitalism,* in which he traced how the unintended consequences of Puritanism led to the development of a capitalist ethos.[10] The matter is so well known as to require no extensive elaboration here. Suffice it to note that Weber also elaborated his original study of capitalism by carrying out a series of "experiments," that is, comparative studies, each seeking to elucidate the unintended consequences of certain value patterns or religions for economic and social development and institutionalization and vice versa. These studies, taken as a whole, comprise Weber's efforts to present an example of an empirical science of history.[11] At their most general and abstract level these studies indicated the relationship between institutionalized values and socioeconomic formations.

WEBER'S THEORY OF SOCIAL CHANGE

Unlike a science of history, a theory of social change is an effort to provide a timeless explanation which underlies recurrent social processes. Although Teggart expresses some doubt about a timeless sociology, his theory of social change, centered in the concept of "release," is just such a timeless explanation. The supposition that sociology can provide a single theory of social change is, however, chimerical, although some theories of social change have been incredibly amibitious, for example, Marx's theory of the significance of the economic substructure, whereby all social change is understood in terms of the conflicts which stem from the social relations of production;[12] or Talcott Parsons's theory of structural differentiation, whereby specialized structures emerge as adaptations to tensions in the social system;[13] or Pitirim Sorokin's vast and invisible pendulum that ineluctably swings all civilizations through a grand sweep from "ideational" to "sensate."[14]

A theory of social change properly associated with a sociology of the absurd[15] is modestly adapted from Weber's theory of social change. The absurdist theory of social change begins with recognition of the significance of Weber's discussion of leadership. A principal consequence of charismatic leadership is the emergence of new obligations, new roles, new role relationships, new orientations toward authority, and new outlets for the expression of sentiment and feeling. Just how these new obligations are brought about is a particular contribution of empirical studies in the sociology of the absurd, and these studies would constitute its most important contribution to the elaboration of a theory of social change.

Max Weber is certainly a precursor of the idea of the absurd.[16] For Weber, as for sociologists associated with the idea of the absurd, reality is infinite and can be divided up in an infinity of ways.[17] Following Weber, we, or anyone, may freely construct one-sided exaggerations of reality—that is, ideal types—if these permit us to elevate our understanding.[18] Like Weber, but unlike Marx, Parsons, and other nonabsurdists, we do not believe that there are definite, unambiguous, central structural mechanisms that are necessary for understanding the essential features of the social world. In other words, following in the spirit of Weber, the sociology of the absurd rejects the positivist goal of discovering sets of general laws, and we further reject the claim made by nonabsurdists that certain structures in society or certain mechanisms are always present and always salient to the same degree in every society.

Weber's theory of social change is organized around the phenomenon of charisma and its routinization. Charisma and its routinization are for Weber the two engines of social change.[19] So also for the absurdist theory of change.

Absurdity can be located at two quite distinct levels. At one level—that of the philosopher or of the sociologist about to perform a study—the absurd, with its emphasis on the notion of an essentially meaningless world, is a way of posing the problem of social order. Thus, the sociologist of the absurd, starting with the assumption of an ultimately meaningless world, immediately notes that everywhere the world has meaning. The paradox that is thus made manifest—an essentially meaningless world that is always meaningful—provides the basic problem for which his particular sociological investigation is constructed. The sociologist of the absurd seeks to uncover how it is possible for ordinary as well as extraordinary people to convert the meaningless world into one that is meaningful and to do so without a conscious philosophy or elaborated praxis to guide them.

At quite a different level, however, one can discuss absurdity as a category of members' knowledge. This is a somewhat philosophical way of pointing to the occasionally experienced social fact of absurdity. This is to say that absurdity—in the form of irreconcilable contradictions, unresolved paradoxes and a felt sense of meaninglessness—can be a feature of any persons's perception. The meaningless world is, hence, not only a philosophical assumption or an heuristic device, it is also recognized and recognizable as a phenomenon among ordinary people "out there in the world." The experience of absurdity is, however, uncomfortable. Those who find themselves in an absurd situation, that is, a situation characterized by seemingly unresolvable contradiction, absolute meaninglessness or gnawing anomie, will try to obviate the absurdist elements from it, or, failing that, they might try to remove themselves from the absurd situation. However, even when it is impossible to extricate oneself from a situation whose absurdity has become clear or to modify the situation so as to remove the absurdity, it is usually possible *to imagine* what would be required to end the condition of absurdity. This is the sense that things would be all right, "if only. . . ."

The perception of absurdity, then, is a potential feature of the ordinary world. To be sure it is only *a* feature and it is experienced only by some. Moreover, the perception of absurdity is temporal, that is to say, it occurs occasionally and unpredictably, and therefore it cannot be predicted with the same degree of accuracy as those phenomena that are foreseen by predictive social scientific theories. However, it is sometimes the case that the experience of absurdity, when not allowed to remain merely personal and private, will not only receive a wide hearing but create a following. This is often the case because others are experiencing the same kind of irreconcilable contradictions but are unable to articulate them with the clarity voiced by the original perceiver of the absurd condition. It follows then that the announcement of the existential presence of the absurd is likely to create a kind of excitement and contagion and, following this, to constitute the basis for the emergence of charisma.

Charisma is more than a characteristic attributable to an individual. The person who can give voice to his experience of absurdity is filled with a dynamism that permits him literally to "charm" his audience. *Charm* here refers both to the magical aspects inherent in that term and to the dramatic expression and effect that Stanislavsky has pointed to in his discussions of charm in acting.[20] A person capable of "charming" an audience is like one who is possessed, and when one who is possessed "charms" an audience, he is capable of making it feel possessed as well. Like some remarkable actors and awe-inspiring leaders, the charismatic person may *express* the absurdity felt inarticulately by his audience but not *experience* it in himself.

Much of the effect of the charismatic figure is derived from nonsymbolic communication. The audience—those who listen to the charismatic figure as he makes meaningful the meaningless world—feel as if a new force is entering them; they lose their ordinary role vigilance and give up personal control. As an event in group psychology the effect of the charismatic leader on his followers may be compared to hypnotism. The charismatic leader uses his "charm" to hypnotize his audience. The audience in turn feels itself to be "charmed." A magical force has taken over and entered into them. They are as it were in a trance, and in this trance they are in a position to realize new identities, new roles, new role relations, or, indeed, a new world.

"Charm," then, that emerges from this personal and, shall we say, aesthetic confrontation with absurdity, is the basis of the hypnotic power that the charismatic leader exercises over his followers. The charismatic leader gives voice first to the experience of meaninglessness, and then he points out the line of conduct and thought that will reduce the anxiety of that absurdity. Those who have been hypnotized or "charmed" by the charismatic leader may then become "reborn" in terms of that leader's resolute interpretation of the situation. In other words absurdity as a condition of human existence constitutes a basis for the emergence of the charismatic leader; in turn, his "charm" provides the energy and catalyst for the mobilization of a collectivity.

The absurd is a limbo land in which few care to live. When his own land is experienced as this limbo land of absurdity the individual will seek out something to relieve this condition and remove him from the land of meaninglessness. The absurd situation, then—a situation of irreconcilable contradiction—may lead inter alia to a challenge to authority, especially when the structure of or personnel in authority is believed to be the very source for and maintenance of the absurd situation. The collectivity, aroused by its desire to end existence in absurdity, will then engage in a struggle and, by its actions, hope to remove the source of authority and thereby remove themselves from limbo.

The charismatic aspects of social change and its relation to the reduction of absurdity have been exemplified recently by Bryan Wilson in his fine study, *The Noble Savages: The Primitive Origins of Charisma and Its Contemporary Survival*.[21] Wilson points to the peculiar significance of conquest, imperialism and colonialism for generating a recognition of an absurd condition among the natives. It is, for example, after the imposition of European ways upon the land and life of the Amerindian aborigines that we find emergence of charismatic leaders and fateful confrontations. Moreover, in the very content of their speech these charismatic leaders voice their perception of paradox and give instruction in new and sometimes magical lines of conduct. These noble savages, as Wilson calls them, are charismatic leaders of the first order, and, indeed, they possess and are possessed by "charm." In turn they possess their followers who, believing themselves to be magically protected by their own collective charisma, reorganize their lives, formulate an attack and move haplessly toward a terrible fate.

The absurdist theory of social change notes then that both actions and character are reconstructed to form new social meanings, and through these actions and these new characters the condition of absurdity is transcended. Contrary to the belief of certain critics of the sociology of the absurd, the theory does provide a generalizable or timeless theory of social change. It is a theory which assumes that absurdity is not only a philosophical orientation or a methodological decision but also and more importantly a realizable and occasionally realized human condition. Once this human condition has been sensed and been given expression and will, there will come not merely the pressure for change but change itself.

NOTES

I am indebted to Guy Oakes, Marvin B. Scott and Arthur J. Vidich for criticism and advice on this essay and to Ronald Glassman for the invitation to present it at the Fourth Annual Max Weber Colloquium, October 31, 1980.

1. See Frederick J. Teggart, "World History," *Scientia*, 69 (January, 1941), pp. 30-35.

2. Frederick J. Teggart, *Rome and China: A Study of Correlations in Historical Events* (Berkeley: University of California Press, 1939).

3. See Stanford M. Lyman, "The Acceptance, Rejection, and Reconstruction of Histories: On Some Controversies in the Study of Social and Cultural Change," in Richard Harvey Brown and Stanford M. Lyman, eds., *Structure, Consciousness and History* (Cambridge: Cambridge University Press, 1978), pp. 53-105.

4. Robert A. Nisbet, *Social Change and History: Aspects of the Western Theory of Development* (New York: Oxford University Press, 1969).

5. Frederick J. Teggart, *Theory and Processes of History* (Berkeley: University of California Press, 1941), pp. 191-92.

6. Ibid., pp. 149-50, 196-97, 272-96, 307-12.

7. See Alfred Schutz, *Collected Papers II: Studies in Social Theory,* ed. Arvid Brodersen (The Hague: Martinus Nijhoff, 1964), pp. 73-78, 95-101, 122-23, 251; and Alfred Schutz and Thomas Luckmann, *The Structures of the Life-World,* trans. Richard M. Zaner and H. Tristram Engelhardt, Jr. (Evanston: Northwestern University Press, 1973), pp. 15, 107-10, 136, 225-26, 271, 284, 311-12.

8. See Harold Garfinkel, *Studies in Ethnomethodology* (Englewood Cliffs: Prentice-Hall, 1967). Garfinkel and his colleagues have emphasized microecological studies of public order and eschewed the issues of history and social change. However, a neglected intellectual ancestor of the persepective that Garfinkel claims to have originated, Frank Hamilton Cushing (1857-1900), employed a variant of ethnomethods—"reproductive

archaeology" and "manual concepts"—to discover the bases of civiliza-
tion and its development. See Stanford M. Lyman, "Two Neglected
Pioneers of Civilizational Analysis: R. Stewart Culin and Frank Hamilton
Cushing," *Social Research* in press.

9. Weber, too, emphasized the elements of irrational mystery that
formed the primordial base of any system giving priority to the significance
of race, ethnicity, blood, etc. See Max Weber, "Ethnic Groups," in his
Economy and Society: An Outline of Interpretive Sociology, ed. Guenther
Roth and Claus Wittich (New York: Bedminster Press, 1968), I, pp. 385-98.

10. Max Weber, *The Protestant Ethic and the Spirit of Capitalism,*
trans. Talcott Parsons (New York: Charles Scribner's Sons, 1930).

11. See four works by Max Weber, *Ancient Judaism,* tr. and ed. Hans
H. Gerth and Don Martindale (Glencoe: The Free Press, 1952); *The
Religion of China: Confucianism and Taoism,* tr. and ed. Hans H. Gerth
(Glencoe: The Free Press, 1951); *The Religion of India: The Sociology of
Hinduism and Buddhism,* tr. and ed. Hans H. Gerth and Don Martindale
(Glencoe: The Free Press, 1958); *The Sociology of Religion,* tr. Ephraim
Fischoff (Boston: Beacon Press, 1963).

12. Karl Marx and Friedrich Engels, *Basic Writings on Politics and
Philosophy,* ed. Lewis S. Feuer (Garden City: Doubleday Anchor, 1959),
pp. 246-61.

13. Talcott Parsons, *The Social System* (Glencoe: The Free Press, 1951),
pp. 480-535.

14. Pitirim Sorokin, *Social and Cultural Dynamics: A Study of Change
in Major Systems of Art, Truth, Ethics, Law and Social Relationships,*
rev., abr. ed. (Boston: Porter Sargent, 1957).

15. Stanford M. Lyman and Marvin B. Scott, *A Sociology of the Absurd*
(New York: Appleton-Century-Crofts, 1970).

16. On this point see Marvin B. Scott and Stanford M. Lyman, *The
Revolt of the Students* (Columbus: Charles Merrill, 1970), pp. 128-32; and
Stanford M. Lyman and Marvin B. Scott, *The Drama of Social Reality*
(New York: Oxford University Press, 1975), pp. 13, 55-56, 98-99, 159-61.

17. See Max Weber, *The Methodology of the Social Sciences,* tr. and ed.
Edward A. Shils and Henry A. Finch (New York: Free Press, 1949),
pp. 80-81.

18. Ibid., pp. 72-112.

19. See Weber, *Economy and Society,* III, pp. 1111-1211, 1375-80.

20. See Constantin Stanislavski, *An Actor's Handbook,* ed. and trans.
Elizabeth Reynolds Hapgood (New York: Theatre Arts Books, 1963),
pp. 34-35.

21. Bryan Wilson, *The Noble Savages: The Primitive Origins of
Charisma and Its Contemporary Survival* (Berkeley: University of
California Press, 1975).

11

REVOLUTION AND CHARISMA IN A RATIONALIZED WORLD: WEBER REVISITED AND EXTENDED

William H. Swatos, Jr.

There is at least one sense in which it is simpler to treat Max Weber on revolution than on other topics: He never wrote his projected "theory of revolution" chapter for *Economy and Society*. Most of what has been written about Weber and revolution is drawn from his discussion of charisma. However, he also speaks of both "traditionalist revolution" and the "revolutionary force" of bureaucratic rationalization (1968: 277, 1116). Whereas it is correct to say that for Weber genuine charisma is "the specifically creative revolutionary force in history" (1968: 244), it is not correct to claim that all revolutions must be based in the figure of a charismatic leader. A lack of proper consideration of these other two types of revolution has perhaps been the source, at least in part, for much misguided debate on charisma.

RATIONALIZATION AND DISENCHANTMENT

Weber's sociology is united by one overarching thematic element, the constant refrain of the nature, causes, and effects of *Rationalität* (rationalization). The disenchantment (*Entzauberung*) of the world—a phrase that Weber takes from Schiller—is the opposite side of the rationalization process and refers to the progressive demystifying or "desuperempiricalizing" that is a concomitant of rationalization at the systemic level (see Abramowski, 1966; Little, 1974; Mueller, 1977).

Weber clearly intends to use disenchantment in a "value-free" analytical way. Disenchantment is not a subjective feeling-state, but a potentially measurable "objective" social reality in the modern world. Yet it is hard to deny that there is also a connotation of loss in the use of the phrase. Though he professes himself "unmusical" in religious matters, one still gets a very strong feeling from reading Weber that the mystical quality of existence to which religion has addressed itself as a social institution throughout history has value. That value is the price paid for rationalization. Yet—and this is the critically important Weberian paradox— rationalization also has value, for it frees the intellect from the repression of "demonic" forces (Mommsen, 1965: 24). Weber agonized regularly over the relative worth of the rationalization-disenchantment tradeoff, hoping for the best but often overcome by the fear of the worst.

While rationalization–disenchantment is a global concept for civilizational analysis, it never loses specific application in the lives of concrete human beings. Weber is neither antirationalistic nor pro-religious. This, then, is Weber's curse: He dreaded the old gods of the pre–Judeo-Christian era, but he feared that the ultimate consequence of Judeo-Christianity as it had developed in Western history was an equally barbaric, mechanized bureaucracy in which the old gods would reappear "disenchanted" as impersonal forces striving to gain power in our lives, destroying our freedom and creativity in the process. The Weberian is cursed because he must live in the ambiguity—dare we say anomie?—between an intellectual sacrifice to religion and a similar one to uncontrolled bureaucracy. In his many pessimistic moments, Weber seems sure that people will take one option or the other, with little difference in the results.

CHARISMA AND ITS TRANSFORMATIONS

Use of the concept of charisma today is so sloppy that it is easy to despair of ever recalling its roots in Weber. Yet it is important to realize that however the term is used today, it is used because of Weber. A generation of social and political scientists, journalists, and media experts has somewhere along its educational career found out about charisma. Whatever it is, they have learned, charisma is what makes leaders leaders. Popes and presidents are elected because of their "charisma." A football player or musician who doesn't have charisma won't make it to stardom. Favorite ministers and professors are said to have charisma, and in some of the most bureaucratic churches there is an active "charismatic movement." Some sociologists have even suggested that corporations and brands have charisma. As a result there must be an effort, among sociologists at least, to unearth within the rough ground of Weber's own work the meaning of this concept and its place in his typology of authority/domination.

As with rationalization–disenchantment, so here too Weber's interest lay in types of social authority or domination and *not* in the psychological profiles of leaders. Weber's charismatic authority type is not to be identified with the psychohistorical "great man" tradition. *Charisma is fundamentally social.* First, although formally always a leader's claim to obedience by followers as a duty, as an objective legitimate system of domination charisma is always subject to validation by the followers that the leader is what he or she claims to be. Thus charisma is always contingent upon a shared belief on the part of both leader and followers in the genuineness of the leader's charismatic possession. Furthermore, the "activation" of charisma, according to Weber, is predicated on "extraordinary" *social* circumstances. The case is not one of a person arising in everyday activity to proclaim himself, or even be proclaimed, a new leader—much less the so-called charisma of theatrical, musical, or sports personalities.[1] Rather, the extraordinary nature of the times calls forth a charismatic authority structure. The leader is but a part—albeit a critically important part—of a *structure* of domination. Real-world authority structures corresponding comparatively closely to this pure type Weber refers to as based upon "genuine charisma." Charisma here, then, is "the specifically creative revolutionary force of history," but it exists only briefly, "*in statu nascendi*," before being transformed or routinized into some more stable form (Weber, 1968: 1130-1133; see Friedland, 1964).

Transformed Charisma

It is at this point that confusion arises in many attempts at Weberian analysis, that is, the failure to understand that Weber makes a consistent distinction between "genuine charisma" and routinized or transformed "stable" forms. Genuine charisma is revolutionary in nature and short-lived. Routinized charisma—

whether hereditary, democratic, or the "charisma of office"—is a stable form of domination that enters into a mix with either traditional or rational-legal structures (see Dow, 1969). Since the charismatic structure is in a sense the source of all authority, various transformations and routinizations will appear in both traditional and rational-legal types of societies. The hereditary "charismatic" leader is to be understood as succeeding from and existing in reference to some "genuine" charismatic leader who preceded him or her, but in no sense are the two to be identified. It is thus possible and correct to speak of persons as "charismatic" figures within traditional or rational-legal systems *in varying degrees,* because pure type systems are methodological constructs rather than empirical realities. Dow (1969), following Berger (1963) and Runciman (1963), gives several examples of this, and Constas (1961) speaks of "charismatic bureaucracy." Such "charismatic" figures, however, must be carefully distinguished from the "genuine" charismatic leader and his or her revolutionary significance. The difference, then, is between charismatic figures or elements in noncharismatic authority structures and the charismatic type of domination per se. My concern here is with the latter. Admittedly many figures or events in both traditionalistic—primarily patrimonial—and rational-legal systems have charismatic qualities, but this is transformed charisma routinized into an authority structure corresponding to a different type of domination.

The confusion on this point reaches its most difficult stage in an essay by E. A. Shils and the work it has spawned. Shils finds charisma almost everywhere he looks and claims in virtually direct contradiction of Weber that "the charismatic propensity is a function of the need for order" (1965: 203). Dow argues perceptively that "Shils' attempt to attribute charismatic elements to a wide range of ordinary secular roles, institutions, and strata of persons" creates a setting in which "charisma ceases to have any independent descriptive or analytic value" (1969: 317). Shils vitiates the critical defining component of a special "gift of grace," a gift that is by its very nature inexplicable in empirical terms.[2] The charismatic figure—or the charismatic bond—is enchanted, and without enchantment genuine charisma is impossible. This, of course, does not mean that charisma will appear within channels of institutionalized religion. Rather, it is more likely that charisma will often appear irreligious in the eyes of the "legitimate religious structures." It is for this very reason that I prefer to speak of it in terms of enchantment (*Zauberung*), rather than religion. Thus it follows that in a rationalized world charismatic revolution is impossible, as is the appearance of genuine charisma—at least with respect to the ideal-typical context. In Weber's use charisma is irrational. Genuine charisma depends upon the mysterious above-and-beyond, and this is neither the mere ability to confuse or deceive nor speculative "scientific" insight into the potentially knowable empirical future (see Wilson, 1975, 1976).

Manufactured Pseudocharisma

Weber (1968: 1129-30) indicated—perhaps more prophetically than he realized—the possibility that bureaucratic structures in a democratic society might have to use "mass effects" and the "charisma of rhetoric" to create "charismatic hero worship" in order to build the emotional support necessary for the maintenance of power. In short, charisma might have to be *manufactured*; rationality might have to "create" irrationality (see Glassman, 1975). From the viewpoint of the creators, then, this would be a completely *rational* act intended to remain within certain clearly nonrevolutionary bounds. It would maintain the status quo rather than overthrow it; hence it could hardly be identified with either genuine charisma or its transformations. Here we should follow Bensman and Givant's (1975) reference to this as "pseudocharisma"[3] and recognize that it is a step beyond the regular transformations of charisma to which Weber refers. Pseudocharisma is not an incorporation of charismatic elements into a more structured everyday form, but the calculated rational construction of superficial charismatic "signals" to maintain everyday forms. Paradoxically, pseudocharisma uses revolutionary signals, rhetoric, and effects to prevent genuine revolution. It is a rationalization of social science prophecy—i.e., man's dependence on charisma, emotional and irrational signals of supermundane power, for survival. Pseudocharisma is an unforeseen, and probably unfortunate, byproduct of Weber's own research. His demonstration of the place of charisma in the history of human societies and his delineation of its empirical features have not been without their applications by skillful political "advisers." The production of "charisma" (i.e., pseudocharisma) is now an established part of applied political science. This has been noted most eloquently and with application to mass culture by writers like Lowenthal (1968), Adorno (1978), Marcuse (1964), and even Boorstin (1978).

Weber was not aware of the telecommunications revolution as he wrote, or of its impact upon Western culture. He died before radio had reached its heyday, and television, computerization, satellite transmission, and the like were mere glimmers in the eyes of a handful of scientists. The possibilities for the manufacture of charisma through these means seem limitless. Yet Glassman (1975) suggests that ironically the increasingly sophisticated technology in its very rationality is potentially "decharismatizing." The control of the media is critical here. In societies where control is completely in the hands of the power structure, the manufacture of charisma by those in power, while at the same time those without power are systematically excluded, can extend almost beyond imagination. Small wonder that the first target for revolutionaries in these societies is often the national broadcasting facilities. In societies where some measure of democratic control is exercised through either or both the public or private sectors, on the other hand, the media can have a tremendously decharismatizing effect by providing "instant analysis"—i.e., criticism—of any figure or event. The extraordinary and the everyday are so merged here as to become indistinguishable, and of course, one may at any time turn the dial elsewhere or the tube off.

Karl Lowenstein thus observes correctly that although

democratization has strengthened beyond all expectations the plebiscitary components in the power process . . . at the same time it has decidedly diminished the chances for the development and operation of true charisma. . . . The leader who shows himself daily . . . is less magical and magnetic than the leader who is not seen at all, or only rarely on occasions especially favorable to him. Far from reinforcing charisma and spreading its magic in a wider context, the mass media in an open society act as disenchantments. . . . It would appear that charisma . . . has become a victim of modern technology. In the last analysis, as a basis of rule, it possesses a historical reality. Or, to put it differently: charismatic authority in politics is a phenomenon of the pre-Cartesian world. (1966: 84-86)

TRADITIONALIST REVOLUTION

Weber does not say a great deal about traditionalist revolution. It is perhaps sufficient that he indicates that "it is directed against the master or his servant personally, the accusation being that he failed to observe the traditional limits of his power," rather than being "directed against the system as such" (1968: 227). Since Weber introduces this concept under the section "Traditional Authority" in the chapter "Types of Legitimate Domination," he apparently does not think that charismatic leadership is a necessary condition here. Indeed, elsewhere he explicitly distinguishes the charismatic claim from traditional bases of authority:

Since it is "extraordinary," charismatic authority is sharply opposed to . . . traditional authority, whether in its patriarchal, patrimonial, or estate variants, all of which are everyday forms of domination; while the charismatic type is the direct antithesis of this. . . . Traditional authority is bound to the precedents handed down from the past and to this extent is also oriented to rules. Within the sphere of its claims, charismatic authority repudiates the past, and is in this sense a specifically revolutionary force. (1968:243-44, 115)

Unlike charisma, traditionalism as a political force is not necessarily dependent upon enchantment. Personal loyalty to a leader—patrimony, or sultanism in its extreme form—may arise from purely secular origins. Tradition-bureaucracy cannot be reduced to a sacred-secular dichotomy. *Both* tradition *and* bureaucracy are essentially secular routinizations of the extraordinary demonstration of authority that is the cornerstone of charisma. "The disenchantment of the world," then, does not mean a decline of the authority structures that Weber discusses as traditional. Just as it is possible to speak of the Roman Empire as a bureaucratic authority structure (see Antonio, 1979), while not denying the extreme rationalizations of our own era, so one may not use the term *premodern* to imply that traditionalism or traditionalist revolution cannot occur in contemporary postindustrial society. Traditional authority structures can and do make use of modern technology apart from ideal-typical bureaucratic rationalizations. From a Weberian standpoint, it is very possible to speak of traditionalist revolution in modern society without engaging in either typological or semantic confusion. The relationship among nostalgia, tradition, and fascist revolution must be discussed in this context. Consideration of this question is forced on us not merely academically but because of the tremendous similarities that pertain between our own society and pre-Nazi Europe (see Weber, 1958a: 137-56; Holland, 1977; Bancroft, 1979; Buck, 1979). Here we must first struggle to separate fascism as an authority structure from Hitler's personal insanity. If we do so, fascism appears as a basically traditionalist form of domination, essentially patrimonial, with certain elements of manufactured charisma.

Fascist leaders promise a return to *the way things were.* Though they ostensibly criticize the current system more than the ideal-type would suggest, their criticism is ultimately of the people who embody the system. Their remedy is a return to the "traditional" system as it was before the current power-people came into domination. To this end they generate personal loyalty from their followers, while often identifying the hated power-people as a class. Displacement of that class of usurpers of the "tradition" becomes the primary goal of the revolution.

Viewed from this perspective, fascism represents a live possibility for traditionalist revolution in our times. Such a revolution would *not* be charismatic in its essential nature. The only "charisma" its patrimonial leadership would have is what it manufactured as a result of the technical resources generated by modern industrial society. It is, however, possible that such a traditionalist revolution, if sufficiently comprehensive and prolonged, might bring a certain level of reenchantment in its wake—the personality of the leader being ascribed god-like qualities, for example. Then, with an irony Weber would have appreciated, it would once again be possible for charismatic leadership to arise and a charismatic revolution to follow.

BUREAUCRATIC REVOLUTION

The bureaucratic form of revolution is explicitly compared and contrasted with charismatic revolution as an antitraditional force. Bureaucracy, Weber says, revolutionizes with technical means . . . "from without": It *first* changes the material and social orders, and through them the people, by changing the conditions of adaptation, and perhaps the opportunities of means and ends. By contrast, the power of charisma rests upon the belief in revelation and heroes, upon the conviction that certain manifestations . . . are important and valuable. . . . Charismatic belief revolutionizes man "from within" and shapes material and social conditions according to its revolutionary will. (1968: 1115-16)

It is tempting here to think by way of example of the industrial revolution. But it is much more important and instructive to realize that virtually all "modern socialist"—i.e., Marxist and neo-Marxist—revolutions are of this type. Although there is a large theoretical literature within Marxism that has absorbed Weber's overarching concern with bureaucratic routinization and has become self-critical, nevertheless the primary intent of such revolutions in practice is to impose a new system that will alter the mode of production and the nature of social organization. It is rational calculation that is at the core of liberal ideology, of which Marxism—even if not Marx himself—is but one strain.

Romantic socialists often overlook the fundamentally bureaucratic nature of actual socialist societies. This is epitomized clearly, for example, in the term that the Soviets use for their ruling cadre—the Polit*bureau*.

In spite of constant complaints, contemporary American society is less bureaucratized than it seems. Personal considerations often enter into decision making. Weber himself points out that the elected officials of our government—and to an extent their administrative staffs as well—represent routinized charisma. "They are not 'bureaucratic types.' . . . Such an administrative structure as that of the U.S. is greatly inferior as a precision instrument compared to the bureaucratic type with its appointed officials" (1968:267). Although local representatives of federal agencies and their immediate superiors appear as "bureaucrats," their ultimate responsibility is to elected officials and to rules made with considerations other than those of technical efficiency in mind. The American system is a mixed type in which rational administration is sought for purposes that *include* personal considerations. Irritation with "bureaucracy" may well reflect the structural constraints of such a system, as well as the larger question of whether human beings can ever approximate a social order based upon a mechanical model.

THE FUTURE PRESENT

Weber did not move beyond his excellent analysis of bureaucratic domination and instrumental rationality to critical reflection about how they can be controlled or at least how their destructive effects could be softened. Weber simply did not solve the problems unfolding from even his own commitment to modern rationalism, in spite of his assertion in *Economy and Society* that the extreme instrumental rationality of modernity is linked to great substantive irrationality. The commitment of the scientist to the certainty of uncertainty that he applauds in "Science as a Vocation" is a clue but cannot resolve this contradiction—particularly as Weber correctly limits science to the sphere of instrumental rationality.

Weber recognizes the sociological sense—made explicit, for example, by Berger and Luckmann in *The Social Construction of Reality* (1967)—that human nature is a historically relative concept. Yet he also asserts that bureaucratic rationalization spreads at the cost of "love, hatred, and all purely personal, irrational and emotional elements which escape calculation." Instrumental rationality advances, to some degree, as other action orientations shrink in importance; in so doing it limits the range of human experience—a sense of loss and alienation results. The disenchanted world is thus often portrayed as a sad one in which unrelenting bureaucratization reduces creativity, spontaneity, and freedom to meaninglessness. We constantly seek "experiences" but are left unfulfilled. In some of Weber's writings this pessimistic *Weltanschauung* has no corrective; yet such a position is clearly un-Weberian in its determinism. If history is totally controlled by rationalization, then there is nothing to commend Weber's work over that of Marx or any other deterministic "force" theorist. Voluntarism gives man more credit for his destiny, without being historically naive. Our future is conditioned by our past, but to speak of driving forces is to lose touch with our ability to recreate the nature and meaning of human existence. The quest for experience, then, and its lack of fulfillment become in part definitive for human nature in our time and space—the preconditions for the permanent suspension of the natural attitude that Ernest Gellner refers to as the "second secularization" (1974: 195). The two options for resolution that appear most obvious—traditionalist or bureaucratic revolution—both constitute *mauvais foi:* nostalgia for a world that can never be because it never was, or capitulation before a mechanized system of action that denies the irrational and transcendent potential of human existence.

Although Weber is vague in setting it out, one cannot help but think that he looked toward still another option, a more profound idea of the movement of modern reason that provides a basis for hope. This option, far more revolutionary in its consequences should it be effected, is living with a rational and thoroughly disenchanted awareness of the inevitability of unfulfillment that is at the same time fully cognizant of and unwilling to exploit the irrational elements of our personalities. Such an attitude has neither the eerie nor exciting, mysterious nor miserable, possibilities of quests for "final solutions." It also radically distinguishes our time and potential future from all of human existence heretofore. At all times in the past a society could look with confidence toward an above-and-beyond system of meaning that would provide ultimate answers. Neither the United States nor, even less, the world-system can do so today.

It is an oversimplification to say that there are no answers. The truth is that we make our own answers. A full and deep consciousness of this elementary fact of life in a rationalized-disenchanted world opens a wide horizon for creativity, even as it forces us back upon our own tragically wounded and terribly mortal existence (see Berger, 1970, 1979). Clearly neither tradition nor bureaucracy will serve us well here, and charisma has been disenchanted into a product-for-sale without revolutionary significance. Yet Weber never lived to put any plan—if he had one—into effect.

As social scientists we cannot give the metaphysical guarantees Weber rightly criticized the "rostrum prophets" of his own day for attempting to create. But we can make explicit the meaning systems of the different institutions of our complex society and champion the importance to human civilization of what Berger and Neuhaus (1977) have termed mediating structures—family, religion, voluntary associations, and the like. This approach—rather than trying to find a "wholeness" that is not there—places individual experience and consciousness into an empirical sociocultural framework that makes responsible decision making possible even in the face of the certainty of uncertainty. It denies neither irrationality nor transcendence but places them in a perspective that makes rationality work for rather than against a humane social order. In short, we need a deification of rationality that celebrates its human roots and thus grasps limitation as a principle for action rather than as nonsense that "will not compute." The goal here is not "intellectual sacrifice" (see Weber, 1958a: 154) but intellectual *struggle*.

Here the stage will be set for a purposive and participatory construction of a world view that gives meaning to the simple fact that life does go on, in spite of disenchantment. Instead of a search for "new mysteries," we recognize that the mystery is in the search itself. This here-and-now (rather than above-and-beyond) can never be sought, but can always be lived. Specifically it requires commitment to an ethic of limitation—to a frank and fresh awareness that we will never have or never know all that there is—and to an ethic of human worth. Given scarcity as a basic principle, the personal, social, and cultural development of the individual as he or she lives with others takes on renewed importance. We must teach and urge people to live for the future present—never to deny today because of the glories of tomorrow, but never to waste today so that there is no tomorrow.

Weber's lack of faith in the doctrine of progress thus stands ultimately vindicated. The era of mindless expansion appears increasingly as an anomaly across the broad sweep of history. The technological advances that have come with it have obvious destructive as well as productive potentials. The task is to develop a new system of authority that is historically sensitive to the abysses that lie on either side of us. The social and cultural sciences offer to those who will hear the potential for a new construction of reality. Surely Weber would not mind if it were to make his typology henceforth less than complete.

NOTES

The author wishes to express appreciation to Vatro Murvar, Bill Mayrl, Jerry Stark, Ron Glassman, and Ted Long for their comments on earlier drafts.

1. Weber's use of *charisma* is in connection with forms of legitimate domination. The "electric personalities" of popular entertainment figures, for example, have no relationship to the general intention of his work— unless they carry over into the political sphere directly. It is, of course, possible to speak of a charismatic figure in (e.g.) the arts in the Weberian sense, if one means by that some person who brings about fundamental change in "the way things are done." Such a person is not likely to be a *political* hero, however.

2. Thus Vinson (1977) is mistaken when, following Shils, he says that I.B.M. has "charisma." What I.B.M. has is technical competence, not only in what they produce, but also in management, service, and advertising. At most, this is the "charisma of office," but even this is stretching a genuinely bureaucratic element—the virtue of efficiency—too far.

3. Here Bensman and Givant are following Merton's equally insightful use of *pseudo-Gemeinschaft*.

REFERENCES

Abramowski, Günter
    1966   Das Geschichtsbild Max Webers. Stuttgart: Klett.
Adorno, Theodor
    1978   Minima Moralia: Reflections from Damaged Life. New York: Schocken.
Antonio, Robert J.
    1979   "The contradiction of domination and production in bureaucracy: the contribution of organizational efficiency to the decline of the Roman Empire." American Sociological Review 44: 895-912.
Bancroft, Nancy
    1979   "American fascism: religious and secular analyses and response." Paper delivered at the annual meeting of the Society for the Scientific Study of Religion, San Antonio, Texas.
Bensman, Joseph and Michael Givant
    1975   "Charisma and modernity." Social Research 42: 570-614.
Berger, Peter L.
    1963   "Charisma and religious innovation." American Sociological Review 28: 940-50.
    1970   A Rumor of Angels. Garden City, N.Y.: Doubleday.
    1979   The Heretical Imperative. Garden City, N.Y.: Doubleday.
Berger, Peter L. and Thomas Luckmann
    1967   The Social Construction of Reality. Garden City, N.Y.: Doubleday.

Berger, Peter L. and Richard Neuhaus
    1977   To Empower People: The Role of Mediating Structures in
              Public Policy. Washington, D.C.: American Enterprise
              Institute.
Boorstin, Daniel J.
    1978   The Republic of Technology. New York: Harper & Row.
Buck, Roy
    1979   "Power of 'the word' in tourism promotion." Paper
              presented at the Tourism in the Next Decade symposium,
              George Washington University, Washington, D.C.
Constas, Helen
    1961   "The U.S.S.R.—from charismatic sect to bureaucratic
              society." Administrative Science Quarterly 6: 282-98.
Dow, Thomas
    1969   "The theory of charisma." Sociological Quarterly 10:
              306-18.
Friedland, William E.
    1964   "For a sociological concept of charisma." Social Forces
              43: 18-26.
Gellner, Ernest
    1974   Legitimation of Belief. New York: Cambridge.
Glassman, Donald
    1976   "Legitimacy and manufactured charisma." Social
              Research 42: 615-36.
Holland, Joe
    1977   The American Journey. New York: IDOC.
Little, David
    1974   "Max Weber and the comparative study of religious
              ethics." Journal of Religious Ethics 2: 5-40.
Lowenstein, Karl
    1966   Max Weber's Political Ideas in the Perspective of Our
              Time. Amherst: University of Massachusetts.
Lowenthal, Leo
    1968   Literature, Popular Culture and Society. Palo Alto, Calif.:
              Pacific Books.
Marcuse, Herbert
    1964   One-Dimensional Man. Boston: Beacon.
Mommsen, Wolfgang
    1965   "Max Weber's political sociology and his philosophy of
              world history." International Social Science Journal 17:
              23-45.
    1974   The Age of Bureaucracy. Oxford: Blackwell.

Mueller, Gert H.
    1977   "The notion of rationality in the work of Max Weber."
                Paper presented to the Colloquia and Symposia on Max
                Weber, University of Wisconsin-Milwaukee.
Runciman, W. G.
    1963   "Charismatic legitimacy and one-party rule in Ghana."
                Archives Européenes de Sociologie 4: 148-65.
Shils, Edward
    1965   "Charisma, order, and status." American Sociological
                Review 30: 199-213.
Weber, Max
    1958   From Max Weber. New York: Oxford.
    1968   Economy and Society. Totowa, N.J.: Bedminster.
Wilson, Bryan R.
    1975   The Noble Savages. Berkeley: University of California.
    1976   Contemporary Transformations of Religion. New York:
                Oxford.

12

MANUFACTURED CHARISMA AND LEGITIMACY

Ronald M. Glassman

Max Weber focused his attention upon three kinds of human political leadership: power leadership, charismatic leadership, and administrative leadership. Though power leadership, or what he called "ceasarism," figures clearly in his political sociology, his major contributions in this regard involve his conceptions of charismatic leadership and administrative bureaucracy.

For Weber, as Reinhard Bendix has suggested, charisma was more than a sociological category. In his despair over the trends he saw emerging in the modern world, he turned to charisma as a potential savior.[1] However, Weber was always the realist, and he described two anticharismatic trends in the contemporary world which I wish to analyze in this essay. That is, Weber described the "depersonalization" of charisma[2] (that occurs after the routinization of charisma), as well as the "disenchantment"[3] with charisma (that emerges from a rational world view).

The manufacture of "depersonalized" charisma and the inhibition of "pure" charisma in today's rationalized world will be the focus of this analysis. I shall argue that depersonalized charisma, a *"manufactured"* form of charisma, becomes critical in the legitimation processes of contemporary political systems of all kinds. The influence of the mass media on mass populations becomes a central factor—a factor which Weber could not have foreseen but which fits in neatly as an extension of his theoretical formulations.

ADMINISTRATIVE LEADERSHIP

In terms of human political leadership, let us at the outset differentiate between "task" leadership and "charismatic" leadership.

Task leadership is based purely on the skill of an individual at a given task, a task which the group needs to accomplish. There will be many leaders in a group depending on the number of tasks necessitated and the specific differential skills of the individuals in the group. This kind of leadership is never absent from human polities.

Bureaucracy, in its essence, represents the total institutionalization of task leadership. It is an effective, if not always an efficient, way to organize and accomplish specific tasks in large-scale, complex societies. Weber has described its structure,[4] Mumford its origins.[5] But since task-accomplishment is never one of the central issues of the political process, humans are always singularly unimpressed by task-officialdom. This attitude is a mixture of blasé acceptance of the necessity of task-officialdom and annoyance when this officialdom impinges upon them and prods them to accomplish some specific task. Bureaucracy gains legitimacy simply because people accept the fact that complex tasks need to be done in large-scale societies.

In fact, bureaucracy is always attached to some other legitimation system. Historically, it has been attached to traditional kingly authority and to legal-democratic authority. It has also been attached to Communist party power in contemporary Communist states. Whether bureaucratic leadership can stand alone as a fully legitimated "power elite"[6] in a future technocratic-industrial society, we cannot yet know, though this may be one of the critical questions of our age.

CHARISMATIC LEADERSHIP

Two other more critical processes characterize leadership and politics. The first is power, that is, the need to maintain external protection and territoriality and the need to maintain internal order and distribute life needs (food, shelter, sexuality, childcare). Weber considered power leadership to be a form of *nonlegitimate domination*. But, of course, he recognized that "ceasarism" could be long-lived and that the use of excess force could characterize a political system for decades.[7] However, instability would necessarily plague such a political system, since the "acquiescence" engendered by the fear of force could give way to rebellion at any moment within a system wherein the population does not recognize the right of the leadership to rule. One need only read Machiavelli's

Prince[8] to gain a clear idea of the instability and resulting need for the use of escalating violence necessitated by a system of nonlegitimate power leadership.

Second, there is leadership based on morale boosting of the individual and of the group, and group cohesion. This kind of leadership is not related to some specific task, nor is it based on physical force. It is leadership dependent upon that special gift that certain individuals posses of being able to rouse other individuals to greater feats than they thought possible in difficult situations, being able to rouse people from their lethargy when they are depressed or frightened, being able to impart confidence to the group when it is collectively anxious, being able to make the group function as one when conflicts divide it, being able to help the group face crisis situations and face the unknown with courage and optimism. Weber defines charismatic leadership in this way:

> The term *charisma* will be applied to a certain quality of an individual personality by virtue of which he is considered extraordinary and treated as endowed with supernatural, superhuman, or at least specifically exceptional powers or qualities. These are such as are not accessible to the ordinary person, but are regarded as of divine origin or as exemplary, and on the basis of them the individual concerned is treated as a "leader."[9]

TRANSFERABLE, HERITABLE, "MANUFACTURED," AND INSTITUTIONAL CHARISMA

Whether charisma is transferable may seem like a contradictory question. Technically, of course, charisma should not be transferable. Either an individual has the gift or he does not. In practice, close association with the charismatic leader often confers charisma onto others. This is so much the case that at the death of a charismatic leader the group will often turn for leadership to one of the individuals closely associated with the charismatic leader. In this sense charisma is transferable, and it is often the case that those close to a charismatic leader can succeed that leader.

In early human society a close relative or friend of a leader was usually that leader's associate. In fact, the individual most like the leader and closest to the leader was probably a relative rather than a friend. A brother, a near uncle, a son, where leadership was male-monopolized, would often succeed to charismatic leadership. Sometimes a mother or daughter or wife would succeed to such leadership where it was not male-monopolized.[10] This process of the transference of charisma becomes important in human society in terms of the problem of succession to leadership positions. For we are faced with the irony that hereditary succession to charismatic leadership—which should be impossible in principle—becomes possible in actuality. Early human societies often came to charismatize a whole family, even a large clan, because of some past association with a great charismatic leader. Weber called this latter "clan charisma."[11] In this way, succession struggles were eliminated in advance, because anyone born into a charismatic family would possess a certain amount of charisma by the fact of association.

In late tribal and early agricultural society, where size and complexity of the human societies grew, succession struggles became more extreme. In such societies clan charisma or hereditary charisma was maintained through artificial attempts at stage-managing the charismatic process. The key element in this process was that a leader could be made to appear charismatic, not through his or her personal qualities of leadership but through artificial, manufactured means. Let us look at the ramifications of manufactured charisma on leadership, succession, and legitimacy.

The critical operation involved in the manufacture of charisma was the successful creation of physical and psychic grandeur through which *any* individual could *appear* charismatic. Special clothing, masks, headdresses, and ornaments which conferred a spectacular appearance upon any individual wearing them were created. If grandeur and beauty were not enough, size and mystery and flair could be added to the charismatizing garb.

If grandiose and beautiful jewel-bedecked clothing were not enough to create an aura of charisma for anyone wearing it, then padding and stilts could be used to make the individual look huge, and masks and giant headgear could be used to make the individual appear frightening, mysterious, even mystical. Magic symbols like animal skins, carved objects, and rare vegetation could be used to evoke awe. In this way, the *office itself*, rather than the specific leader, was charismatized institutionally. That is, the office—with its manufactured charismatic symbols—preexisted any individual who succeeded to it.[12]

But as societies grew larger and more differentiated, access to office and the stage management of the charismatic effects became even more limited to fewer and fewer individuals from clearly specified clans, classes, professions, age grades, or sexes.

When charisma is extended to only a select segment of a society, then the traditionalized charismatization of leadership roles not only produces the charismatic effect of group cohesion and morale boosting, but alienation and resentment also occur, especially among those individuals who aspire to leadership but cannot achieve it because they do not fit the traditionalized succession pattern. Such individuals may become delegitimated from the traditional managed charismatization process and attempt to develop a following of their own against the traditional leadership.

To counteract this latter possibility and to maintain internal order in these larger, more complex societies, the established leadership introduced cooptation, ideological manipulation, force, and terror. Pure charismatic leadership—that is, real or personal charismatic leadership—then became a revolutionary force in traditional societies.[13]

MANUFACTURED CHARISMA AND POLITICAL LEGITIMACY

Manufactured charisma cannot be understood in its entirety if it is not seen as a component of the legitimacy process. Legitimacy can be roughly defined as "consent to be led."[14] The process of legitimation, or consent giving, in regard to leadership and dominance among group animals, is specific to human groups. Humans have consciousness—that is, the ability to think and reflect together. These capacities lead to what Weber called the "rationality" of humans in their approach to natural and social life, and I shall shortly show that this rationality leads to what I shall call the rational components of legitimacy.[15] But consciousness is a double-edged sword, for it also leads to a marked irrationality in human behavior.

It is the search for meaning in a seemingly incomprehensible world which produces certain irrational aspects of consciousness. Ironically, the process of attempting to find meanings for life and world and attempting to alleviate feelings of despair and depression is quite rational indeed. Nonetheless, since rational solutions to this endemic existential problem are probably impossible, irrational solutions are turned to for relief.[16]

This dual nature of humans leads to a conflicting result. Because of the rational component of consciousness, human individuals have the ability to be the least dominated and freest of all animals with group structures, but yet, because of the irrational component of consciousness, humans also can be subjugated more slavishly than all other animals. Let us look at the rational components of legitimacy first, remembering that legitimacy is that human process best defined as "consent to be led" and that there may be many different ways for leaders to gain such consent.

The rational components of legitimacy can be separated into several categories: (1) participation in decision making, rule making, rule interpretation, and the selection of leaders and access to leadership offices; (2) limitation of the power, and the tenure of leaders (including recall); (3) and law (legal authority) involving debatable, amendable rules for the maintenance of group order, constitutional-law guidelines for leaders, and protection for citizens.

There is a direct link between what I have called the rational components of legitimacy and democracy. But democracy is not fully coexistensive with the rational components of legitimacy. Irrational elements also abound in democracy. Cooptation through gifts and through ideological manipulation and myth building and coercion through police, military, and judicial institutions are parts of democratic political systems. Democracy however, in its ideal form, strives toward purely rational legitimation, whereas kingship, say, or oligarchy, or dictatorship does not.

Given the fact that humans are prone to irrational as well as rational acts of consciousness, one should not be surprised to find that there are numerous ways of engendering consent through irrational means and the processes of irrational consent getting are as commonly found in human societies as are the rational factors. The irrational components of legitimacy can be summarized as follows: pure charisma; manufactured charisma; ideological manipulation; cooptation (the buying of consent through direct political, economic, or social gifts); and coercion (the use of psychological terror or force or both).

This last category, coercion, is not technically a component of legitimacy. Obviously, coercion does not produce voluntary consent, whereas all the other components of legitimacy—rational and irrational—do. There is a debate over whether a system of terror and force can be called a legitimate political structure. E. V. Walter, in *Terror and Resistance,*[17] takes the position that it can be so called simply because of the longevity of such systems and the relative ineffectualness of, and minority participation in, resistance to such leadership. Here let me suggest that terror and force are not really mechanisms of true legitimacy. Leaders resort to them only when all else fails. Leaders always desperately attempt to produce other processes of consent getting which will engender the desired voluntary lending of consent by the group. Terror and force are too difficult and costly to maintain. Retaliation by the group becomes a nightmare to the leader, disturbing his status desires and inculcating real fears and paranoiac delusions of resistance and rebellion.

No leadership clique maintains itself for long by terror and force alone, but continued use of terror and force may accompany the legitimacy processes, especially where total voluntary consent is never achieved, or where the polity is so large and diverse and complex that some subgroups within the larger society will inevitably be left out of the legitimacy system or will opt out of it. But those societies in which rational and irrational processes of consent giving are operating effectively will use much less coercion than those societies in which legitimacy processes are ineffectual.

In times of massive social change, of course, all legitimacy systems may break down, and the use of terror and force may temporarily emerge as the dominant factor in leadership.[18] But even in such cases, the rise of a great charismatic leader may ease the transition and eliminate the necessity of massive coercion.

CHARISMA AND IRRATIONAL LEGITIMACY

Pure or genuine charisma is the perfect example of an irrational consent relationship between leader and led. Each individual within the charismatizing group feels a special personal relationship with the leader—even if he has never met the leader. This personal relationship creates a bond between the individual and the leader such that the individual fully trusts the leader and consents to the leader in all phases of his leadership.

A charismatic leader can usurp enormous amounts of privilege, wealth, and power, yet because of his special, almost superhuman status, the charismatizing group not only will fully consent to this but will approve of it. For every outward sign that the leader is, in truth, superhuman raises the group's confidence in the leader and tends to justify the irrational faith which the charismatizing group places in this leader.

Because personal charismatic leadership is the only kind of leadership which combines massive usurpation with total consent giving, and because charisma is transferable, as I have suggested, it is no wonder that attempts to manufacture charisma in order to create permanent leadership offices, with carefully designated succession to such offices, were successfully institutionalized.

Undoubtedly, the leadership clans, classes, and cliques surrounding the manufactured charismatic leader came to perceive the power relationship in a more rational fashion than the majority of the group. They, after all, often trained the leader and knew him in a close personal way. Further, they participated in the manufacturing process, making sure that robes, scepters, insignias, myths, ideologies, and ceremonies strictly and carefully surrounded the leader at all times. Nevertheless, such elites often believed in the charisma that they manufactured. There is no doubt, too, that the leader himself often fully believed that his charisma was real—especially if the belief was inculcated from childhood. No one could have been more bewildered than a divine king when his divinity was stripped away. Often an entire leadership stratum would react in such a way.

In agricultural societies the manufacture of charisma essentially took the form of the combination of aristocratic-clan charisma with the leadership offices of war chief and shaman. The larger populations of agricultural societies and the specialization of labor gave rise to non–food-producing strata for the first time. The war chiefs eventually became a whole stratum of non–food-producing "knights" or full-time warriors. The shamans, too, became a whole stratum of non–food-producing priests.

These strata of priests and knights had their succession lines linked directly to, and limited to, the aristocratic clans. Thus true aristocratic classes emerged which dominated all leadership roles in agricultural societies. These aristocratic classes utilized manufactured charisma to the fullest.

It is impossible to go into detail here except to say that, though these two aristocratic classes were early in deadly conflict with each other, the eventual union of the two upper classes produced the ultimate in manufactured charisma, a creation never before equaled in the annals of humankind. This was the divine kingship— the divine emperor, the sultanate, and similar leaders.

Here the zenith of manufactured charismatic irrationality was reached, for the charismatizing group projected onto the divine king that which it always wanted to project onto a personal charismatic leader anyway, superhuman divinity. The leader became God—not a mediator between humans and gods, but God himself. The led cringed, trembled, crawled, bowed, kissed the feet of, looked away from, the God-leader. Yet the actual human shrouded in a manufactured charismatic veil might be a moron, an incompetent, a child, a senile elder, a woman.

Further, as the aristocratic classes became leisure classes, and as the wealth and complexity of agricultural society increased, a class of noncharismatic task officials was coopted into the leadership structure. Bureaucracy, as a structure of administrative leadership, emerged. A host of bureaucratic officials filled permanently institutionalized offices and performed the functions of task leadership. The charismatic functions of leadership—morale boosting and social cohesion—were still performed by the aristocratic-charismatic classes and the office of the divine kingship.

Thus bureaucracy and bureaucratic strata existed under the mantle of traditional authority and manufactured charismatic leadership. In some societies, such as in China, the bureaucratic stratum itself developed at least some measure of legitimate authority and even a religious ideology to further legitimate it.[19] Yet even in China, the mandarins, though revered and legitimated beyond any bureaucratic stratum elsewhere, could never gain anything like total consent or full legitimacy but had to hide under the manufactured-charismatic veil of the divine kingship. Stripped of this veil, even the centuries-old mandarin-Confucian legitimation structure proved totally inadequate to justify bureaucratic domination.

In agricultural society, small leadership cliques surrounding the divine king and deified from (or not responding to) the manufactured charisma of the deified leader emerged as stage managers of political leadership and partook of—and protected and extended—the usurpations. This leadership clique, or elite, was drawn primarily from the aristocratic classes but also came to include members of the bureaucratic stratum and eventually members of the emerging merchant stratum.

The political center or court of the divine king, then, became a separate political arena where elite leadership asserted itself—in a manipulative, usurpative way—and wherein political struggles took on a character of their own, beyond the broader political struggles of the society as a whole.

Thus two levels of politics existed in late agricultural society: the politics of the total society involving all the factors of leadership and legitimacy; and the politics of the elite, courtly, inner circle, which operated outside the legitimacy structure but was protected by the manufactured-charismatic structure, of which the elite now became caretakers. This process took centuries to develop. However, once the elite court cliques emerged, manipulation of the legitimacy processes and consciously usurpative activites became parts of human politics.

MEDIA-MANUFACTURED CHARISMA IN THE MODERN WORLD

Although traditional forms of manufactured charisma have probably disappeared forever, leadership's elites will continue to exploit new techniques of manufacturing charisma both to achieve societal integration and to legitimize their usurpation of power. We are acutely conscious today of the role of the mass media in manufacturing charisma. Indeed, leadership elites have employed specially trained social science teams to "package" the new media-manufactured charismatic leader in the most successful way.

Newspapers, magazines, and printed posters create an atmosphere in which the political leader seems ever-present and larger than life. Since the charismatic relationship functions best when the group feels a personal, trusting, infantilizing bond with the leader, the constant presence—in bright images—helps manufacture such leader-led relationships.

Radio is also a medium through which very successful charisma-manufacture can and has occurred. Great and passionate oratory is one of the key ways in which charisma can be generated by a leader. The intersubjective communication or oratorical language can create a spell in which humans can become swayed and charismatically linked to a leader. Radio amplifies this oratorical linkage.

Hitler and Castro, Roosevelt and Churchill, used radio to raise oratorical charisma to new media-manufactured heights.

Now all the leaders mentioned above were also genuine or "pure" charismatic leaders. Since charisma is transferable and heritable, their successors have used and will use media-manufactured techniques to insure the transfer of charisma to nonnatural heirs. Stalin, for instance, used these techniques to create charisma for himself, where none had existed in the natural sense.

Movies are spectacular in their ability to create manufactured charisma. Just as microphones create an oratory greater than life, so movies create physical beauty and strength far greater than life. Technicolor splendor transforms men and women into gods and goddesses possessing sensuality and strength of charismatic proportions. The movies are larger than life, the voices are smooth and beautiful. Further, the darkness of the theater puts the individual into a dream state in which fantasy projections and identifications become easy to attain.

Television is still in its infancy, but it may develop a potential for manufactured-charismatic manipulations more far-reaching than any of the other media. Three different processes are already discernible in terms of television's impact on charismatic leadership. First, television, through its newscasts, can de-charismatize pure charismatic leaders, as well as enhance their charisma. Second, television helps create manufactured charismatic leaders where pure charisma is lacking, and, third, television (along with movies) creates its own media-manufactured charismatic figures—stars— who then become national celebrities in their own right. Let us look at each of these processes.

A test of a political leader's charisma in the modern world is whether his or her charisma can be projected through the media. The kind of charismatic techniques that worked well in the era of public speaking, microphones, and radio do not usually translate well in a television appearance.

That is, as MacLuhan has pointed out brilliantly,[20] television is a "cool" medium in which "hot" oratory looks out of place—it becomes annoying, grating. The gesticulations seem too flamboyant, facial expressions too twisted and forced, and the voice too small to justify such bodily histrionics. Therefore, the "great orator" does not do well on television. In fact, such oratory is rarely shown directly. Instead, with the speaker in the background and the speaker's voice tuned out, the television newsperson summarizes the main points of the speech with only a few sentences of the actual speech allowed to go on the air directly. Not only is the oratorical charisma neutralized, but the newscaster's interpretation of the main points of the speech is all that is conveyed. Only the president, and less often, party chiefs, get uninterrupted speech time on the media, and even then the commentators engage in "instant analysis" and critical summations of the address.

Furthermore, television is unkind to many leaders in that the close-up lens tends to highlight blemishes, pimples, and other physical imperfections. Leaders, used to "the stump," but unskilled in the media, often look furrowed, pockmarked, and uncertain on television. Very often they look smaller than life, as opposed to the media stars, who appear larger than life. The lack of media skill, along with a clinging to older oratorical styles can decharismatize a candidate who cannot adapt to the era of television. Television in this sense can be a de-charismatizing medium.

Some candidates, of course, have just the right combination of good looks, oratorical restraint, wit, and style which works well on the new medium. John Kennedy's looks and style were so well suited to television that he became charismatized through it. The projection of pure charisma through the medium is not impossible, then, but demands a different set of techniques than those which enhanced charisma prior to television.

Few political leaders have been able to imitate Kennedy's success. There is good reason for this, having to do with television coverage of political leaders rather than the leaders' failure to imitate Kennedy. Certain further de-charismatizing processes have become typical in the television medium.

It is now evident that even if a political leader learns to master television technique, if the television networks wish to de-charismatize such a candidate, they very often can. The television newspeople tend to be cynical and often attempt to debunk a candidate. They can be formidable opponents in this regard because *they* manipulate the media situation. They may set out on a careful campaign of slandering the leader's programs, impugning his judgments and his choice of aids and friends and uncovering embarrassing incidents from his or her personal life. They may ask hostile questions during interviews, put the leader on the defensive, and never ask the questions which would allow the leader to present his or her own point of view.

It is because of these problems that modern political leaders have had to learn how to utilize the media to their advantage. They have had to learn how to present themselves on television when in spontaneous or arranged situations, and they have had to hire public relations "imagemakers" and Madison Avenue "marketing experts" to create televison commercials wherein their image, their message, and the television situation can be manipulated in their behalf.

Madison Avenue image making and political commercials are now commonplace phenomena. Media experts can make or break a candidate. "Packaged" versions of candidates are presented to the public regularly. All of these image-making processes represent attempts at media-manufactured charisma. The real candidate is hidden behind the facade as surely as the kings were hidden behind their crowns, robes, and scepters.

This is a "rationalized" world, of course, and therefore the candidates' actions and policies can be analyzed beyond their manufactured images. Thus, sometimes the image-making works, and sometimes it does not. But in either case, the presentation of the leader in today's media-dominated world is often a packaged product.

Television then, inhibits the projection of pure charisma and sometimes debunks it when it does emerge, while at the same time structurally encouraging the manufacture of charisma through media techniques.

Finally, if television debunks the pure charisma of political leaders, it also produces charismatic figures of its own. That is, television, like movies, produces stars. The television stars are, of course, packaged personalities. We do not know much about the "real" person. The star possesses some modicum of charm, beauty, or other characteristic of importance in that not everyone who is packaged catches on. But the greater part of the personality is manufactured image.

Stars have become potentially powerful as political leaders. C. Wright Mills, so far ahead of his time, wrote of the celebrities, and how easily they mingled with the politically powerful figures of the United States. He was so right when he suggested that the "power elite" would include figures from the world of the celebrities.[21]

Figures like Ronald Reagan, Jane Fonda, and Ed Asner have already emerged as political leaders. Even before Ronald Reagan became president, people were talking about Walter Cronkite as a possible candidate. In fact, when Carter ran against Ford, the general feeling in the nation was that Cronkite would be more trustworthy than either of them.

Media celebrities, be they movie stars, television stars, sports figures (like Jack Kemp) or astronauts (like John Glenn) are taken seriously as political leaders even though they have no political experience. They are taken seriously because they possess media-manufactured charisma. This manufactured charisma produces an irrational bond between such a leader and a mass audience in typical charismatic fashion. This irrational bond can be utilized to create mass acceptance in the political sphere.

The example of Walter Cronkite brings us to the topic of the newscasters themselves as stars in their own right. As media celebrities emerged as political leaders, television newscasters themselves began to stand out as stars—and therefore as potential political leaders.

As television news ratings skyrocketed and news shows expanded from one half-hour to two hours and from morning to evening to nighttime (with slots in between), the newscasters themselves have been manufactured into stars. Their faces are everywhere, they command prime time and they "chaperone" every critical event of the moment. Not only do they enhance or debunk the charisma of political leaders, but they can become political leaders themselves. If they do, they will do so as television celebrities.

The age of television is truly in its infancy. Size, color, and cable if newly combined could produce a "hot" medium of the future in which the manufacture of charisma could reach heady heights again. Television technology, on the other hand, instead of leading toward "1984" media-manufactured charismatic political leadership, could lead toward a new kind of rational legitimacy process. Through local and national cable TV hook-ups, a new kind of participation could be generated in which media-monitored town meetings and debates could create a new kind of democratic politics.

I am not suggesting that the media are neutral entities through which we can do whatever we existentially will—this is not the case, these media definitely affect the process of human interaction. But the use of the media is often variable rather than rigidly singular, and human input and intent are as critical in media adaptation as the structure and effect of the media themselves. The media are only half the message;[22] human participation and will potential are the other half.

SOME IMPEDIMENTS TO THE MANUFACTURE OF CHARISMA IN THE MODERN WORLD

The impediments to the media-manufacture of charisma in the modern world all come under Weber's heading of "rationality." TV commentators in their cynical and probing style (and newspaper reporters and columnists) tend to produce a kind of debunking rationality in the approach to political life.

Science and social science produce a rational, skeptical, empirical kind of world view in which humans become an object to themselves, an object of study. Therefore, attempts at manufactured charisma are analyzed and unveiled by the constant probing and analytical process of the rational scientific world view.

Of course, at the same time scientists and social scientists are also coopted by elites and utilized to help create manufactured charisma and new media through which to manufacture charisma. Nonetheless, there will always be other scientists who are not coopted and who will continue to analyze such processes rationally. Thus the attempts to manufacture charisma and to unmask such manufactured charisma will both occur in the scientific community.

As a world view, science itself produces the kind of rationality in which the "average" individual becomes cynical and decharismatized easily, even though media and audience manipulation become ever more sophisticated.

Another factor which makes the media-manufacture of charisma difficult is that modern society is a multigroup, multiclass society. Because of this any charismatic leader will fail to charismatize certain portions of the population. Such a leader can be, then, decharismatized through active propaganda used against him or her. This process did occur in traditional societies, but it is greatly heightened by the rationality of modern groups and by the possibilities of quick travel and media communications. Repression can be used against such sensitiveness, but repression does not charismatize the repressed, and so the effect of manufactured charisma is never total in multigroup societies of any kind.

Finally, the rise and extension of bureaucratic political organization creates a situation in which charisma is purposefully eliminated from leadership roles and creates a structure instead in which leadership offices are divided and subdivided and organized in a maze of hierarchies in which charismatic leadership is not necessary for cohesion and in which charismatic leadership is discouraged.

But bureaucratic political leadership creates no legitimacy structure of its own except in terms of performance evaluation, and the alienation and lack of cohesion humans feel when confronted with or absorbed into bureaucratic organizations often drive them toward the desire for charismatic leadership. Thus, bureaucratic political organization actively devalues and destroys charismatic leadership, yet it produces the concomitant longing for charismatic leadership in those individuals alienated by the structure of bureaucracy itself.

Historically, bureaucracy as a political system has never been able to exist separate from some form of charismatic leadership. Thus it may be that the use of bureaucratic organization in all modern societies, capitalist or Communist, may drive people toward the easy acceptance of charismatic leadership. However, the rationality of the modern world makes it difficult for individuals to charismatize any leader.

Not only does bureaucracy eliminate and limit charismatic leadership, but bureaucracy also limits the effectiveness of the rational political procedures. That is, bureaucracy has a rationality of its own and a hierarchical structure that is anathema to rational forms of political participation, leadership choice, and leadership limitation. Specialization, compartmentalization, and hierarchy—these are the rational structures of bureaucracy, but their rationality is different from that of rational political consent getting.[23]

Thus it is that bureaucratic organization inhibits both irrational charismatic leadership and rational democratic leadership. Because of this it leaves the individual in a state of alienation and low morale. Undoubtedly some other forms of political action and consent will have to emerge beyond the modern, purely bureaucratic political and economic organization.

In Communist societies the media-manufacture of charisma is consciously and carefully stage managed by the bureaucratic elite of the Communist party. There, bureaucratic political organization is combined with the cult of the media-manufactured charismatic leader. This was very effective in the modernizing period, when traditional populations remained the most populous grouping in society. Now that scientific, technocratic, and bureaucratic classes are beginning to become majority classes, and as television spreads, the same kind of impediments to the manufacture of charisma as emerged in the West are appearing.

In Western societies, the rational processes of consent getting are declining as corporate and government bureaucracies increasingly come to dominate political action.[24] Alienation is increasing, and parliamentary democracy is no longer seen as a real vehicle for rational participation by large segments of these societies. A turn toward media-packaged leaders has emerged. But these attempts have been met, so far, with cynicism. Again, whether these media-packaged leaders will gain charismatic currency or whether new forms of rational political leadership procedures will emerge is unclear.

CONCLUSION

Two contradictory trends are emerging powerfully in the modern world: the rational, de-charismatizing trend, demanding active participation in the political process and producing alienation where this does not fully occur; and the irrational, infantile trend toward desiring a charismatic leader, genuine or manufactured, who will take care of the individual totally and reintegrate society into a single, loving, cohesive, cooperative group.

The tension between the rational and the irrational processes of political action will always exist, and the outcome of this tension can produce very different political structures even in techno-logically similar societies, depending on the historical, cultural, and structural circumstances of those societies at a given time and upon the existential desires of the individuals within those societies if they choose to act beyond the limitations which culture, structure, and history impose.

Nonetheless, the cohesion problems of large-scale societies are so complex that pressures toward some kind of irrational unification figure or symbol become almost necessary if anomie and social conflict are to be reduced to manageable levels. It is still possible that rational processes of consent getting can be revived and innovated such that the irrational processes can be minimized, if not discarded, and reciprocal and cooperative rather than usurpative and coercive relationships can exist between the people and their leaders.

NOTES

1. Reinhard Bendix, "Reflections on Charismatic Leadership," in *State and Society* (Boston: Little, Brown, 1968).

2. Max Weber, *Economy and Society,* ed. Guenther Roth and Claus Wittich (New York: Bedminster Press, 1968).

3. William H. Swatos, Jr., "Revolution and Charisma in a Rationalized World" (in this volume).

4. Weber, *Economy and Society*, pp. 956-1002.

5. Lewis Mumford, *The Myth of the Machine* (New York: Harcourt, Brace and World, 1966), pp. 188-212.

6. C. Wright Mills, *The Power Elite* (New York: Oxford University Press, 1956). See also Milovan Djilas, *The New Class* (New York: Praeger, 1974).

7. Weber, *Economy and Society,* pp. 1006-68, 1159, 1212-1363.

8. Niccolo Machiavelli, *The Prince* (New York: New American Library, 1952).

9. Weber, *Economy and Society,* pp. 241-42.

10. Examples of this phenomenon abound. In the modern world, Bobby Kennedy, Raul Castro, and Mao Dse Dung's wife come to mind.

11. Weber, *Economy and Society,* p. 1135.

12. Shils, "Charisma, Order, and Status," *American Sociological Review,* Vol. 30, 1965.

13. Joseph Bensman and H. Givant, "Charisma and Modernity: The Use and Abuse of a Concept," *Social Research,* Spring 1978.

14. Claude Levi Strauss, "The Social Psychological Aspects of Chieftainship," in *Museum of Natural History Source Book,* ed. Ronald Cohen and John Middleton (Garden City, N.Y.: Natural History Press, 1967).

15. Weber, *Economy and Society,* p. 941, 641-76.

16. Peter Berger, *The Sacred Canopy* (Garden City, N.Y.: Doubleday, 1969).

17. E. V. Walter, *Terror and Resistance* (New York: Oxford University Press, 1972).

18. During periods of anarchy (and anomie) orgies of violence do emerge. It is difficult to explain such violence without involving some theory of animal aggression. However, one must always do so in the context of a *balanced* conception of "human nature" which includes the conscious mind of humans and the cultural norms and values of human societies, along with the animal side of our being. The biosociologists and sociobiologists do not emphasize the human side of human nature, therefore their theories are as incomplete as those social theories which ignore the animal nature of human beings. We do not need a revival of "social Darwinism," nor should we accept an "oversocialized" conception of human beings (Dennis Wrong, "The Oversocialized Conception of Man," in Lewis Coser and Bernard Roserberg, eds., *Sociological Theory,* 4th ed. (New York: Macmillan, 1976).

19. Max Weber, *The Religion of China* (New York: Free Press, 1951).

20. Marshall McLuhan, *Understanding Media* (New York: McGraw-Hill, 1965); Marshall McLuhan; *The Medium is the Message* (New York: Bantam Books, 1967).

21. Mills, *Power Elite.*

22. McLuhan, *Understanding Media;* McLuhan, *The Medium is the Message.*

23. Ronald Glassman, "Conflicts Between Legal and Bureaucratic Authority," in Arthur J. Vidich and Ronald M. Glassman, *Conflict and Control: The Challenge to Legitimacy of Modern Governments* (Beverly Hills, Calif.: Sage Publications, 1979).

24. Mills, *Power Elite.*

EPILOGUE

MAX WEBER AND THE TWO NONREVOLUTIONARY EVENTS IN RUSSIA 1917: SCIENTIFIC ACHIEVEMENTS OR PROPHETIC FAILURES?

Vatro Murvar

The purpose of this essay is to reexamine Weber's analyses of Russia's striving for liberation from tsarist patrimonialism during the first two decades of the twentieth century, especially from the 1905 revolution to his death in 1920. These writings are little known or at times dismissed as instant journalism, being so close to the events as he was, and they also are with a few exceptions untranslated. Weber's monumental analysis of patrimonialism, of which Chinese and Russian rulerships are perhaps the most significant case studies, is currently more utilized and appreciated even as a tool applicable to the modern phenomena of power concentration and not just to past centuries.

Some commentators have selected and translated within their own writings a few choice statements by Weber on Russia, the selection being made on the basis of the author's own perception of the issues Weber discussed, his attitudes toward Weber and the 1917 events in Russia, and his own intellectual needs and pursuits. Everyone seems to have his own set of preconceived notions of Weber's alleged legacy. However, this "legacy" has been misinterpreted with remarkable thoroughness, and some of the misinterpretations have enjoyed such longevity as to become orthodoxy. On the other hand plenty of references to his works amount to no more than lip service. Therefore, some highly significant aspects of his opus remain unknown or misconstrued.

There are at least five pieces (four articles and one lecture) on Russia of the twentieth century in addition to some pages in other writings of his.* Lionel Kochan labeled one piece as truly remarkable (1966:212). As time passes and more materials become available on the Russian experience—now well into the seventh decade—Weber's articles appear strikingly accurate today.

Since Weber was repeatedly accused of rampant Russophobia, it is necessary first, before his propositions are analyzed, to note Weber's vehemence and the biting language and style he used almost regularly when discussing not only the Russian but also the German ruling elites and their imperialistic politics. His articles on Russia are evidently considered by themselves alone for his criticism directed against the Russian ruling circles, tsarist and post-tsarist, has never been compared with his more devastating attacks against the German imperialistic establishment and its defenders of before and during World War I.

Additionally, some of his remarks on the Russian development were taken entirely out of the context in which he had at the same time expressed his admiration for what he called the Russian liberation movement, namely the various revolutionary groups, however conflicting they were with each other. This practice of omission was almost common even among those scholars who rejected the unwarranted accusations of Russophobia. In one particular instance only the first part of a very complimentary sentence on the Russian struggle for freedom is cited, and the rest of it, certainly more apt than what was quoted, was simply dropped (Beetham, 1974).

Indeed, commenting on the behavior of the tsar, his dynasty and the ruling structure surrounding him and dominating him, Weber frequently applied words such as vanity, stubbornness, and stupidity, but he was also highly critical of the inability of the anti-tsarist groups to cope with the opportunities available to them before and especially after the tsardom's collapse.

---

*All Weber (and Heuss) materials used or quoted here are translated by the author with one exception: Weber 1946 citations are translated by H. H. Gerth and C. W. Mills. For major misconceptions of Weber's legacy, see Murvar 1983: 3-30.

To put it all into proper perspective, a brief comment is in order on Weber's attitudes toward the German ruling elites, which he heartily detested. His hatred for oppression anywhere is perhaps most intensive and visible when he speaks of the German oppressors: the kaiser, the Junkers, the industrialists separately and the entire German power structure in general. As Baumgarten said, "Power, typically German power, was the actual object of hatred, of Weber's national self-hatred" (1971:124). Weber wrote in 1911 in a letter to Graf Keyserling that the Germans are not a civilized nation or people with a refined politically sophisticated culture simply because "we never have had the nerve to behead one of our monarchs," as the civilized nations have, presumably France, England, and others. He felt that such an emotional experience in the German cultural heritage would have been a good lesson for all the future rulers of Germany. In 1917 during the war Weber again attacked the kaiser and at the same time ridiculed the concept of master race (*Herrenvolk*): "We are not a master race for we put up with our monarch."

The first president of the German Bundesrepublic after World War II, T. Heuss, recalls how many leading intellectuals and statesmen of Weber's era were profoundly shaken by Weber's continuous and implacable attacks against Wilhelm II, not only during but even after the war, when Weber himself too said that it was not "gentlemanly" to use "harsh" words against the deposed monarch (1971:xvi). Heuss also said that modern readers still will be shocked with Weber's rage (*die grimmige Wut*)—nary any word expresses it—when he, who in those fatal years was so basically disturbed with the German foreign policy, attacked the decision makers of (German) Prussia's domestic policies (1971:xix).

Many of these statements were given wide publicity and in turn created a great deal of hostile German public opinion against Weber. With the accusation that "Max Weber is a disgrace to the nation" people from the right and left canceled subscriptions to the journals and newspapers in which Weber published. Heuss said that *Die Frankfurter Zeitung* always welcomed whatever Weber wished to say: it became Weber's "organ" (1971:xxiv). Ludendorff, one of the military chiefs, who had an emotional confrontation with Weber, as reported by Heuss (1971:xxviii), told Baumgarten after the war that Weber was a traitor to his country. In spite of all this, the accusations of his alleged German chauvinism and imperialism, contempt for democracy, etc., which all make his alleged Russophobia self-evident, are still very much current.

Deeply committed to his personal values of liberty, basic human rights and self-determination for all nations, Weber paid to the Russian liberation movement a touchingly eloquent tribute:

Never has a liberation movement been carried out under such difficult circumstances after all and never with such a high measure of almost reckless readiness for martyrdom as the Russian, for which it seems to me the German who finds in himself some remains of the idealism of his forefathers must possess very deep sympathy. (1906b:398)

In the same article, written after the 1905 revolution, Weber expressed his fears that the prospects for the success of Russian liberation movement were not too promising, but he warned his German readers not to assume that this was due to the alleged "Russians' immaturity for the constitutional government," as it was fashionable to believe in Germany. Any future failure would be entirely ascribed to the unusually harsh conditions of political life under despotism in Russia. He also attacked the cynicism of the German establishment, who in their reactionary insensitivity for long-range relationships preferred an unstable Russia as an easy prey for German imperialist purposes. Again in 1917 Weber spoke of his "very strong sympathies for the Russian liberation movement" (1971:197). That this was not empty rhetoric is best documented when Weber in total despair criticized various Russian groups, whether the Constitutional Democrats (Kadets), Zemstvo, the practically nonexisting proletariat, or the extremely weak, nonfunctioning bourgeoisie, for their failures to push harder toward their goals.

If Weber's propositions on 1917 Russia are substantiated by modern historical research, certain faulty conceptualizations and terminology have to be removed or revised accordingly.

(Due to the thirteen days difference between the Julian and Gregorian calendars, the first event takes place in February according to the Julian calendar and in March following the Gregorian one. The second event happened in October or November, respectively. When the Soviet Union celebrates these two events as the source for the legitimacy of their power structure the celebration takes place in March and November. The October event is honored with sumptuous festivities in November, and the February event to a lesser degree in March. For these reasons this essay will consistently refer to the March and November events.)

THE MARCH 1917 NONREVOLUTIONARY EVENT

"Not a 'revolution' but merely a simple 'elimination' of an incapable monarch is all that has happened in Russia until now." This Weber wrote (1971:210) in an article published April 26, 1917, a month after an almost natural collapse of tsarism in March 1917. He italicized the entire sentence for added significance.

The Provisional Government (*PG*) replacing tsarism was indeed transitional. At least half of the real power structure, Weber noted, was still in the hands of the monarchically oriented circles, who pretended to participate in the republican swindle, because to their immense chagrin the tsar was still in March unable to understand the political realities. This old ruling elite easily dominated the political scene after the collapse of tsarism, and due to their presence the Mensheviks and the Narodniki in the PG were forced into the role of "hangers on." The Narodniki and the Mensheviks "gave the masses of people the illusion" that the new government was really "revolutionary." Of course, however, despicable to the old ruling elite this illusion was, they were pleased with it and promoted it as necessary for the time being. However, according to their strategy, as soon as order was established, the army would be used anyway at the first opportunity to remove the Narodniki and Mensheviks from the PG.

It is actually irrelevant, Weber added, whether the "republic" thanks to the stupidities and inferiority (*Minderwertigkeit*) of the dynasty would be established for a longer time, perhaps even permanently, and this the dominant ruling circles certainly did not want to happen. The only decisive question is whether or not the real "democratic" elements could win the power: the peasants, craftsmen, and industrial workers *outside* the war industry. This would not be impossible, he said, but at this moment anyway it was not yet the case.

This almost permanently fixed instability of the PG, Weber suggested, was caused by a most serious conflict between the peasantry—by far the most numerous potential political power structure—and the industrialists and the workers who depended on them, a very small group indeed in comparison with the peasants (1971:207).

Only a month after the collapse of tsarism, Weber offered a keen observation on the Narodniki, the true representatives of the peasantry: "The only way to remove all the enormous difficulties facing the PG would be a *coup d'état* and a durable if not permanent dictatorship by the Narodniki" (1971:207). As it is now history, only less than eight months later an entirely different *coup d'état* by a tiny minority was to fill the power vacuum by occupying the empty throne. More about this in the section below on the November nonrevolutionary event.

Still in April 1917 Weber passionately defended the Narodniki—as the best bet—from many accusations fabricated by the monarchists, Kadets, Social Democrats, both Menshevik and Bolshevik, and others. The Narodnik, Weber argued, was not a sort of wild or savage politician but simply a realist who pays no attention to the concept of the holiness of private property in land. Anyway this concept of the sacredness of landed private property is very weak, very recent, in many regions totally new, in Russia (1971:207).

While the PG never promised a Constituent Assembly, Weber said, the mythology glorifying the Constituent Assembly could become a partial reality only if (1) genuinely free elections took place in Russia and (2) prior to that the peasants would receive realistic information on the domestic and foreign situation. Surely then without failure such an election would bring a huge majority of peasant representatives into the Constituent Assembly. This massive majority would push for partitioning of the land, rescinding government debts and concluding peace (1971:209).

However, the ruling landowning strata and commanding army officers as well as the great domestic and foreign financial powers (*Geldmächte*) were interested in the first place in offering to the peasants only fraudulent and false information and secondly, if the first, the fraud, did not work (and the election took place bringing about a huge peasant majority) they would keep postponing the meeting of the Constituent Assembly as long as feasible. But above all, Weber added, under no circumstances would the masses of strongest peasants, serving presently in the army, be permitted to participate in the election. Curiously enough this is precisely what the Bolsheviks did and what Weber said the landlords and the military would do.

Weber also feared that many representatives of the Russian industrial workers, the Mensheviks and the Bolsheviks, could never be seriously enthusiastic about any of the three points of the peasants' program (1971:209). To the Marxist Social Democrats, especially to Menshevik Plekhanov, Weber continued, the real hopes of the peasants appear today just as utopian and "backward" as they were in 1905.

Plekhanov and similar ethicists being Marxist evolutionists are the sworn enemies of all "petty-bourgeois, peasants' ideals of equality and sharing of land" (Weber, 1971:209). To those ideological points, Weber said, the material, practical considerations are to be added: the workers demanding highest prices for their products and cheap bread at the same time, and the peasants holding their wheat back resisting with force whenever they could. Any success of the realistic demands of the peasants could slow down the capitalist industrial development of Russia for many years.

When speaking of the Narodniki's *coup d'état* and their durable dictatorship to follow as the only logical/rational solution to the unsurmountable problems, Weber concluded rather pessimistically: "Are the personalities capable of accomplishing this enormous task available in Russia at the present moment—I do not know" (1971:206). Probably Weber here had in mind two basically different kinds of political animals capable of successfully exercising a durable dictatorship of the Narodniki on behalf of the huge majority, the peasants: (1) a charismatic leader with his exceptional gifts of grace; or (2) a patrimonialist ruler with his political skills to manipulate his bureaucracy and subjects.

Of course, in this article Weber did not make any reference to his famous typology of rulership and legitimacy, of which the two types are very significant and almost universally evidenced types, especially outside the West. Still it is relevant here that the patrimonialist political skills, including the successful manufacturing of pseudo-charisma of several Russian actors in this—to use Weber's phrase—"breathless Russian drama" from March to November 1917, have not been sufficiently studied.

Instead, almost indiscriminately the genuine gifts of charismatic graces have been attributed to most of them in spite of suspicion that genuine charisma as opposed to manufactured charisma is disappearing from the modern age: Supposedly advanced modern societies are not a suitable environment for it.

Is it possible to expect that even some speculative statements of Weber are seemingly based on facts? His "choice" of what kind of dictatorship would hit Russia in 1917 appears factual and realistic today as well as even for that time: The fundamental difficulties of the PG were not eliminated with the November *coup d'état*, but they have plagued all the subsequent dictatorships since 1917 to present. As will be pointed out later, the use of plural *dictatorships* is in order. Contrary to all claims it is a pure illusion, one of many in this context, and a segment of an elaborate mythology to insist on the continuity when four different sorts of dictatorships were separated by roughly five-year periods each of three transitional collective leaderships always within the same process of recapturing the empty throne.

Finally, Weber's "choice" would have been even prophetic if the events between March and November 1917 in Russia had not taken an unrealistic turn. However, Weber qualified it by expressing serious doubts as to its feasibility.

Modern Research

Several of Weber's propositions concerning the March 1917 nonrevolutionary event are firmly supported by recent reinvestigations of the original materials. First, his statement, "Not a revolution," then his frequent references to an abundance of illusions of various sorts in this context are substantiated.

"The old Tsarist regime collapsed throughout the country at one and the same time" in March 1917. Pethybridge continues: "The speed at which this happened, and the universality of the phenomenon, proved just how rotten the old system was: but it did not prove that a new, cohesive community had replaced it" (1967:111). Comparing the Russian and German imperialist regimes before World War I, Mosse said that both "disappeared virtually overnight without a blow being struck in their defense" (1967:100). And Chamberlin agreed: "The sequel to the fall of the tsar was a huge political vacuum in Russia. . . . the tsar disappeared from the scene" (1965:4). Pethybridge also speaks of a massive power vacuum in Russia from March 1917 until 1921, and especially between March 1917 and March 1918 (1967:110).

The specialists are discovering the impact of the unrealistic but ideologically supported powerful illusions on the Russian liberation movement. In "1917—A Year of Illusion," Riha analyzes the political situation of the decade or so before 1917: "The hothouse conditions of those years helped to create and maintain many illusions: it would have taken more than a few months of 1917 to destroy these" (1967:121).

Perhaps it would be more appropriate to consider as major sources of illusions an entire century of revolutionary messianism beginning with the Decembrists of 1825, who too were preceded by several centuries of religious messianic movements of the sects before and after the Old Believers of 1666, which handicapped the entire Russian liberation movement. As this author (1971) has suggested, the contents of illusionary expectations seem identical in both religious and revolutionary messianic movements.

The Continuity of Imperialism

The most significant, at least in this author's evaluation, and at the same time most neglected aspects are Weber's analyses within the Russian cultural context of basic human rights, freedom for minorities, democracy and self-determination for submerged nations, which all seem to be increasingly endangered by modernization and economic-technological advancement. Here Weber most persistently criticized the continuity of Russian imperialism, which was to him clearly evidenced in the performance of the PG in that short period from March to April 1917 (1971:199-200).

This so-called new and revolutionary government, he said, shared with the just-collapsed tsarist government an identical foreign policy and war goals. What particularly frightened Weber were the formal warmongering pronouncements and actual activities of the PG refusing to conclude an early peace. Of course, there were other aspects of the PG which were identical with those of the tsarist government. As a German patriot Weber anticipated that the new PG would conclude a peace which could benefit the German as well as the Russian people. He makes this point clear here as well as in the introductory statement to this essay when he spoke of "people in both countries and not the imperialist German and Russian governments" (1971:197).

Above and beyond his justified concern for peace between these two traditional enemies, Weber raised the question of the many submerged or nonstate nations that were within the Austro-Hungarian, Russian and Turkish empires (1971:199-200). Both the tsarist and the Provisional governments shared the same alleged goals of war, which were still highly advertised but not taken seriously by either government, Weber said, namely the goals to recapture Constantinople for Christianity and to liberate all the Slavic peoples not only in Turkey but also in Austro-Hungary. The many Slavic and non-Slavic nonfree nations in Russia are not considered, however:

Constantinople and the so-called liberation of the Slavic peoples means in practice their total domination by the Great Russian national bureaucracy; these new goals have now completely replaced the earlier revolutionary empty rhetorics on "human rights" and an election for "Constitutional Assembly." The total Great Russian mythology is still very much alive today. Especially rampantly alive among the bourgeois intelligentsia during the entire liberation movement is the claim to Great Russian domination [over all non-Russian nations] within the old Russian empire. Also even before the smallest possible guaranties for their own striving for freedom's progress have been reached, almost all the leading personalities of the "liberation organization" have already in 1905 their eyes glued on Constantinople and western borders. The leadership of the same organization denied the existence of the Ukrainian nation, while Polish autonomy was handled strictly from the point of view of the future expansion of Russia toward the outside to create "friends on the western borders." The liberation of all peoples possible was declared by the same leadership as the task of Great Russiandom specifically—while in their own house practically everything remains to be liberated. (1971:199-200)

Strong convictions as to the "unavoidable" collapse of the Austro-Hungarian Empire and the weakening of Turkey in the Balkan War swelled the hopes of this imperialist intelligentsia to the extreme. In agreement with J. Haller, Weber continued: "The burning political issue of the national autonomies within the Russian Empire was the most significant means in the hands of the tsarist government to destroy all democratic opposition by the awakening of Great Russian nationalism" (1971:200-201). Weber argues that this is precisely what the PG was doing. He could have added more explicitly what he frequently implied when he sharply criticized the

Kadets, the liberal party, for their warmongering and their chauvinism against nonstate nations in Russia, that in all likelihood all the Russian governments of the near future would do the same irrespective of their political composition, whether liberal, radical or conservative, bourgeois or socialist. Almost seven decades later the accuracy of this "prophecy" is simply devastating. And his insistence that under all those particular conditions of political reality in Russia no liberal, democratic government would likely survive is also substantiated by subsequent events.

THE NOVEMBER 1917
NONREVOLUTIONARY EVENT

Only three months after Lenin's *coup d'état* against the PG in November and barely a month after Lenin's sealing of the doors of the Constituent Assembly on January 6, 1918, Weber made some astonishing propositions in a newspaper article. While they have survived the test of time, the confusion created by numerous commentators who have rendered only certain fragments of their own choice from this untranslated article has not abated. Time and time again they commit the same blunder when quoting Weber's very first and crucial comment, that is, his comment on the duration of Lenin's seizure of power. Like many before, Beetham also said that the longest Weber expected the Bolshevik regime to last was a few months (1974:201). However, what Weber actually wrote is entirely different: "From their own personal observations the best informed and most unprejudiced (radical-socialist) experts, as far as I know, give Bolshevism a power-duration which counts in months only" (1971:292). The very next sentence starts: "Trifft dies zu" and he continues:

In any event Bolshevism is a government of a very small minority. Above all it is leaning on large segments of the war-tired army. As a matter of fact (and quite independently from the candidness of its ideology) Bolshevism is from sheer necessity forced into a pure *military dictatorship,* though not one of generals, but of *corporals.* It is pure nonsense to foster the impression that "class-conscious" proletarian masses of the Western European sort stand behind Bolshevism. The *soldier* proletariat stands behind it. And this has its consequences. Whatever purposes the Petersburg literati may pursue, their own power structure apparatus, that is the soldiers, expect and demand above all *reward* and *loot.* And this is peremptory over all other considerations. The well-paid Red Guards have no interest in peace, which would deprive them of any sources of income. (Original emphasis.) (1971:292-93)

Indeed, if one recalls that Lenin actually ordered the liquidation of precisely those small military groups who put him in power because they demanded higher pay and other material privileges, then Weber's remarks were not too far off and should not be labeled hostile, just unpleasantly factual. Weber believed that revolutionary parasites, those who lived "not for but off the revolution," were very influential among the Bolsheviks: They were more interested in perpetuating the image of revolution, which gave them a very good living, than in realizing goals of the revolution. To Weber this was the "essence of Bolshevism." As when commenting on Weber in another context, Dunn said, "Cruelly put though it was, [Weber] did express a profound and dreadful truth" which is still ringing today "like a funeral knell" (1979:91-92) throughout the consciousness of modern man: "It is the purest militarism which ever existed anywhere until the present time. Everything else is, objectively, a swindle, irrespective of whether or not the leadership only pretends to profess the revolutionary goals or perhaps subjectively really and sincerely may believe in the same goals" (Weber, 1971:293).

Sealing the Doors of the Constituent Assembly

Only a month after this event Weber stated: "The Constituent Assembly, the only—at least formally through democratic elections—accredited Russian authority, has been destroyed by force" (1971:293). This happened not because of differences in immediate goals: The majority party also declared to hold a ceasefire and to continue with peace negotiations, as did the Bolshevik minority. The real reason was to prevent the new bread givers from sharing rewards and loot among the new bodyguards, the new bureaucratic and military staff. Obviously Weber had in mind the Assembly's 76.4 percent majority facing the Bolsheviks who had in November 1917 captured the power in only two capital cities, Moscow and Petrograd, but received only 23.6 percent of the total national vote. The Bolshevik electoral strength was in Moscow and Petrograd: They received 46.3 percent in the two capital cities, which represented only two districts of the country's total of sixty districts. If several districts which were unable to vote were to be included in the total national vote, the Bolshevik vote percentage would have dramatically decreased further.

In evaluating Weber's propositions on this event these two crucial factors cannot be emphasized enough: (1) The Bolshevik capture of power and subsequent control did not extend beyond or outside of Moscow and Petrograd; and (2) precisely in these two capital cities the Bolsheviks claimed popular support, real and imaginary. Going back to the election results, out of that anti-Bolshevik 76.4 percent, the Narodniki held 40.9 percent, the non-Russian nationalities 20.1 percent, the Kadets 4.8 percent, the Mensheviks 3.0 percent, and divided among several minor parties 7.6 percent.

Even if the Kadets were excluded, Weber was correct in saying that the majority shared with the Bolshevik minority the principle of a ceasefire and separate peace negotiations and that the real issue, the one and only issue, was who would control the power through the differential system of rewards and penalties to manipulate their own military and bureaucratic staff. In practice this would mean that the Narodniki and their allies within that majority would replace the Bolshevik bodyguards, military units, etc. with their own guards selected among their supporters. This is one of the major, if not most fundamental, attributes of the patrimonialist power structure and legitimacy, traditionalist as well as modern. Immediately after the seizure of power, the Bolsheviks commenced to arrest the leaders and to shut down the newspapers of all other parties, however their rage was directed especially against the Narodniki and Mensheviks. This fulfilled at least in part Weber's prophecy that the Narodniki and Mensheviks would be the chief victims of conservative-monarchist *coup d'état* because they were the true revolutionaries. They indeed were the victims, but of another coup.

As reported by Melgunov, Trotsky said that during the first days, if not hours, after the capture of power, Lenin decided not to hold the Constituent Assembly because "life has already bypassed this stage" and the Assembly was "an old fairy-tale" (1972:186). Lenin representing a minority of one was finally persuaded by those who feared that to announce this decision now would disappoint the supporters and outrage the opponents in view of the strong commitment of the Bolshevik press and daily speakers for the Assembly. Some voiced the fear that the nonfighting opponents might decide to use force to secure the Assembly, especially the Narodniki and Mensheviks, who commanded large support but who decided to wait for the opening day. As a matter of fact the Bolsheviks accused the Narodniki and Mensheviks daily, steadily and unanimously of conspiring with the bourgeoisie to prevent the opening of the Assembly.

The evidence here is not questionable: it is overwhelming. Already on November 8, 1917, a day after the coup, at a Bolshevik strategy meeting in Petrograd, Melgunov recorded that one of the leaders, Volodarsky, predicted that "perhaps we shall be forced to disperse the Constituent Assembly with bayonets." To which a low-ranking Bolshevik commented, "Wouldn't it then be best not to hold a Constituent Assembly? The power is in our hands." Volodarsky's reply was: "If Petrograd were all Russia, then, of course, we would refrain from convening the Constituent Assembly" (1972:186).

On January 5, 1918, and the entire night, the Assembly met for its one and only session, a unique experience in Russian history, never before and never again. With Lenin watching in the gallery, the Bolshevik guards began turning off the lights and heat and refused to serve food and drinks in order to get the representatives out after they rejected the Bolshevik agenda for the proceedings by a 237 to 136 vote. (Of the total of 520 delegates, the Bolsheviks held only 161 seats, while the Narodniki had an absolute majority with 267 seats.) It was already morning when, exhausted from the unending enthusiasm and excitement of its first session, the Assembly members left. They returned the same evening of January 6 with plenty of candles, sandwiches, blankets, and drinks to resist for another day the Bolshevik manipulation, to which some historians have commented with a touch of sadness that that was the only resistance they displayed. They were met by the guards, who said softly: "*Batyushka* (good old dear little father), go home, the Constituent Assembly is no more."

The Continuity of Imperialism

In this analysis of the November event once again Weber goes back to the submerged nations' quest for independence: "Under the pretext of 'liberating' Ukraine, Finland, and other non-Russian nations, the soldiers move in there (as they do in Russia proper) and collect imposed contributions.'' Their alleged revolutionary goals, ''as with every Russian intellectual without exception, are totally '*imperialistic*''' (his emphasis). Then he makes his major point:

> It is then not true that the only imperialism in existence is bourgeois imperialism when also someone who out *of greed for power* under ideal excuses interferes with the affairs of foreign nations even before any semblance of order is established in his own house can be labeled imperialist. As long as Bolshevik soldier imperialism exists it endangers the security and self-determination of all the nations at its borders. (Original emphasis.) (1971:293)

Weber's proposition in 1918 on the continuity of Russian imperialism from the tsarist, to the Provisional, to the Bolshevik government could have been dismissed at that time as too premature or biased, but in the ending days of Brezhnev's era it was more substantiated than ever before. The Russian imperialist goals today are not only celebrated as mankind's progress, they are also successfully expanding, at least in part. Since 1972 Brezhnev's seemingly new, but not quite new, imperialist ploy is in full operation. It is an all-encompassing, long-range program according to which a brand-new *Soviet nation* will in name and substance replace the Russian as well as all other non-Russian nations. Tudjman offers a substantive review of the Soviet literature (1981:219-31) and shows that Brezhnev's new ''theoretical'' propositions are hailed ''as an enrichment of Marxist teaching'' and that ''in the Soviet Union the national question had not only been solved definitely on Marxist-Leninist principles but also a higher level had been attained—the creation of the Soviet nation'' (220-21).

In the present political context the Russian national name can certainly be dropped for a shorter or longer period of time, but not the crucial attributes of Russian nationhood, namely language along with literature and art, the entire Russian cultural heritage, especially the patrimonialist power structure and legitimacy.

In the entire literature on what makes a nation a nation from Renan in 1882, to Weber and up to the present, as this author has reported (1982), there is a consensus that some attributes are more significant than others in various cases and that there is a differential ranking of them in almost every case study. On the basis of this it can then be scientifically predicted that the final result of the process of making a new Soviet nation will be the total destruction of all non-Russian nations. The Russian attributes being more crucial and overwhelming in number will easily dominate all others. Curiously there is an inkling of this in Soviet literature for, as Tudjman shows, some interpreters of Brezhnev's propositions are more zealous or unsubtle than others:

In the Soviet Union the Russian language has a status of official state language; the compulsory teaching of Russian . . . was instituted a long time ago in all non-Russian nations . . . with the aim that it should become not merely a second language but also a mother tongue for all the Soviet population. In the conditions of mature socialism, the Russian language, which expresses a "cultural wealth and spiritual treasure house," is becoming an "international language" of general harmonization. As "every nation and nationality wants to adopt the Russian language in its own interests" . . . in the last few years a "real movement" for adopting the Russian language has grown up. (1981:224)

As suggested above this imperialist ploy of replacing the name was attempted before. After the murder of three elected Croat representatives (and wounding of several others) during a session of parliament in 1928, the Kingdom of Serbs, Croats, and Slovenes was declared the Kingdom of Yugoslavia by a new "constitution" which prohibited all three national names. However, the Serbian Orthodox church, always a department of the state, was exempted, permitting the oppressor nation to use its name, flag, shield, anthem, and all other Serbian national symbols.

In sharp contradistinction to these imperialist goals and actions at the close of the twentieth century, of special significance is Weber's defense, in the first two decades of the same century, of smaller nations, whether already free (Denmark, Netherlands, Norway, Switzerland) or still submerged (Croatia, Ireland, Ukraine; also Finland and Poland before 1918), of their rights to self-determination and protection against genocide. He forcefully pointed to smaller nations' original creativity in various spheres of human growth and argued for an absolute equality of their distinctive cultural values with those of all other nations. As

Beetham recognized, to Weber "distinctiveness was more valuable than uniformity, . . . [the] capacity to articulate distinctive values was among the highest human achievements" (1974:127).

Charismatic Gifts or Patrimonialist Political Skills?

Weber's conceptualizations of charismatic and patrimonialist rulerships and legitimacies are most pertinent here for the absence of (at least successful) charisma within the 1917 events and for the continuous presence of four subsequent personalized modern patrimonialist rulerships in Soviet Russia ever since 1917.

Charismatic leadership as perceived by Weber is not identical with revolution or with political power success. Many (Worsley, 1968:ix; Willner and Willner, 1965:78; Tucker, 1968:740; Hirschman, 1968:933-35, and others) have pointed out how frequently in the 1960s, especially in the developing world, the sudden fashionableness of the concept of charisma was directly correlated to "the rapid emergence of nationalist movements" and appearance of "personally popular" or "magnetic," revolution-promising, skillful politicians. At that time "nearly every leader with marked popular appeal, especially those of new states, [was] indiscriminately tagged as charismatic." In some instances the process of manufacturing the exalted leader's charisma had already started before the capture of power and invariably intensified after the seizure through the monopoly of all means of communication, education, sports, and other state activities. Now after they have gone from the political scene, there is uncontrovertible evidence that a huge majority of them were modern patrimonialist "bosses" who skillfully manipulated the differential system of rewards and penalties and successfully camouflaged their personalized patrimonialist regimes with manufactured charismatic images and plenty of revolutionary programs, claims and pretenses.

What is urgently needed, as this author has already suggested, is an analysis of the leadership attributes of the major actors in that "breathless Russian drama," especially in comparison with the evidence from the recently liberated or new states, which are in many aspects of their development today similar to Russia just before and after 1917. In addition to the currently familiar literature, there are some relatively new materials, which are not too well known. The personal diaries, memoirs, letters, notes, etc. written by the actors themselves, their closest associates and disciples as well as their former associates and fiercest competitors have not been analyzed from that particular vantage of the charismatic versus patrimonialist rulership's attributes. If the participants in these events (Volsky, Sukhanov, Plekhanov, Kerensky, Chernov, Miliukov, Katkov, Vernadsky, Berdyaev, and many others), all from different personal and political value perspectives, seem to point in the same direction when describing certain crucial pieces of action in 1917 and before, then some facts based on this unusual consensus should be clearly recognizable.

It has been said many times that before the November event there were many powerful actors on the scene, but after there was only Lenin. A number of these eyewitness accounts seem to offer an entirely new panorama of Lenin's unquestionably superb political skills, which are now, in post-Weber research, identified as patrimonialist political skills. They also seem to cast a shadow of doubt, when describing some happenings in which Lenin partici-pated, on Lenin's alleged charismatic attributes, ascribed to him by his admirers and certainly in general much later after his capture of power. According to the same eyewitness accounts his two major competitors, Kerensky and Chernov, leaders of the Narodniki, appear much closer to the model and attributes of genuine charisma than Lenin. If this happens to be supported by solid research, then Hirschman's speculative statement that Lenin is "a particularly fascinating example" of a leader who can somehow accommodate both skills and charisma will have to be reexamined. He added, "Such an even blend of charisma and skill is most uncommon. Usually any one leader is likely to be better either at charisma or at skills, precisely because these two qualities are in part based on opposite deviations from the norm." He strongly emphasizes the contradiction between the two and how they "are often at loggerheads" (1968:934-35). Finally, Hirschman seems to agree with Tucker, who warns, "we run greater risk of error in identifying a given leader as charismatic" after he and his supporters have captured power than before, "for power is a source of phenomena that resembles the effects of charisma without actually being such. It brings prestige and, especially in modern technological conditions, possibilities of artificial inducement or simulation of mass adulation of a leader" (1968:740).

Even before his capture of power, Lenin's exceptional political skills were brought sharply into focus by a number of events, especially the 1903 meeting which permanently split the Social Democrats into the Menshevik majority and Bolshevik minority. Lenin was so successfully in charge that after the majority left, under the impression that the meeting was over, he declared the rights of his small minority to speak for the entire Social Democratic party, labeling the majority *Mensheviks* meaning the smaller, minor, backward part, and his own group *Bolsheviks*, meaning the larger, major, progressive part. While his opponents did not take him seriously, his labels and his claims stuck permanently. Subsequently Lenin started a most careful selection of his future administrative staff from among his supporters, which after his successful seizure of power developed into a typically patrimonialist bureaucracy.

Indeed, Weber was very much cognizant of these patrimonialist characteristics of Lenin's power structure without using the term (1971:529, 556-57). In spite of an early translation (1946:99-100, 115, 119, 121-22,125) students in general have seemingly overlooked these brilliantly precise attributes, perhaps because Weber buried them as examples in a lengthy piece. There he analyzed the power structure based on "purely personal retinues" (*rein persönliche Gefolgschaften*), that is, the bodies of retainers, vassals or followers who accompany, serve and protect the leader, the "boss" or whoever, but always within the connotation of the absolute father's domination. Concerning this basic attribute, Weber compared the medieval city's political parties, the Guelfs and the Ghibellines, with the Bolsheviks. Juxtaposing the use of violence and the blueprints for the perfect society, Weber stressed the ruler's dependence on his human apparatus (the term he used):

He who wants to establish absolute justice on earth by force requires a following, a human "machine." He must hold out the necessary internal and external premiums, heavenly or worldly reward, to this "machine" or else the machine will not function. Under the conditions of the modern class struggle, the internal premiums consist of the satisfying of hatred and the craving for revenge; above all, resentment and the need for pseudo-ethical self-righteousness: The opponents must be slandered and accused of heresy. The external rewards are adventure, victory, booty, power, and spoils. The leader and his success are completely dependent upon the functioning of his machine and hence not on his own motives. Therefore he also depends upon whether or not the premiums can be *permanently* granted to the following, that is, to the Red Guard, the informers, the agitators, whom he needs. What he actually attains under the conditions of his work is therefore not in his hand, but is prescribed to him by the following's motives, which, if viewed ethically, are predominantly base. (1946:125)

After the capture of power the human apparatus of a revolutionary hero, the believer in the sacred cause, now practically a new ruling elite, normally and quite easily tends to degenerate into the quite common phenomenon of spoilsmen. Their belief in his person and his cause

even when subjectively sincere, is in a very great number of cases really no more than an ethical "legitimation" of cravings for revenge, power, booty, and spoils. We shall not be deceived about this verbiage; the materialist interpretation of history is no cab to be taken at will; it does not stop short of the promoters of revolutions. Emotional revolutionism is followed by the traditionalist routine of everyday life; the crusading leader and the faith itself fade away, or, what is even more effective, the faith becomes part of the conventional phraseology of political Philistines and banausic technicians. (1946:125)

"This development," Weber concluded, "is especially rapid with struggles of faith because they are usually led or inspired by genuine leaders, that is, prophets of revolution." Here without elaborating in detail Weber clearly recognized how and why the revolutionary regimes after successfully capturing power become very quickly the archconservative defenders of the new status quo, namely new totalist patrimonialist governments. While today there is abundant evidence for this, Weber in his day simply observed that one of the conditions for success is the necessity imposed on the leader's human machine to perform routine everyday tasks, which in turn inevitably pushes exalted revolutionary goals into a very distant and eventually permanent future. Of course this happens gradually and slowly, without any public admission. Weber called it "the depersonalization and routinization," or "the psychic proletarianization," all in the interest of discipline for all, the rulers and the ruled. Whatever the sincerity of the leader, his actual helplessness due to his total dependence on his human apparatus not only handicaps but eventually destroys any semblance of reaching the original revolutionary goals.

Patrimonialist Bureaucracy and Rationality

Weber's concepts of bureaucracy and rationality have been commonly misinterpreted as only limited to the legal-rational type of rulership and legitimacy as its major, exclusive, almost inseparable attributes. In spite of available translations of his (1951, 1968) brilliant analyses of Chinese, Islamic, Russian, and other patrimonialist power structures, the concept of patrimonialist bureaucracy and certain rationalistic features within patrimonialism have not attained the currency comparable to some of his perhaps less seminal works. This in turn caused much confusion when Weber's writings on Russia were discussed.

The October 1905 manifesto promising some political reforms was extracted from a most reluctant tsar by the impact of the 1905 revolution, which incidentally Weber considered a genuine revolution. This also explains why he was so bitterly disappointed with the two subsequent nonrevolutionary events. Not only must Weber's observations be placed within the context of tsarist patrimonialism, but they were made almost immediately after the election and subsequent dismissal of the elected Assembly in August 1906. Once again tsarist patrimonialism apparently was triumphant. Even in the title of this essay Weber (1906b:171 ff; 1971:70-71) labeled tsarist attempts toward a constitutional monarchy as pseudo or sham constitutionalism which would create only illusions of change without giving up any fundamental elements of power and would only provide a breathing space for pro-tsarist forces to recover and regroup. That was the tsarist response to the 1905 revolution.

In considerable detail Weber explained how this pseudo constitutionalism is more dangerous than naked repression, because it formally grants some rights on one hand, while it actually takes them away with the other (1906b:228-33; 1971:76-82). In practice the only reforms which are expected to succeed are those that will undermine chances for liberties even further. Traditional tsarism consisted of separate "satrapies," each answerable to the tsar. Since they were usually at war with each other, this situation created enough obstructionism to make life somewhat more tolerable for the subjects. From the perspective of human freedom every obstruction provided some sort of protection for the human dignity of the subjects. The alleged reforms were to create a modern centralized bureaucracy under a single ministerial council directly responsible to the tsar. This represents a much worse situation for the subjects. The entire Russian society stands as one man, Weber said, with the exception of the industrialists and the bankers, against this transmutation of an ancient absolutism into a modern rational bureaucracy. Another question to be asked today is whether this opposition was in the long run successful.

Pseudo constitutionalism represented to Weber "the definitive bureaucratic rationalization of the autocracy within the entire area of internal policies" (1906b:228). This statement does not justify Pipes imputing to Weber a conclusion he certainly did not draw: "Its net result was the *shift from the crown to the bureaucracy*" (original emphasis) (1955:386, 396). Pipes continued to criticize Weber by saying that what actually did happen was "the very opposite of what Weber had anticipated":

Between 1906 and 1917, the Russian bureaucracy neither usurped the authority of the crown, nor attempted to do so. It did its very best to serve the monarchy, but it became so thoroughly demoralized by the crown's irresponsible behavior that in March 1917, when the dynasty fell, it vanished from the political stage without so much as a token show of resistance. . . . the power of the monarchy remained undiminished, while that of the bureaucracy declined at an alarming rate. (1955:396)

Pipes's "argument" sounds like an affirmation that a properly running patrimonialist bureaucracy was safely under the control of the tsarist court, and his statement on the tsarism's "vanishing act" in March 1917 certainly supports Weber's analysis of the same event. Contradictory to it is Pipes's own total rejection of Weber's analysis of the two nonrevolutionary events (1955:396). It is based on a number of currently surviving grand illusions of that time, among them illusions of believing that the nonexistent "industrial proletariat" and the small bands of war-tired sailors and soldiers, who put Lenin in power, were "popular forces." Finally, Lenin's bitter complaint about the indestructibility of the tsarist bureaucracy he inherited did not warrant the statement on the bureaucracy's alleged decline "at an alarming rate."

Before he suffered his final stroke, in a speech of January 23, 1923, Lenin voiced his deep disenchantement with the events subsequent to his capture of power: "With the exception of the People's Commissariat for Foreign Affairs, our state apparatus is very largely a survival of the old one, and has least of all undergone serious change. It has only been slightly repainted on the surface, but in all other things it is a typical relic of our old state apparatus" (1937:382). As usual the official Moscow-approved selected works of Lenin (from which this quote is taken) omitted Lenin's further comments made in the same context, on Russia's return to *Aziashchina* and "Oriental" or "Asiatic despotism," which he feared was inevitably happening even before his demise and which he was unable to stop due to his progressing illness. Among other reliable old Bolshevik witnesses, Khrushchev in his infamous "de-Stalinization" speech confirmed these statements of Lenin and also that they were made in the context suggested above.

Modern Research

Based on those two aspects of Weber's work on Russia and supported by most recent research, it is proposed that the November 1917 event bears in the best tradition of patrimonialism all the attributes of a typically patrimonialist *coup d'état* based on surprise and, initially, a small military force. It did fill the power vacuum created by the March 1917 event of the collapse of tsarism, or as some say, it did occupy the vacant throne. The November event, more precisely, did affirm the successful beginning of the end of the "Time of Troubles" from the early twentieth century to the final establishment of the new government sometime after the Civil War in the 1920s. Russian historians almost uniformly use the term "Time of Troubles" for the protracted periods of general insecurity and patriotic unhappiness between outgoing and incoming dynasties or regimes, because there was no real rulership when the seat of power, the throne, was not occupied, if only temporarily.

The patrimonialist attributes of the November 1917 event are strikingly similar to many previous instances of power transfer from one sacred rulership to another equally sacred in Russian, Chinese and other patrimonialist empires. Weber frequently noticed that in these instances of power struggle there is a sort of charismatic claim based on the charisma of success: successfully occupying the position of power is at the same time the source of and proof for its legitimacy. Whoever occupies the position of power, and for as long as he does so successfully, will command the loyalty of the subjects and achieve unquestioned legitimacy. Said Wolfe, who rather understated "the influence of the Russian imperial heritage" on the Bolshevik power structure and legitimacy:

Lenin seized power, not in a land "ripe for socialism," but in a land ripe for seizing power. "It was as easy," he wrote, "as lifting up a feather." His coup was supposed to touch off a European socialist revolution; but while his revolution "matured," there was an opportunity to take power in the great Russian empire. "The point of the uprising," he chided his hesitant associates, uncertain about Russia's "ripeness" for his blueprint, "is the seizure of power. Afterwards, we will see what we can do with it" (1963:21).

Hindus quotes Lenin as saying, "If 40,000 landlords [actually the ruler's patrimonialist staff, not the feudal lords v.m.] could rule Russia so could 40,000 Bolsheviks" (1953:28). A political precedent of the past, Hindus concluded, was to be a model for the future.

There is much support for this in recent research. An increasing number of specialists seem to emphasize now more frequently than before the continuity of the old, tsarist, with the new, Soviet Russia in many crucial aspects of political power structure and legitimacy. Several of them find it attractive to go back to an old formula innocently expressed in a travelogue. Except for his name, an almost unknown Italian traveler throughout early imperial (Petrine and post-Petrine) Russia, Caracciolo (or Caroccilo) picked up the essence of Weber's charisma of success when he reported: "The Russian throne is neither hereditary nor elective. It is occupative." This was in reference to the almost regular violent removal of the reigning monarch by a successful usurper whose legitimacy was never challenged until he was replaced by another successful usurper. Among several others Katkov eloquently presents evidence on the continuity of the Russian power structure and legitimacy, tsarist and Soviet. Without specifying or even labeling any of the numerous evolutionary theories, which still enjoy great popularity, Katkov clearly directs his general disdain against all of them, be they the old "laws of history" or the modern functionalist and Marxist. Assuming uniform development everywhere and an almost identical process of modernization in all countries irrespective of their varying cultural heritages, they all effectively becloud the evidence of the continuity of the power structure and legitimacy of the old with the new and their common attributes. When these "modernization" theories are applied to today's Russia the result is, Katkov said, an almost indestructable

assumption that autocracy as a form of government was obsolete, and doomed to disappear in Russia, as it had in the other Western countries. . . . The experience of the Soviet regime . . . has taught us that there was no foundation either for the analogy with the West European monarchies or for the belief that autocracy in Russia was obsolete, for autocracy persisted despite the revolution. (1967:424)

The patterns of succession in old Russia are also astonishingly similar to the well-known and now solidly documented Soviet succession games. The entire syndrome of succession in both, tsarist and Soviet Russia, is a typical patrimonialist political experience between the two regimes while the throne is temporarily vacant. The only new aspects are the enhanced sophistication in the contents of beliefs for the new legitimacy—now an ideology with a potential international appeal which has replaced the old popular mythologies based on religious doctrine—and superior technology including the means of communication used exclusively for the lasting benefit of the new patrimonialist power structure.

The record is surprisingly simple: Within six and a half decades there were four extremely successful patrimonialist rulerships, separated by three short-lived "Times of Troubles," now attractively labeled collective leadership, which lasted only until the new patrimonialist ruler successfully defeated all the potential and actual competitors. It took Stalin and Khrushchev each precisely five years to liquidate the pretense of collective leadership, while Brezhnev needed somewhat less time (depending on when the *actual* removal of Prime Minister Kosygin took place). And all three periods of "collective leadership" were indeed "Times of Troubles." But the charisma of success almost automatically established and safeguarded the unquestionable legitimacy of the new chief as long as he successfully maintained himself in power. With Andropov's instant and apparently smooth climb to supreme rulership the decision was presumably made in the Kremlin that under present circumstances another Collective Leadership or "Time of Troubles" might be strategically (time, money, emotions) too costly and perhaps also too embarrassing in the watchful world's public opinion. Of course, this does not mean that the new Chief could safely disregard his primary task of delivering the proof of his continuous legitimacy by firmly maintaining his charisma of success, i.e. holding his power intact.

It could be candidly said that Lenin's seizure of power and subsequent regime did not last, that it was replaced by another typically patrimonialist *coup d'état* and a subsequent power structure which lasted much longer. The coup was executed in a gradually accelerated motion by that greatest manufacturer of pseudo charisma ever, Stalin, who over two decades firmly recreated a patrimonialist empire par excellence. Scholarship is unanimous on this, irrespective of the terminology used.

Stalin's coup, of course, was not directly aimed at Lenin, who was incapacitated progressively over protracted periods of time. Still during his illness Lenin was continuously pictured in the official pronouncements and activities as "the revolutionary hero, believer in the sacred cause" (Weber 1946:125) by Stalin and his staff with the sole purpose of promoting the future legitimacy of Lenin's one and only true disciple-successor, Stalin. But most definitely Stalin's coup was directed against Lenin's choice of his successor, against his closest associates and against his wife, a dedicated revolutionary. Perhaps, if Khrushchev is to be taken seriously on this, it was also directed against Lenin's particular program, which according to Khrushchev was allegedly different from Stalin's.

The patrimonialist reality of life under Stalin, Khrushchev and Brezhnev was certainly the source of inspiration and justification for bitter criticisms against the Soviet Union's "bureaucratic despotism" and "state capitalism" by numerous anti-Stalinist Marxists of the 1950s and 1960s. However, the patterns of succession games and other attributes here are typical not only of Russia, whether tsarist or soviet, but of all other patrimonialist regimes, traditional and modern. There is an immense amount of literature which appears without using this term supportive of the concept of modern patrimonialism as applicable to both the economically and technologically advanced as well as the developing societies. One of the closest analyses to that of Weber is Wolpert's on modern caesarism (1950:690-92).

To the inveterate enthusiasts of Lenin the best consolation the facts offer is that in spite of all his exceptional gifts of political skills Lenin was simply unable to remove all those "insurmountable difficulties"—those which Weber not only clearly substantiated but also cited to "prophesy" that they will destroy the ambitious goals of the Russian liberation movement no matter who is in charge.

The political power vacuum of 1917 has been documented above. But there is another, in this context most pertinent, vacuum of a somewhat different sort: a social-structural vacuum throughout Russian history. Over a long period of time first many native eyewitnesses and foreign visitors, then later historical specialists have in various ways "discovered" this vacuum, which is especially striking if compared with West European and some other social structures. When all these observations are cumulatively considered a strong consensus on this matter appears unquestionable. It points to a long-lasting Russian political tradition which is at the same time not only a byproduct but also a major source of strength of the patrimonialist power structure and its legitimacy. The famous Russian historian Kliuchevsky is usually credited with "the idea of . . . the extreme simplicity of the Russian social structure. . . . In Western Europe, no matter how authoritarian and undemocratic society might have been, there always existed some solid interest groups which could give substance and practical meaning to the generalized protest of the intellectuals" (Malia, 1961:16). But Kliuchevsky is neither the first nor the only one in this. To social critic Tikhomirov "the extreme simplicity" indicated an element of truth in the famous patriotic claim of the

Slavophiles: There are only two forces in Russia—the tsar and the people (1886:161). Much earlier a French aristocrat, after visiting Russia as the tsar's special guest, was almost miraculously healed of his hatred of the French revolution; Custine said: "In the history of Russia no one except the emperor has performed his part. The nobles, the clergy, and all other classes of society, have each failed in their own" (1843:I:185ff).

Throughout his opus Weber indeed extensively analyzed all these Russian "classes" which failed to perform their political functions as the West European classes had done. However, only two aspects are to be briefly examined now, namely, as indicated above, the practically nonexisting proletariat and the extremely weak, non-functioning bourgeoisie.

In general Weber discussed the frailty of the liberation movement in Russia, which was due to a number of missing foundations, not only economic, but also political, religious, etc. (1906a,b). There is a clearly noticeable tendency among some commentators to ignore the latter two and to overemphasize the first, which does create the impression that Weber was a sort of economic determinist. Weber evaluated the support the Western religious doctrines and structures extended over a long period of time for the growth of free institutions in the West (1906a:280). This is even more true of Weber's analysis of the political doctrines and structures. Just as those developments were absent from the Russian historical experience, also missing, Weber said, were all the periods of development which in the West positioned strong economic interests of the owners' strata in support of the Western free city's liberation from the jurisdiction of the ruler (1906b:397-98).

The minute percent of industrial proletariat at that time, he continued, predicts extremely little about the future. In spite of a substantial increase in number, the proletariat in 1917 remained relatively small, still less than 2 percent of the population. And the Narodniki's (the huge peasant majority) blueprints are located in spite of everything in an unreal world, a land of fantasy. Modern research supports Weber on the Narodniki as discussed above (Schapiro, 1956:147ff; Mosse, 1967:102; and others). Only an improbable alliance of the proletariat and the bourgeoisie could bring tsarism down, Weber said in 1906.

In Russia the label bourgeoisie, Weber suggested, is applicable only if it is used not in the sense of an economic class, but in the sense of a style of life in general and higher degree of education—that is, the so-called Russian bourgeois intelligentsia (1906a:244-45). They are highly educated idealists committed to reform, but without any trace of power, political or economic (money). The actual (*eigentliche*) "bourgeoisie," especially the large industrialists and financiers, instead of helping, actively opposed the "bourgeois" idealists' liberation structures. This absence of capitalists from the ranks of "bourgeois intelligentsia" is striking. No industrialists or bankers ever joined the Russian liberal parties or liberation movements as regularly happened in the West; instead they supported the pro-tsarist groups and the tsarist bureaucracy. And the small ("petty") burghers with their religiously inspired traditional anti-Semitism joined the ranks of the archreactionaries, the Black Hundreds. In general, Weber said, the ardent desire of the owners, big and small, for law and order was much stronger than their zeal for constitutional rights. They were willing to accept a routine denial of civil liberties provided that profit be given free hand (1906a:342; 1906b:233).

In comparison with modern research, Weber's views in 1906 were relatively more encouraging concerning the slim chances for the development in Russia of both, proletariat and bourgeoisie, than are the more negative findings today. As Derek Scott put it: "As there was hardly any proletariat, so also there was hardly any bourgeoisie" (1961:29). Florinsky speaks of the "almost complete nonexistence of a middle class in the sense in which this term is used in Western Europe" (1931:118). Karpovich said that in spite of the wealth of individual merchants "their status remained an inferior one" and without any share of political power. He added that "no strong and influential bourgeoisie of the West European type existed" (1932:12-13). As Riha said: "The importance of the bourgeoisie and the petty bourgeoisie in Russia had been inflated by ideology, but also by the artificial political situation of the decade before 1917" (1967:121).

The significance of the proletariat in Russia also has been highly exaggerated by ideology. The Menshevik inability to act in spite of support by the industrial workers was conditioned by their realistic and quite orthodox Marxist interpretation that it is necessary to wait for the proletariat to emerge. The two chief antagonists in the Provisional Government, Kerensky and Miliukov, respectively, were in retrospect almost unanimous in their analysis of what was missing and why the short-lived experiment in pluralism, March to November 1917 failed:

For a number of historical reasons Russia entered the imperial period of its history under conditions which prevented the rise of the middle class, the very social force which in Western Europe sprang up in between the feudal aristocracy and lower orders. (Kerensky, 1934:25-26, 29ff)

There was no bourgeoisie in Russia worthy the name. The dependence of the Russian trading and commercial class on the government was still greater that that of the gentry; and this could but be expected, since the cherishing and fostering of Russian industries are entirely due to state measures. . . . *There was on the stage no social force which could influence political life and take part in the development of political ideas.* (Emphasis added.) (Miliukov, 1905:558)

These are only a few selections from the abundant post-Weber research which clearly support his major theoretical propositions and in general increase the validity of his theoretical paradigm on modernization and patrimonialism. But the disturbingly recurrent question is why some specialists on Russia still approach Weber's work with the old-fashioned pattern of sheer superficiality established by their predecessors and thus in turn reinforce the inherited pre-packaged images of Weber? Some recent publications affirm that this is not confined to the past and few observations relevant for future research in this area seem very appropriate to conclude this essay. Out of several recent instances only two important works will be noted.

Pipes wrote about "Weber's assumption that Russia had no political history—that it was a *tabula rasa*"—and of "his . . . inexplicable disregard of Russia's whole political tradition, and . . . his unfounded hope in Russia's ability to produce an entirely new civilization 'from the ground up' " (1955:398). Beetham and others showed that "Pipes is wrong when he says that Weber was looking to Russia for entirely new possibilities of freedom which existed nowhere else" (1974:183). But neither Pipes nor his imitators ever found it necessary to retract this pure phantasm. Pipes does not quote any of Weber's major works (1927, 1951, 1956) in which Russian history is amply sifted. Indeed, tsarist patrimonialism was a significant major case study perhaps second only to Chinese imperial patrimonialism, which lasted over 2,500 years. Still in his recent work Pipes actually ignores Weber's entire conceptualization of patrimonialism for he made only one single reference to it: "the term 'patrimonial regime' was revived and introduced into current usage by Max Weber" (1974:22). Only the label of patrimonialism is used in several chapter titles without analyzing at all any of the major attributes of Russian patrimonialism.

Skocpol (1979) is justly credited with solid historical narratives on three revolutions, French, Russian and Chinese. She convincingly rejects most of the current theorizing on revolution as too speculative without supportive historical evidence. Incidentally her historical data are destructive of much of the popular Russian revolutionary mythology as are Weber's and post-Weberian materials presented in this essay. Still she seems to be unable to free herself from some of those lingering myths and accompanying rhetoric. But the deep disappointment with her work is that she, like her predecessors, totally ignores both Weber's analyses of Russian patrimonialism and modernization in his major works and his essays on the 1917 events discussed here.

While Pipes makes use of the term alone, Skocpol in all three segments on tsarism and the subsequent events does not have a single reference to it (1979:81-99, 128-140, and 206-235). In this light her lone footnote reference to Weber (1968, chaps. 9-13), to a total of 210 pages, is purely perfunctory. In the very same footnote Skocpol criticizes Weber twice for serious flaws if not scientific failure, which is simply fictional. Similar accusations are originally found in the fabricated images and forged legacies of Weber as prepackaged by the various academic establishments. Skocpol said: "Weber tended to theorize about major forms of political structures" and "he tended to use categories that referred to political forms alone, in isolation from socioeconomic structures" (1979:304, n. 4). In total contradiction to this is a compliment paid to Weber for his steady efforts toward the closest possible attention to "socioeconomic" structures by those who attempted, of course unsuccessfully, to misinterpret Weber as an up-to-date, sophisticated Marxist. But more seriously, by using some of

Weber's Russian materials, theoretical and substantive, Pipes and Skocpol could have lightened their individual burdens of attempting to do what Weber had already done so well. Among other useful propositions Weber's superb dichotomy of patrimonialism versus feudalism would have facilitated (and shortened) the confusing presentation by Pipes and Skocpol of the contradictory phenomena of (patrimonialist) Russian and (feudal) Western European rulership and legitimacy.

There is much more of major contemporary significance in Weber's Russian studies than this Epilogue can adequately convey. At least three additional propositions, not reported here, would support this essay in its entirety: Weber's comparison of the twentieth century Russian monarchy with Oriental despotism; his reasons why the French Revolution is not comparable to the 1905 Russian revolution; and his changing views on the so-called process of "westernization" of Russia from the earlier more enthusiastic to the later, based on the 1917 events, more pessimistic and restrained evaluation of the actual success of the liberation programs. If this Epilogue's basic propositions are documented and generally accepted, then a re-examination of the commonly used conceptualizations and even terminology in this configuration will be necessary.

It is sincerely anticipated that this entire volume will contribute toward the process of at least slowing down the frequency and the extent of numerous misconceptions within and misinterpretations of the living legacy of Max Weber.

REFERENCES

Baumgarten, Eduard
    1971   "Discussion on Max Weber and Power-Politics." In
              Stammer, Otto (ed.), Max Weber and Sociology Today.
              New York: Harper and Row, pp. 122-27.
Beetham, David
    1974   Max Weber and the Theory of Modern Politics. London:
              Allen and Unwin.
Berdyaev, Nicholas
    1961   The Russian Revolution. Ann Arbor: The University of
              Michigan Press.

1948   The Origins of Russian Communism. London: Blas.

Chamberlin, William Henry
1965   The Russian Revolution, 1917-1921. 2 vols. New York: Grosset and Dunlap. (Reprint of the 1935 original.)

Chernov, Victor
1936   The Great Russian Revolution. New Haven: Yale University Press.

Custine, A.
1843   The Empire of the Czar. Vol. 1. London: Longman.

Dunn, John
1979   Western Political Theory in the Face of the Future. Cambridge University Press.

Florinsky, M. T.
1931   The End of the Russian Empire. New Haven, Conn.: Yale University Press.

Heuss, Theodore
1971   "Max Weber in seiner Gegenwart." In Max Weber, Gesammelte Politische Schriften. Tübingen: Mohr, pp. vii-xxxi.

Hindus, Maurice
1953   Crisis in the Kremlin. New York.

Hirschman, Albert O.
1968   "Underdevelopment, Obstacles to the Perception of Change, and Leadership." Daedalus 97 (Summer): 925-37.

Karpovich, Michael M.
1932   Imperial Russia. New York: Berkshire Studies.

Katkov, George
1967   Russia 1917: February Revolution. New York: Harper.

Kerensky, Alexander
1934   The Crucifixion of Liberty. New York.

Kochan, Lionel
1966   Russia in Revolution, 1890-1918. New York.

Lenin, V. I.
1937   Selected Works. Vol. 9. New York: International Publishers.

Malia, Martin
1961   "What is the Intelligentsia? Daedalus (Summer): 441-58

Melgunov, Sergei Petrovich
1972   The Bolshevik Seizure of Power. Santa Barbara: ABC Clio.

Miliukov, Paul N.
1942   Outlines of Russian Culture. Part 1: Religion and the Church in Russia. University of Pennsylvania Press.

1905   Russia and Its Crisis. Chicago: The University of Chicago Press.

Mosse, W. E.
1967   "The February Regime: Prerequisites of Success." Soviet Studies 19 (July): 100-108.

Murvar, Vatro
1983   Max Weber Today: An Introduction to a Living Legacy and Selected Bibliography. Max Weber Colloquia & Symposia at the University of Wisconsin. Brookfield, Wisconsin.
1982   Submerged Nations: An Invitation to Theory. Department of Sociology: The University of Wisconsin-Milwaukee.
1979   "Integrative and Revolutionary Capabilities of Religion." In Johnson, Harry M. (ed.), Religious Change and Continuity: Sociological Perspectives. San Francisco: Jossey-Bass, pp. 74-86.
1971   "Messianism in Russia: Religious and Revolutionary." Journal for Scientific Study of Religion 10 (Winter): 277-338.
1967   "Max Weber's Urban Typology and Russia." Sociological Quarterly 8:481-94.

Pethybridge, Roger
1967   "The Significance of Communications in 1917." Soviet Studies 19:109-14

Pipes, Richard
1974   Russia under the Old Regime. New York.
1955   "Max Weber and Russia." World Politics 7:371-401.

Riha, Thomas
1969   A Russian European: Paul Miliukov in Russian Politics. University of Notre Dame Press.
1967   "1917—A Year of Illusions." Soviet Studies 19: 115-21.

Schapiro, Leonard
1956   The Origin of the Communist Autocracy: Political Opposition in the Soviet State, First Phase 1917-1922. Harvard University Press.

Scott, Derek, J.
1961   Russian Political Institutions. New York: Praeger.

Skocpol, Theda
1979   States and Social Revolutions: A Comparative Analysis of France, Russia and China. Cambridge University Press.
1976   "Old Regime Legacies and Communist Revolutions in Russia and China." Social Forces 55:284-315.

Stammer, Otto (ed.)
    1971   Max Weber and Sociology Today. New York: Harper and Row.

Sukhanov, N. N.
    1955   The Russian Revolution 1917: Eyewitness Account. 2 vols. Ed. and trans. Joel Carmichael. Oxford University Press.

Tikhomirov, Lev
    1886   La Russie politique et sociale. Paris.

Tucker, Robert C.
    1968   "The Theory of Charismatic Leadership." Daedalus 97 (Summer): 731-56.

Tudjman, Franjo
    1981   Nationalism in Contemporary Europe. Columbia University Press.

Vernadsky, George
    1932   Russian Revolution, 1917-1931. New York: Holt.

Volskii, Nikolai Vladislavovich (Nikolai Valentinov)
    1969   The Early Years of Lenin. Ann Arbor: The University of Michigan Press.
    1968   Encounters with Lenin. Oxford University Press.

Weber, Max
    1971   Gesammelte politische Schriften. 3rd enlarged edition. Ed. Johannes Winckelmann. Tübingen: Mohr (Siebeck).
    1967   Socialism. Trans. H. F. Dickie-Clark. Durban: University of Natal Press.
    1956   Wirtschaft und Gesellschaft. 4^e Auflage. Tübingen: Mohr (Siebeck).
    1946   From Max Weber: Essays in Sociology. Trans and ed. H. H. Gerth and C. W. Mills. New York: Oxford University Press.
    1927   General Economic History. Trans. F. H. Knight. Glencoe, Ill.: The Free Press.
    1906a   "Zur Lage der bürgerlichen Demokratie in Russland." Archiv fur Sozialwissenschaft und Sozialpolitik 4: 234-353.
    1906b   "Russlands Übergang zum Scheinkonstitutionalismus." Archiv fur Sozialwissenschaft und Sozialpolitik 5: 165-401.

Willner, Ann Ruth, and Dorothy Willner
    1965   "The Rise and Role of Charismatic Leaders." The Annals of the American Academy of Political and Social Science 358 (March): 77-88.

Wolfe, Bertram D.
    1963   "Communist Ideology and Soviet Foreign Policy." In

Petersen, William (ed.), The Realities of World Communism. Englewood Cliffs, N.J.: Prentice Hall, pp. 19-40.

Wolpert, Jeremiah F.
1950   "Toward a Sociology of Authority." In A. W. Gouldner, (ed.), Studies in Leadership. New York: Harper, pp. 679-701.

Worsley, Peter
1968   The Trumpet Shall Sound. 2nd. ed. New York: Schocken.

BIBLIOGRAPHY

Abramowski, Günter
1966   Das Geschichtsbild Max Webers. Stuttgart: Klett.
Adorno, Theodor
1978   Minima Moralia: Reflections from Damaged Life. New York: Schocken.
Antoni, Carlo
1962   From History to Sociology. London: Merlin.
Antonio, Robert J.
1979   "The Contradiction of Domination and Production in Bureaucracy: The Contribution of Organizational Efficiency to the Decline of the Roman Empire." American Sociological Review 44:895-912.
Arato, Andrew
1974   "The Neo-Idealist Defense of Subjectivity." Telos 21:108-61.
Aaron, Raymond
1964   German Sociology. Glencoe, Ill.: The Free Press.
1967   Main Currents in Sociological Thought. Vol. 2. New York: Basic Books.
Bancroft, Nancy
1979   "American Fascism: Religious and Secular Analyses and Response." Paper delivered at the annual meeting of the society for the Scientific Study of Religion, San Antonio, Texas.
Batalov, Eduard
1975   The Philosophy of Revolt. Moscow: Progress.
Baumgarten, Eduard
1971   "Discussion on Max Weber and Power-Politics." In

Stammer, Otto (ed.), Max Weber and Sociology Today. New York: Harper and Row, pp. 122-27.

Beetham, David
1974   Max Weber and the Theory of Modern Politics. London: Allen and Unwin.

Bendix, Reinhard
1962   Max Weber: an Intellectual Portrait. New York: Anchor.
1971   Scholarship and Partisanship: Essays on Max Weber. Berkeley: University of California.
1973   State and Society: A Reader in Comparative Political Sociology. Berkeley: University of California Press.

Bensman, Joseph, and Givant, Michael
1975   "Charisma and Modernity." Social Research 42:570-614.

Berdyaev, Nicholas
1948   The Origins of Russian Communism. London: Blas.
1961   The Russian Revolution. Ann Arbor: The University of Michigan Press.

Berger, Peter L.
1963   "Charisma and Religious Innovation." American Sociological Review 28:940-50.
1970   A Rumor of Angels. Garden City, N.Y.: Doubleday.
1979   The Heretical Imperative. Garden City, N.Y.: Doubleday.

Berger, Peter L., and Luckmann, Thomas
1967   The Social Construction of Reality. Garden City, N.Y.: Doubleday.

Berger, Peter L., and Neuhaus, Richard
1977   To Empower People: The Role of Mediating Structures in Public Policy. Washington, D.C.: American Enterprise Institute.

Birnbaum, Norman
1953   "Conflicting Interpretations of the Rise of Capitalism." British Journal of Sociology 4:125-41.

Blau, Peter
1970   "Weber's Theory of Bureaucracy." In Dennis Wrong (ed.), Max Weber. Englewood Cliffs, N.J.: Prentice-Hall.

Blau, Peter M., and Meyer, Marshall W.
1971   Bureaucracy in Modern Society. New York: Random House.

Boorstin, Daniel J.
1970   The Republic of Technology. New York: Harper & Row.

Braverman, Harry
1974   Labor and Monopoly Capital. New York: Monthly Review.

Bruun, H. H.
1972   Science, Values and Politics in Max Weber's Methodology.
          Copenhagen: Munksgaard.

Buck, Roy
1979   "Power of 'the Word' in Tourism Promotion." Paper
          presented at the Tourism in the Next Decade Symposium,
          George Washington University, Washington, D.C.

Burger, Thomas
1976   Max Weber's Theory of Concept Formation: History,
          Laws, Ideal Types. Durham, N.C.: Duke University Press.

Cawelti, John
1970   Six-Gun Mystique. Bowling Green, Ohio: Popular.

Chernov, Victor
1936   The Great Russian Revolution. New Haven, Conn.: Yale
          University Press.

Chamberlin, William Henry
1965   The Russian Revolution, 1917-1921. 2 vols. New York:
          Grosset and Dunlap. (Reprint of the 1935 original.)

Cohen, Jere; Hazelrigg, Lawrence E.; and Pope, Whitney
1975a   "De-Parsonizing Weber: A Critique of Parson's
          Interpretation of Weber's Sociology." American
          Sociological Review 40:229-41.
1975b   "Reply to Parsons." American Sociological Review
          40:670-74.

Collins, Randall
1980   "Weber's Last Theory of Capitalism: A Systematization."
          American Sociological Review 45:925-42.

Constas, Helen
1961   "The U.S.S.R.—From Charismatic Sect to Bureaucratic
          Society." Administrative Science Quarterly 6:282-98.

Crozier, Michael
1971   The World of the Office Workers. Chicago: University of
          Chicago Press.

Custine, A.
1843   The Empire of the Czar. Vol. 1 London: Longman.

Dibble, Vernon K.
1968   "Social Science and Political Commitment in the Young
          Max Weber." Archives européennes de sociologie
          9:92-110.

Dorpalen, A.
1957   Heinrich von Treitschke. New Haven, Conn.: Yale
          University Press.

Dow, Thomas
    1969   "The Theory of Charisma." Sociological Quarterly
            10:306-18.
Dronberger, Illse
    1971   "Introduction." In J. J. Loubser, Rainer C. Baum,
            Andrew Effrat, and Victor Meyer Lidz (eds.), Explorations
            in General Theory in Social Science (Vol. 2). New York:
            Macmillan.
Dunn, John
    1979   Western Political Theory in the Face of the Future. New
            York: Cambridge University Press.
Eden, R.
    1983   Political Leadership and Nihilism: A Study of Weber and
            Nietzsche. Tampa: University Presses of Florida.
Eliot, T. S.
    1968   Christianity and Culture: The Idea of a Christian Society
            and Notes Towards the Definition of Culture. New York:
            Harcourt Brace Jovanovich, Harvest Book.
Ferrarotti, Franco
    1982   Max Weber and the Destiny of Reason. Armonk, New
            York: M. E. Sharpe.
Fischoff, Ephraim
    1944   "The Protestant Ethic and the Spirit of Capitalism." Social
            Research 2:61-77.
Florinsky, M. T.
    1931   The End of the Russian Empire. New Haven, Conn.: Yale
            University Press.
Freund, Julien
    1968   The Sociology of Max Weber (Mary Ilford, trans.). New
            York: Vintage.
Friedland, William H.
    1964   "For a Sociological Concept of Charisma." Social Forces
            43:18-26.
Gellner, Ernest
    1974   Legitimation of Belief. New York: Cambridge University
            Press.
Gerth, H. H., and C. Wright Mills
    1946   From Max Weber: Essays in Sociology. New York: Oxford
            University Press.
Giddens, Anthony
    1971   Capitalism and Modern Social Theory. Cambridge:
            Cambridge University Press.

1972   Politics and Sociology in the Thought of Max Weber. London: Macmillan.

1977   Studies in Social and Political Theory. New York: Basic.

Glassman, Ronald
1973   "Legitimacy and Manufactured Charisma." Social Research 42:615-36.

Gustafson, Paul M.
1967   "UO-US-PS-PO." Journal for the Scientific Study of Religion 6:64-68.

Gvishiani, D.
1972   Organization and Management. Moscow: Progress.

Habermas, Jurgen
1967   Zur Logik der Sozialwissenschaften. Tübingen: Mohr.

Hättich, Manfred
1967   "Der begriff des politischen bei Max Weber." Politische Vierteljahresschrift 8:40-50.

Hayek, F. A.
1960   The Constitution of Liberty. Chicago: University of Chicago Press.

Heuss, Theodore
1971   "Max Weber in seiner Gegenwart." In Max Weber, Gesammelte Politische Schriften. Tübingen: Mohr, pp. vii-xxx.

Hill, Michael
1973   The Religious Order. London: Heinemann.

Hills, R. Jean
1976   "The Organization as a Component in the Structure of Society. In Jan J. Loubser, Rainer C. Baum, Andrew Effrat, and Victor Meyer Lidz (eds.), Explorations in General Theory in Social Science (Vol. 2). New York: Macmillan.

Hindus, Maurice
1953   Crisis in the Kremlin. New York.

Hirschman, Albert O.
1968   "Underdevelopment, Obstacles to the Perception of Change, and Leadership." Daedalus 97 (Summer): 925-37.

Holland, Josiah Gilbert
1860   The American Journey. New York: Scribner.

Honigsheim, Paul
1968   On Max Weber. New York: Free Press.

Horkheimer, Max
1974   Critique of Instrumental Reason (Matthew J. O'Connell and others, trans.). New York: Seabury.

Hughes, H. S.
1958   Consciousness and Society. New York: Random House.
Jaspers, Karl
1964   Three Essays: Leonardo, Descartes, Max Weber. New York: Harcourt, Brace and World.
Karpovich, Michael M.
1932   Imperial Russia. New York: Berkshire Studies.
Kasler, D. (ed.)
1972   Max Weber. Munich: Nimphenburger Verlagshandlung.
Katkov, George
1967   Russia 1917: February Revolution. New York: Harper.
Kerensky, Alexander
1934   The Crucifixion of Liberty. New York.
Kimball, Solon T. and McClellan, James E., Jr.
1962   Education and the New America. New York: Random House.
Kochan, Lionel
1966   Russia in Revolution, 1890-1918. New York.
Lachmann, L. M.
1970   The Legacy of Max Weber: Three Essays. London: Heinemann.
Lefort, Claude
1974/75   "What Is Bureaucracy?" Telos 22:31-65.
Lenin, V. I.
1937   Selected Works. Vol. 9. New York: International Publishers.
Little, David
1974   "Max Weber and the Comparative Study of Religious Ethics." Journal of Religious Ethics 2:5-40.
Loewenstein, Karl
1966   Max Weber's Political Ideas in the Perspective of Our Time. Amherst: University of Massachusetts Press.
Lowith, Karl
1960   "Max Weber und Karl Marx." In Gessammelte Abhandlungen. Stuttgart: Kohlhammer.
MacRae, Donald G.
1974   Weber. London: Fontana
Malia, Martin
1961   "What is the Intelligentsia?" Daedalus (Summer): 441-58.
Marcuse, Herbert
1964   One-Dimensional Man. Boston: Beacon.
Marx, Karl, and Friedrich Engels
1973   Werke. Berlin: Dietz.

Mayer, J. P.
1956   Max Weber and German Politics. London: Faber & Faber.
Melgunov, Sergei Petrovich
1972   The Bolshevik Seizure of Power. Santa Barbara: ABC Clio.
Merton, Robert K.
1957   Social Theory and Social Structure. Glencoe, Ill.: Free
         Press.
Miliukov, Paul N.
1905   Russia and Its Crisis. Chicago: The University of Chicago
         Press.
1942   Outlines of Russian Culture. Part 1: Religion and the
         Church in Russia. University of Pennsylvania Press.
Mitzman, Arthur
1970   The Iron Cage: An Historical Interpretation of Max
         Weber. New York: Knopf.
Mommsen, Wolfgang
1963   "Zum Begriff der 'plebiszitaren Fuhrerdemokratie' bei
         Max Weber." Kolner Zeitschrift 15.
1965a   "Max Weber's Political Sociology and His Philosophy of
         World History." International Social Science Journal
         17:23-45.
1965b   "Universalgeschichtliches und politisches Denken bei Max
         Weber." Historische Zeitschrift 201.
1974a   The Age of Bureaucracy: Perspectives on the Political
         Sociology of Max Weber. New York: Harper & Row.
1974b   Max Weber und die deutsche Politik, 1890-1920. Tübingen:
         Mohr.
Mosse, W. E.
1967   "The February Regime: Prerequisites of Success." Soviet
         Studies 19 (July): 100-108.
Mueller, Gert H.
1977   "The Notion of Rationality in the Work of Max Weber."
         Paper presented to the Colloquia and Symposia on Max
         Weber, University of Wisconsin—Milwaukee.
Murvar, Vatro
1967   "Max Weber's Urban Typology and Russia." Sociological
         Quarterly 8:481-94.
1971a   "Messianism in Russia: Religious and Revolutionary."
         Journal for Scientific Study of Religion 10 (Winter):
         277-338.
1971b   "Patrimonial-feudal Dichotomy and Political Structure in
         Pre-revolutionary Russia: One Aspect of the Dialogue
         Between the Ghost of Karl Marx and Max Weber."

Sociological Quarterly 12 (Autumn):500-524.

1979   "Integrative and Revolutionary Capabilities of Religion."
In Johnson, Harry M. (ed.), Religious Change and
Continuity: Sociological Perspectives. San Francisco:
Jossey-Bass, pp. 74-86.

1982   Submerged Nations: An Invitation to Theory. Department
of Sociology: The University of Wisconsin—Milwaukee.

1983   Max Weber Today: An Introduction to a Living Legacy
and Selected Bibliography. Max Weber Colloquia and
Symposia at the University of Wisconsin—Brookfield.

Naumann, Friedrich

1893   "Der evanqelisch-soziale Kursus in Berlin." Christliche
Welt 7:1083-88, 1151-54, 1249-51.

1895   "Wochenschau." Die Hilfe 1:1-2.

Nelson, Benjamin

1967   "The Early Modern Revolution in Science and Philosophy."
Boston Studies in the Philosophy of Science 3.

1968   "Scholastic Rationales of 'Conscience,' Early Modern Crisis
of Credibility and the Scientific Technocultural Revolutions
of the 17th and 20th Centuries." Journal for the Scientific
Study of Religion 7:157-77.

1969   The Idea of Usury (2d ed.). Chicago: University of Chicago
Press.

1969b   "Conscience and the Making of Early Modern Culture."
Social Research 36:4-21.

1973a   "Civilizational Complexes and Intercivilizational
Encounters." Sociological Analysis 34:79-105.

1973b   "Weber's Protestant Ethic." In C. Y. Glock and P. E.
Hammond (eds.) Beyond the Classics? New York: Harper &
Row.

1974a   "Max Weber's Author's Introduction (1920): A Master Clue
to His Main Aims." Sociological Inquiry 44:269-78.

1974b   "Sciences and Civilizations, 'East' and 'West'." In Boston
Studies, XI. Dordrecht: Reidel.

1975   "Max Weber, Ernst Troeltsch, Georg Jellinek as
Comparative Historical Sociologists." Sociological Analysis
36:3.

1976   "On Orient and Occident in Max Weber." Social Research
43:114-29.

Nelson, John Wiley

1976   Your God Is Alive and Well and Appearing in Popular
Culture. Philadelphia: Westminster.

Nietzsche, Friedrich
1886   (1964) Jenseits von Gut und Böse. Stuttgart: Kröner.
Nobbe, Moritz August
1897   Der Evangelisch-Soziale Kongress und seine Gegner.
            Göttingen: Vandenhoeck.
Parsons, Talcott
1928   "Capitalism in Recent German Literature: Sombart and
            Weber (I)," Journal of Political Economy 36:641-61.
1929   "Capitalism in Recent German Literature: Sombart and
            Weber (II)," Journal of Political Economy 37:31-51.
1960a   "Review Article: 'Max Weber.'" American Sociological
            Review 25:750-52.
1960b   Structure and Process in Modern Societies. Glencoe, Ill.:
            Free Press.
1964a   "Introduction." In Max Weber, The Theory of Social and
            Economic Organization. New York: Free Press.
1964b   "Evolutionary Universals in Society." American
            Sociological Review 29:339-57.
1964c   The Social System. New York: Free Press.
1968   The Structure of Social Action. 2 vols. New York: Free Press.
1971   The System of Modern Societies. Englewood Cliffs, N.J.:
            Prentice-Hall.
1972   "Review of 'Scholarship and Partisanship: Essays on Max
            Weber'." Contemporary Sociology 1:200-03.
1974   Essays in Sociological Theory Pure and Applied. Glencoe,
            Ill.: Free Press.
1975   "Response to De-Parsonizing Weber." American
            Sociological Review 40:666-69.
Parsons, Talcott, and Neil H. Smelser
1965   Economy and Society. New York: Free Press.
Pethybridge, Roger
1967   "The Significance of Communications in 1917." Soviet
            Studies 19:109-14.
Pipes, Richard
1955   "Max Weber and Russia." World Politics 7:371-401.
1974   Russia under the Old Regime. New York.
Rex, John
1971   "Typology and Objectivity: A Comment on Weber's Four
            Sociological Methods." In A. Sahay (ed.) Max Weber and
            Modern Sociology. London: Routledge & Kegan Paul.
Rifkin, Jeremy, with Ted Howard
1979   The Emerging Order. New York: Putnam.

Riha, Thomas
    1967   "1917—A Year of Illusions." Soviet Studies 19:115-21.
    1969   A Russian European: Paul Miliukov in Russian Politics. University of Notre Dame Press.
Robertson, H. M.
    1933   Aspects of the Rise of Economic Individualism. Cambridge: Cambridge University Press.
Roth, Guenther
    1965   "Political Critiques of Max Weber." American Sociological Review 30:213-23.
    1968   "Introduction." In Max Weber, Economy and Society. New York: Bedminster.
    1971   "The Historical Relationship to Marxism." In Reinhard Bendix and Guenther Roth, Scholarship and Partisanship: Essays on Max Weber. Berkeley: University of California Press.
    1975   "Socio-historical Models and Developmental Theory." American Sociological Review 40:148-57.
    1976   "History and Sociology in the Work of Max Weber." British Journal of Sociology 27:306-18.
    1979   "Duration and Rationalization: Fernand Braudel and Max Weber." In Guenther Roth and Wolfgang Schluchter, Max Weber's Vision of History. Berkeley: University of California Press.
Roth, Guenther, and Wolfgang Schluchter
    1979   Max Weber's Vision of History: Ethics and Methods. Berkeley: University of California Press.
Runciman, W. G.
    1963   "Charismatic Legitimacy and One-Party Rule in Ghana." Archives européenes de sociologie 4:148-65.
    1972   A Critique of Max Weber's Philosophy of Social Science. Cambridge: Cambridge University Press.
Sahay, A.
    1971   Max Weber and Modern Society. London: Routledge & Kegan Paul.
Schapiro, Leonard
    1956   The Origin of the Communist Autocracy: Political Opposition in the Soviet State, First Phase 1917-1922. Cambridge, Mass.: Harvard University Press.
Schelting, A. von
    1934   Max Weber's Wissenschaft slehre. Tübingen: Mohr.
Schutz, Alfred
    1967   The Phenomenology of the Social World. (George Walsh

and Frederick Lehnert, trans.) Chicago: Northwestern University Press.

Scott, Derek, J.
1961   Russian Political Institutions. New York: Praeger.

Sheehan, J. J.
1966   The Career of Lujo Brentano. Chicago: University of Chicago Press.

Shils, Edward
1965   "Charisma, Order, and Status." American Sociological Review 30:199-213.

Sica, Alan
1979   "The Unknown Max Weber: A Note on Missing Translations" (unpublished manuscript). University of Kansas.

Skocpol, Theda
1976   "Old Regime Legacies and Communist Revolutions in Russia and China." Social Forces 55:284-315.
1979   States and Social Revolutions: A Comparative Analysis of France, Russia and China. New York: Cambridge University Press.

Spengler, O.
1967   Selected Essays (D. O. White, trans.) Chicago: Henry Regnery.

Sprinzak, Ehud
1972   "Weber's Thesis as an Historical Explanation." History and Theory 11.

Stammer, Otto (ed.)
1971   Max Weber and Sociology Today. New York: Harper & Row.

Stark, Werner
1967   "Max Weber and the Heterogony of Purposes." Social Research 34.

Sukhanov, N. N.
1955   The Russian Revolution 1917: Eyewitness Account. 2 vols. (Joel Carmichael, ed. and trans.) Oxford University Press.

Swatos, William H., Jr.
1979   Into Denominationalism. Storrs, Conn.: Society for the Scientific Study of Religion.

Tawney, R. H.
1956   Religion and the Rise of Capitalism. New York: New American Library.

Tenbruck, F. H.
1975a   "Das Werk Max Webers." Kolner Zeitschrift 27:663-702.

1975b   "Wie gut kennen wir Max Weber." Zeitschrift f.d. ges. Staatswissenschaft 131:719-42.

Tikhomirov, Lev
1886   La Russie Politique et sociale. Paris.

Tönnies, Ferdinand
1897   Der Nietzsche-Kultus: Eine Kritik. Leipzig: Reisland.

Trevor-Roper, H. R.
1969   "Religion, the Reformation and Social Change." In The European Witchcraze. New York: Harper Torchbook.

Tucker, Robert C.
1968   "The Theory of Charismatic Leadership." Daedalus 97 (Summer):731-56.

Tudjman, Franjo
1981   Nationalism in Contemporary Europe. New York: Columbia University Press.

Turner, S. P.
1982   "Bunyan's Cage and Weber's Casing." Sociological inquiry 52:84-87.

Turner, Victor
1974   Dramas, Fields, and Metaphors. Ithaca, N.Y.: Cornell.

Vernadsky, George
1932   Russian Revolution, 1917-1931. New York: Holt.

Vidich, A. J. (ed.)
1975   "Charisma, Legitimacy, Ideology." Social Research 42:4.

Vinson, Donald E.
1977   "Charisma: A Sociological Explanation of Market Leadership." International Journal of Contemporary Sociology 14:269-75.

Volskii, Nikolai Vladislavovich (Nikolai Valentinov)
1968   Encounters with Lenin. New York: Oxford University Press.

1969   The Early Years of Lenin. Ann Arbor: The University of Michigan Press.

Wade, Richard C.
1964   Slavery in the Cities. New York: Oxford.

Wagner, Adolf
1892   Das neue Sozialdemokratische Program. Berlin: Rehtwisch.

Wallerstein, Immanuel
1974   The Modern World-System. New York: Academic.

Weber, Marianne
1975   Max Weber: A Biography. New York: Wiley.

Weber, Max

1927	General Economic History (Frank H. Knight, trans.). Glencoe: Free Press.
1930	The Protestant Ethic and the Spirit of Capitalism. New York: Scribners.
1936	Jugendbriefe (Marianne Weber, ed.). Tübingen: Mohr.
1946	From Max Weber: Essays in Sociology (H. H. Gerth and C. W. Mills, eds.). New York: Oxford.
1949	The Methodology of the Social Sciences (Edward Shils and Henry Finch, trans.). New York: Free Press.
1951	The Religion of China: Confucianism and Taoism (Hans H. Gerth, trans. and ed.). Glencoe: The Free Press.
1952	Ancient Judaism (Hans H. Gerth and Don Martindale, trans. and ed.). Glencoe: The Free Press.
1954	On Law in Economy and Society. New York: Simon and Schuster.
1958a	The City. New York: Free Press.
1958b	The Protestant Ethic and the Spirit of Capitalism (Talcott Parsons, trans.). New York: Scribners.
1958c	The Rational and Social Foundations of Music. Carbondale: Southern Illinois.
1958d	The Religion of India: The Sociology of Hinduism and Buddhism. (Hans H. Gerth and Don Martindale, trans. and ed.). Glencoe: The Free Press.
1961	General Economic History. New York: Collier-Macmillan.
1963	The Sociology of Religion (Ephraim Fischoff, trans.) Boston: Beacon.
1964	The Theory of Social and Economic Organization (Talcott Parsons, trans.). New York: Free Press.
1967	Socialism. Tr. H. F. Dickie-Clark. Durban: University of Natal Press.
1968	Economy and Society (3 vols.) (Guenther Roth and Claus Wittich, eds.). New York: Bedminister. (2d ed., University of California Press, 1978.)
1971	Gesammelte politische Schriften. 3d enlarged edition. (Johannes Winckelmann, ed.) Tübingen: Mohr (Siebeck).
1975	Roscher and Knies: The Logical Problem of Historical Economics (Guy Oakes, trans.). New York: Free Press.
1976	The Agrarian Sociology of Ancient Civilizations (R. I. Frank, trans.). Highlands, N.J.: Humanities Press.
1977	Critique of Stammler (Guy Oakes, trans.). New York: Free Press.

1978   Max Weber: Selections in Translation (W. G. Runciman, ed., and Eric Matthews, trans.). New York: Cambridge University Press.

Weiss, Johannes
1981   Das Werk Max Webers in der marxistischen Rezeption und Kritik. Opladen: Westdeutscher Verlag.

Willner, Ann Ruth, and Dorothy Willner
1965   "The Rise and Role of Charismatic Leaders." The Annals of the American Academy of Political and Social Science 358 (March):77-88.

Wilson, Bryan R.
1966   Religion in Secular Society. London: Watts.
1975   The Noble Savages. Berkeley: University of California Press.
1976   Contemporary Transformations of Religion. New York: Oxford University Press.

Winkel, Harold
1977   Die deutsche Nationalökonomie im 19. Jahrhundert. Darmstadt: Wissenschaftliche Buchgesellschaft.

Wolfe, Bertram D.
1963   "Communist Ideology and Soviet Foreign Policy." In Petersen, William (ed.), The Realities of World Communism. Englewood Cliffs, N.J.: Prentice Hall, pp. 19-40.

Wolf, W. B.
1974   The Basic Barnard: An Introduction to Chester I. Barnard and His Theories of Organization and Management. ILR Paperback No. 14. Ithaca, N.Y.: New York School of Industrial and Labor Relations, Cornell University.

Wolpert, Jeremiah F.
1950   "Toward a Sociology of Authority." In A. W. Gouldner, (ed.), Studies in Leadership. New York: Harper, pp. 679-701.

Worsley, Peter
1968   The Trumpet Shall Sound. 2d. ed. New York: Schocken.

Wrong, Dennis (ed.)
1970   Max Weber. Englewood Cliffs, N.J.: Prentice-Hall.

INDEX

CONTRIBUTORS

Robert Antonio is a professor at the University of Kansas. He has written many essays on the works of Max Weber, among them a seminal piece on the bureaucracy of ancient Rome. He is currently at work on a coauthored volume with Ronald M. Glassman, entitled *A Weber-Marx Dialogue.*

Reinhard Bendix is a professor in the Political Science Department of the University of California at Berkeley. He is the author of the widely known volume *Max Weber: An Intellectual Portrait.* His latest work is *Kings or People: Power and the Mandate to Rule.*

Roslyn Bologh is a professor at St. John's University in New York City. She has written on the works of Marx and Weber and has a special interest in feminist issues as they relate to social theory. Her latest book is *Dialectical Phenomenology: Marx's Method.*

Jose Casanova is Professor of Bilingual Studies at The State University of New Jersey, Passaic. He has written and translated many essays on the works of Max Weber and is currently at work on a volume on the politics of post-Franco Spain.

Regis Factor is a political scientist at the University of South Florida. He is soon to publish a coauthored work with Stephen Turner, entitled *Max Weber and the Dispute of Reason and Values.*

Hans Gerth was, before his death, Professor of Sociology at the University of Wisconsin. He is best known for his works coauthored with C. Wright Mills, such as *From Max Weber* and *Character and Social Structure*. A posthumous collection of his papers has appeared, edited by Joseph Bensman, Arthur Vidich and Nobuko Gerth, entitled *Politics, Character and Culture: Perspectives from Hans Gerth*.

Ernest Kilker is currently at Boston University. His new book focuses on Max Weber's conceptions of democracy, especially on his notion of the plebiscitarian leader.

Stanford Lyman is Professor of Sociology at the New School for Social Research. He is world renowned for his coauthored volume on the existential approach to sociology, *The Sociology of the Absurd,* along with his *The Seven Deadly Sins.* His most recent work, coauthored with Arthur Vidich, describes the relationship between Protestantism and sociological theory in the United States.

Judith Marcus is a professor at the New School for Social Research. She is currently translating a work by Wolfgang Schluchter into English, and has authored a volume of her own dealing with the intellectual relationship between Lukács and Mann, entitled *Foundations of the Frankfurt Schools.*

Lawrence Scaff is a political scientist at the University of Arizona. He has written numerous essays on the works of Max Weber. His most recent essay compares the work of Marx and Weber, especially focusing on the "young Weber."

William Swatos is currently Vicar at St. Mark's Episcopal Church, Silvis, Illinois. He has written papers and articles on the works of Max Weber and is especially interested in charismatic leadership as it manifests itself in the modern world of mass media and bureaucratic stultification.

Zoltan Tar is a professor at the New School for Social Research. He is best known for his works on Lukács and the Frankfurt School. His latest books are *Foundations of the Frankfurt Schools* and *Selected Correspondence of the Young Lukács: A Dialogue with Weber, Simmel, Mannheim and Others.*

Stephen Turner is a sociologist at the University of South Florida. He is soon to publish a coauthored work with Regis Factor, entitled *Max Weber and the Dispute of Reason and Values.*

Dennis Wrong is Professor of Sociology at New York University. He is best known for his essay "The Oversocialized Conception of Man," which has been reprinted in numerous collections, and for his standard text in demography, entitled *Population and Society.*

ABOUT THE EDITORS

Ronald M. Glassman is currently at William Paterson College of the State University of New Jersey. Among his books are *The Political History of Latin America* and *Conflict and Control: The Challenge to Legitimacy of Modern Governments* (coauthored with Arthur Vidich). His most recent books are *Democracy and Despotism in Primitive Society* and *A Weber-Marx Dialogue* (coauthored with Robert Antonio). Professor Glassman is also the president of the section on Comparative Historical Sociology of the American Sociological Association.

Vatro Murvar is Professor of Sociology at the University of Wisconsin at Milwaukee. He is nationally recognized as the founder of the Max Weber Colloquium Series. In this capacity Professor Murvar brought together Weber scholars from all over the country and the world and helped to generate the current "Weber Renaissance." He has also compiled a bibliography of current works on Max Weber which is invaluable for every Weber scholar. His many essays on Max Weber have helped to illuminate Weber's works for a whole new generation of sociologists. Vatro Murvar is also an expert in the study of submerged peoples and is currently engaged in work on the Basques and the Vlachs.